A Frontend
Web Developer's
Guide to Testing

Explore leading web test automation frameworks
and their future driven by low-code and AI

Eran Kinsbruner

BIRMINGHAM—MUMBAI

A Frontend Web Developer's Guide to Testing

Group Product Manager: Pavan Ramchandani
Publishing Product Manager: Bhavya Rao
Senior Editor: Mark D'Souza
Content Development Editor: Feza Shaikh
Technical Editor: Saurabh Kadave
Copy Editor: Safis Editing
Project Coordinator: Manthan Patel
Proofreader: Safis Editing
Indexer: Tejal Daruwale Soni
Production Designer: Roshan Kawale
Marketing Coordinator: Anamika Singh

First published: April 2022
Production reference: 1280322

Published by Packt Publishing Ltd.
Livery Place
35 Livery Street
Birmingham
B3 2PB, UK.

ISBN 978-1-80323-831-9

www.packt.com

This book, which is the fourth of my career, is dedicated to my mother, Rodica Kinsbruner, and my supportive family: my wife, Shikma Kinsbruner, and my two sons, Ariel and Yahly.

– Eran Kinsbruner

Foreword

I have known and worked with **Eran Kinsbruner** for more than 3 years. Eran is a software testing expert in web and mobile applications. He contributes to the community through his speaking engagements and content creation as part of his role as Chief Evangelist at Perfecto by Perforce.

As web applications have become so complex in recent years, test automation needed to advance as well. In this book, Eran picked the top leading open source frameworks that practitioners will find useful in maturing their test automation coverage.

As one of the main contributors to the Cypress testing framework, I can confidently state that by using the insights covered in this book for network control testing, API testing, functional and accessibility testing, visual testing, and more, frontend web application developers can learn a lot and ensure that they are building better apps that can function and perform well across all leading web browsers.

Beyond getting familiarity and getting started with the top testing JavaScript frameworks, you will also learn how to build a solid testing strategy for your web application from the ground up.

In *A Frontend Web Developer's Guide to Testing*, Eran provides a complete and informative guide to both newcomers as well as veteran frontend web application developers around building test automation that works, scales, and provides value to the business.

Lastly, the book is filled with great and simple-to-use code examples, references, and visuals that can help practitioners ramp up quickly with their testing activities.

Gleb Bahmutov

Senior Director of Engineering at Mercari US

Previously VP of Engineering at Cypress.IO

Contributors

About the author

Eran Kinsbruner is a bestselling author, chief evangelist, and senior director at Perforce Software. He was a DevOps evangelist of the year finalist in 2021 for DevOps.com. His published books include the 2016 Amazon bestseller *The Digital Quality Handbook*, *Continuous Testing for DevOps Professionals*, and *Accelerating Software Quality – ML and AI in the Age of DevOps*, which was named the "best new software testing book" by Book Authority. Eran has many years of experience in development and testing at companies such as Sun Microsystems, Neustar, Texas Instruments, and General Electric. Eran is a patent-holding inventor and is active in the software development and testing community. He can be found across social media (LinkedIn – `https://www.linkedin.com/in/erankinsbruner/`, Twitter - `https://twitter.com/ek121268`, Medium Articles – `https://ek121268.medium.com/`) and has his own blog, `http://continuoustesting.dev`.

About the reviewer

Bruno Bosshard is an experienced software quality assurance manager and test automation architect at Pepgo Pty Ltd, based in Sydney, Australia. He has experience in test management, functional testing, and performance testing, working for clients in Europe, the Middle East, and Australia, both on a management level, such as developing test strategies, plans, processes, and templates, as well as on a practical, hands-on level, including development and implementation of automated test frameworks in Agile continuous integration environments. He is a test automation specialist with good development and DevOps knowledge who knows how to implement successful test automation to achieve real business value. Bruno can be contacted via LinkedIn.

Table of Contents

3

Top Web Test Automation Frameworks

4

Matching Personas and Use Cases to Testing Frameworks

5

Introducing the Leading Frontend Web Development Frameworks

Part 2 – Continuous Testing Strategy for Web Application Developers

6

Map the Pillars of a Dev Testing Strategy for Web Applications

7

Core Capabilities of the Leading JavaScript Test Automation Frameworks

8

Measuring Test Coverage of the Web Application

Part 3 – Frontend JavaScript Web Test Automation Framework Guides

9

Working with the Selenium Framework

10

Working with the Cypress Framework

11

Working with the Playwright Framework

12
Working with the Puppeteer Framework

13
Complementing Code-Based Testing with Low-Code Test Automation

14

Wrapping Up

Index

Other Books You May Enjoy

Preface

Testing web applications during a sprint poses a challenge for frontend web app developers, which can be overcome by harnessing the power of new, open source cross-browser test automation frameworks. This book will introduce you to a range of leading, powerful frameworks, such as Selenium, Cypress, Puppeteer, and Playwright, and serve as a guide to using their test coverage capability. You'll learn essential concepts of web testing and get an overview of the different web automation frameworks to be able to integrate them into your frontend development workflow. Throughout the book, you'll explore the unique features of top open source test automation frameworks, as well as their trade-offs, and learn how to set up each of them to create tests that don't break with changes in the app.

By the end of this book, you'll be able to not only choose the framework that best suits your project needs but also create an initial JavaScript-based test automation suite. This will enable fast feedback upon code changes and increase test automation reliability. As the open source market for these frameworks evolves, this guide will help you to continuously validate your project needs and adapt to the changes.

Who this book is for

If you are a frontend developer working with popular frameworks, such as Vue or React, and want to develop testing skills by learning the essentials of test automation, this book is for you. An intermediate-level understanding of JavaScript and frontend development is assumed.

What this book covers

Chapter 1, *Cross-Browser Testing Methodologies*, covers the most advanced web technologies and web application types you will come across, including responsive and progressive types. It is specifically designed to cover the main trends that typically impact web application developers, along with the various testing types that are relevant for such applications.

Chapter 2, Challenges Faced by Frontend Web Application Developers, covers the key challenges modern web application developers face and their root causes. It is specifically designed to cover the constant debate about velocity, quality, and key non-functional challenges that are a pain for developers.

Chapter 3, Top Web Test Automation Frameworks, focuses on the top four leading open source frameworks on the market and provides an intermediate tutorial on how to get started with each of these.

Chapter 4, Matching Personas and Use Cases to Testing Frameworks, provides a set of considerations to help the two main personas within web application development and testing (developers and test automation engineers) to choose the best test automation framework for their needs.

Chapter 5, Introducing the Leading Frontend Web Development Frameworks, looks at the test frameworks from the web development and application perspectives and provides guidelines on how to ensure that your test framework best fits the application type, as well as the web development frameworks used to build these apps.

Chapter 6, Map the Pillars of a Dev Testing Strategy for Web Applications, looks at how to combine the relevant considerations into a testing strategy that covers all quality aspects and continuously meets the end user experience. In addition, it offers frontend developers key metrics that can be used to monitor and measure the success of the strategy.

Chapter 7, Core Capabilities of the Leading JavaScript Test Automation Frameworks, provides an overview of the most critical testing capabilities that are required for web applications and provides the recommended test framework to go with each capability.

Chapter 8, Measuring Test Coverage of the Web Application, provides guidelines for how to complement the quality assessment of your web application with code coverage across the various test automation frameworks featured in this book (Selenium, Cypress, Playwright, and Puppeteer).

Chapter 9, Working with the Selenium Framework, provides you with a deep technical overview of the Selenium framework with a focus on the advanced capabilities, including support for CDP, relative locators, visual testing, cloud testing, **behavior-driven development** (**BDD**) testing, and self-healing add-ons.

Chapter 10, Working with the Cypress Framework, provides a technical overview of the framework with a focus on its advanced capabilities, including time travel, component testing, network control, API testing, supported plugins, and cloud testing.

Chapter 11, Working with the Playwright Framework, offers a technical overview of the framework with a focus on the advanced capabilities of Playwright, such as API testing, network control, visual testing, the retrying mechanism, Inspector, and the code generator tool.

Chapter 12, Working with the Puppeteer Framework, provides a technical overview of the framework with a focus on the advanced capabilities, including HAR file generation and using headless mode for testing. The chapter comes with some code-based examples that can be used out of the box.

Chapter 13, Complementing Code-Based Testing with Low-Code Test Automation, discusses how, while the open source community offers a wide range of coding test frameworks, as highlighted in this book, there are also new and emerging intelligent testing solutions that can combine their record and playback abilities with self-healing machine learning-driven features to provide an additional layer of test automation coverage. In this chapter, we uncover the available options on the market, the relevant places and use cases to use such tools within a development pipeline, and the caveats or pitfalls to be aware of.

Chapter 14, Wrapping Up, concludes the book with a set of references, additional blogs, and websites to bookmark to expand on the content offered in this book.

To get the most out of this book

Software/hardware covered in the book	Operating system requirements
Cypress framework installation	Windows, macOS
Selenium framework (WebDriver)	Visual Studio C
Puppeteer installation	Visual Studio C
Playwright installation	Node.js
PowerShell on Windows	Java Standard Edition
Chrome Driver, Firefox Driver, Edge Driver	
Google HAR Analyzer (`https://toolbox.googleapps.com/apps/har_analyzer/`)	

If you are using the digital version of this book, we advise you to type the code yourself or access the code from the book's GitHub repository (a link is available in the next section). Doing so will help you avoid any potential errors related to the copying and pasting of code.

Download the example code files

You can download the example code files for this book from GitHub at `https://github.com/PacktPublishing/A-Frontend-Web-Developers-Guide-to-Testing`. If there's an update to the code, it will be updated in the GitHub repository.

We also have other code bundles from our rich catalog of books and videos available at `https://github.com/PacktPublishing/`. Check them out!

Download the color images

We also provide a PDF file that has color images of the screenshots and diagrams used in this book. You can download it here: `https://static.packt-cdn.com/downloads/9781803238319_ColorImages.pdf`.

Conventions used

There are a number of text conventions used throughout this book.

`Code in text`: Indicates code words in text, database table names, folder names, filenames, file extensions, pathnames, dummy URLs, user input, and Twitter handles. Here is an example: "Cypress performs most of its API tests via the `cy.request()` method, which serves as a `GET` command to the web server being tested."

A block of code is set as follows:

```
cy
  .get('list')
  .first(); // "select first item in the list "
cy
  .get('list')
  .last(); // "select last item in the list "
cy
  .get('list')
  .eq(2); // "select 2nd item in the list
"
```

When we wish to draw your attention to a particular part of a code block, the relevant lines or items are set in bold:

```
describe("Docket Post Test 2", () => {
    it("Should create a Todo item", () => {
```

```
cy.request({
    method: "POST",
    url:
        "https://docket-test.herokuapp.com/api/Todo/",
    headers: {
        token: "YOUR TOKEN ID",
    },
    body: {
        Body: "Barclays Demo",
    },
})
```

Any command-line input or output is written as follows:

```
npm install axe-puppeteer
```

Bold: Indicates a new term, an important word, or words that you see onscreen. For instance, words in menus or dialog boxes appear in **bold**. Here is an example: "Upon any test launch from the GUI, users will have the ability to click on the **Add New Test** button."

> **Tips or Important Notes**
> Appear like this.

Get in touch

Feedback from our readers is always welcome.

General feedback: If you have questions about any aspect of this book, email us at customercare@packtpub.com and mention the book title in the subject of your message.

Errata: Although we have taken every care to ensure the accuracy of our content, mistakes do happen. If you have found a mistake in this book, we would be grateful if you would report this to us. Please visit www.packtpub.com/support/errata and fill in the form.

Piracy: If you come across any illegal copies of our works in any form on the internet, we would be grateful if you would provide us with the location address or website name. Please contact us at copyright@packt.com with a link to the material.

If you are interested in becoming an author: If there is a topic that you have expertise in and you are interested in either writing or contributing to a book, please visit authors. packtpub.com.

Share Your Thoughts

Once you've read, we'd love to hear your thoughts! Scan the QR code below to go straight to the Amazon review page for this book and share your feedback.

https://packt.link/r/1803238313

Your review is important to us and the tech community and will help us make sure we're delivering excellent quality content.

Part 1 – Frontend Web Testing Overview

Web technology has significantly advanced over the past few years. With mature web apps in the form of responsive and progressive apps, React, and others, developers are being challenged more than ever to ensure the continuous quality of web apps, regardless of which platforms they are being consumed on (mobile, desktop, or both). In the first part of this book, you will be able to catch up on all the important advancements within web technologies, the challenges in building a top-notch web app, the available testing solutions that can help overcome some of these challenges within a development team, and the main differences between the leading web development frameworks that can impact testing strategies.

In this part, we will cover the following chapters:

- *Chapter 1, Cross-Browser Testing Methodologies*
- *Chapter 2, Challenges Faced by Fronted Web Application Developers*
- *Chapter 3, Top Web Test Automation Frameworks*
- *Chapter 4, Matching Personas and Use Cases to Testing Frameworks*
- *Chapter 5, Introducing the Leading Frontend Web Development Frameworks*

1

Cross-Browser Testing Methodologies

Over the past few years, web technology has advanced significantly. End users are now exposed to a whole new level of mature web apps in the form of responsive and progressive apps such as React and Flutter. With these advancements, developers are challenged more than ever with ensuring the continuous quality of their web apps, regardless of which platforms (mobile, desktop, or both) they are being used on.

This chapter covers the most advanced web technologies and web application types you will come across, including responsive and progressive types. It is specifically designed to cover the main trends that typically impact web application developers, along with the various testing types that are relevant for such applications. The web landscape offers developers a wide range of web application types across different application frameworks. Applications such as responsive web, progressive web, Flutter, React Native, and more are only a subset of the range of such applications. In this chapter, we will outline the main application types and what they mean as well as how they differ from each other to help frontend developers consider different testing activities.

This chapter will cover the following main topics:

- An overview of the web landscape
- Understanding web application types
- Testing types for web applications
- Understanding headed and headless browsers within app development and testing

An overview of the web landscape

The web landscape is at its most advanced stage today compared to some years ago. Today, web applications can leverage the unique capabilities of the different web browsers that were simply not available a few years ago. From interaction with location services, cameras, and more to being installed as apps on a smartphone, tablet, or laptop, today, web applications are closer than ever to mobile applications.

With all of this in mind, there are other aspects within the web landscape that are important to understand: web technologies that are available and are constantly changing for web application developers.

Based on Hackr.io (`https://hackr.io/blog/web-development-frameworks`), web developers have a wide array of choices when building their websites. With *ExpressJS*, *Angular*, *React*, *Vue*, *Ember*, and more, developers can choose the most relevant technology for their next web application.

With web technologies growing and running on different omni-channels, the quality and growth of vulnerabilities are also becoming a great challenge. Based on the ongoing monitoring of web trends by the HTTP Archive (`https://httparchive.org/reports/state-of-the-web`), 59.4% of crawled pages contain at least one known third-party JavaScript vulnerability:

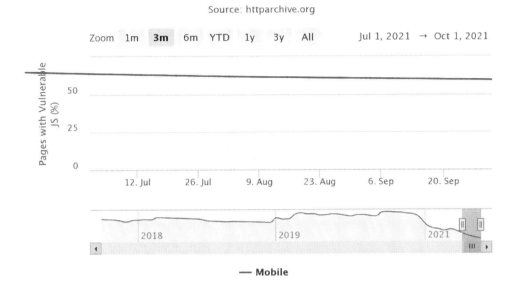

Figure 1.1 – Web pages with vulnerable JavaScript code
(source: https://httparchive.org/reports/state-of-the-web)

In addition to the level of growth of web technologies and maturity of browser capabilities, an additional area that has completely changed in terms of both awareness and importance is web application accessibility compliance. Organizations that build web applications today, and in the future, must adhere to strict accessibility rules across desktop and mobile devices. Not meeting these guidelines, such as section 508, Americans with Disabilities Act (ADA), and Web Content Accessibility Guidelines (WCAG), can result in massive fines and brand damage.

Today, web application developers should be more equipped with the knowledge, tools, and continuous training around web application quality. This is to ensure their apps are solid and don't introduce any kind of business risk to their brand – whether quality-related, security-related, accessibility-related, availability-related, or in terms of compatibility across factors that includes different screen sizes and resolutions.

Now that we've looked at a brief overview of the current web landscape, let's examine the various types of web applications and what each of them mean from a development and testing perspective.

Understanding web application types

When building a web application in the ever-changing digital marketplace, developers have various choices in terms of whether to build a traditional web application, a responsive one, or a progressive application. Each choice comes with advantages, disadvantages, and technology implications, such as the language in which the app is developed, the target platforms on which it will run, and which technology stack would fit such an application. A **progressive web application** (**PWA**) that is intended to run on both web and mobile apps can be developed in JavaScript; however, testing one on real mobile devices and browsers will require a mix of frameworks such as **Selenium**, **Appium**, and more.

Let's learn more about each of the application types.

Traditional web applications

The most basic web application type is one that is developed and designed from the bottom up to run on desktop machines (for example, Windows 11 with the Edge browser and macOS with Safari). While fully supported to run on mobile smartphones and tablets, such applications are not designed to be responsive.

If you navigate from your Windows desktop Chrome browser to the MSN website (`http://msn.com`), you will be able to work through the site, navigate around it, and use it as required. However, if you choose to navigate to the browser menu, under the **More tools** submenu, and select the **Developer tools** option (this one can also be triggered through a click on by pressing the *F12* button on your keyboard), you will see a *Toggle device toolbar* button that is aimed at helping developers and testers to validate their web apps from a responsive standpoint. In this menu option, if a user selects an iPhone device, they will see that the website isn't mobile-ready. As a matter of fact, in the top-level banner of this web application, there is a callout to download a relevant mobile app for both Android and iOS:

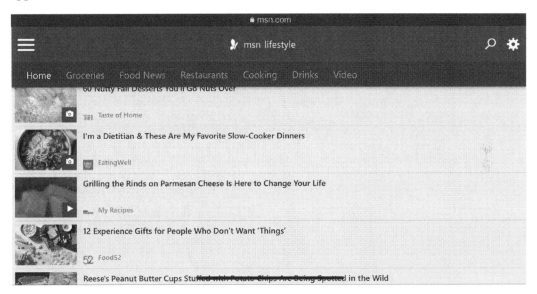

Figure 1.2 – The MSN web application on an iPhone 13 Pro Max in landscape orientation mode

Such a web application type would be developed, tested, and mostly dedicated to desktop web users. Additionally, it will require the organization to maintain a mobile-specific native or hybrid app to ensure a proper user experience across all digital devices.

Responsive web applications

In contrast to traditional web applications, **responsive web applications** are adjustable across most desktop and mobile screen sizes and resolutions. Such a unique design allows web developers to make their apps accessible across the maximum number of digital channels using a single code base and a consistent user experience. However, it is not as simple as that; responsive web apps require, in addition to a unique development workflow, things such as an agreed content strategy that shows customers the most relevant content above and beyond the *fold*. Such visible content across all types of screens needs to be constantly maintained, optimized, and tested to ensure business growth and success:

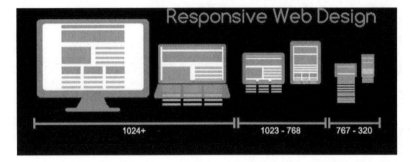

Figure 1.3 – Responsive Web Design for Desktop, Notebook, Tablet and Mobile Phone (originally created by Muhammad Rafizeldi (Mrafizeldi), retrieved from https://commons.wikimedia.org/wiki/File:Responsive_Web_Design_for_Desktop,_Notebook,_Tablet_and_Mobile_Phone.png, licensed and made available under CC BY-SA 3.0 (https://creativecommons.org/licenses/by-sa/3.0/deed.en))

Responsive web apps are a much stronger application type with clear benefits to both the developers and the end users. Maintaining a single code base over time and automatically serving any screen size or resolution are clear cost-efficient software development methods.

New types of digital platforms such as foldable smartphones and home devices, such as Google Hub and Amazon Echo Show, have also entered the market; such applications need to be updated to ensure a continuous user journey across all platforms.

In a nutshell, here is a list of the building blocks of a solid **responsive web design** (**RWD**) test plan that both developers and test engineers should execute continuously:

- Compatibility testing across the most relevant desktop browsers, OS versions, and mobile devices

- Visual testing coverage across different layouts, screen sizes, resolutions, and languages to ensure the proper display of all graphical elements on these platforms

- The end-to-end functional testing of all business flows, links, forms, and other web UI dependencies

- Accessibility of the pages across all different platforms

- Client-side performance testing

- Load testing at peak levels and normal ones

- Testing across different environment conditions (both web and mobile), including networks, working with sensors, incoming events, location-aware events, and more

PWAs

PWAs are one of the most advanced web application types with unique characteristics. Initially developed and led by Google, these application types have been adopted by all the other browser vendors, including Apple, Microsoft, and Mozilla. PWAs are those applications that are built on top of the responsive web app code base, allowing mobile users to install a web link on their Android and iOS devices. Following this, they can interact with these apps offline through different sensors with access to mobile OS functions such as the contact list, camera, location, and more:

Figure 1.4 – PWA icons on a mobile device (Originally titled "Progressive web apps on my home screen." Created by Jeremy Keith, retrieved from https://www.flickr.com/photos/adactio/42535353742, and licensed and made available under CC BY 2.0 (https://creativecommons.org/licenses/by/2.0/))

A PWA can be installed through a link on any mobile iOS or Android device, as well as on Windows hybrid laptops such as Microsoft Surface. Once they are installed, the user can launch them from their mobile device home screen and enjoy the unique features of the app, which are attributed to the *ServiceWorker* component that is built into each PWA. In the preceding screenshot, the **Twitter Lite** icon is the PWA application shortcut that was installed from the web browser on the mobile device.

> **Service Workers**
>
> Service workers are scripts that run in the background of a user's browser, enabling web application developers to add features such as push notifications, offline caching, mobile device sensor engagement, and a proxy that can handle various network requests from your web application. PWAs utilize service workers to enrich web applications running on mobile devices.

PWAs offer users from a single code base the ability to consume a web application on any desktop screen or mobile device screen with the additional features of offline caching, push notifications, sensor support (such as location, camera, and audio), and contact list access. With such reach supported capabilities, web application developers can deploy their apps easily, immediately, and bypass the mobile application stores.

Google and other browser vendors provide tools to validate the PWAs via their browser developer tool capabilities that are available from within the browser, as well as other guidelines and recommended practices. Developers can generate `MANIFEST.MF` files and JavaScript service worker scripts, which will be added to their web applications. Many enterprise web applications (`https://www.pwastats.com/`) across market verticals such as *Instagram*, *Lyft*, *Twitter*, *eBay*, and others, have already adopted this technology and are seeing many benefits daily. As the leader behind these types of applications, *Google* has created a great baseline (`https://web.dev/progressive-web-apps/`) and checklist for complying with the PWA requirements.

The building blocks of a PWA test plan include those of the solid RWD that were mentioned earlier, along with the following *PWA-specific scenarios*:

- The validation of PWA manifests file correctness (pointing to the home URL, theme, icon, and more).

- The validation of the PWA service workers, which comprises critical components of the PWA application, includes registering for push notifications, caching abilities, and more.

- PWA installation and functionality across the platform and in parallel with the native applications.

- PWAs provide a custom offline page to serve users when they are offline.

- PWAs work with any input type such as a mouse, keyboard, stylus, or touch.

- PWAs work fine with all mobile device sensors such as location services, audio, camera, and more.

- PWAs should be tested against all third-party dependencies such as social media integrations (for instance, Facebook and LinkedIn), other APIs, analytics services, and more.

- The PWA testing of security, privacy policies, and permissions of the app to adhere to Apple and Google requirements.

As you might have gathered, this is a superset of the pillars of an RWD plan with additional PWA-specific testing considerations.

The following code snippet demonstrates a basic service worker registration in JavaScript as part of building the foundation of a PWA application:

```
If ('serviceWorker' in navigator) {
window.addEventListener('load',function(){
navigator.serviceWorker.regisdter('/sw.js').then(function(
   registration) {
//Registration was successful
console.log('ServiceWorker registration with scope:'
            ,registration.scope);
} function(err){
//registration failed 🙁
console.log('ServiceWorker registration failed:',err);
});
});
```

Now that we've established the main web application types that are available for application developers, let's go through the key testing types that need to be considered upon each web application release.

Testing types for web applications

Software testing consists of various types: functional, API, integration, non-functional, unit, accessibility, and ad hoc exploratory testing. In this chapter, we will only discuss the high-level functional and non-functional testing types, while later in the book, we will also cover API testing and other types of testing as part of the specific test automation framework overview. Each of these types can be divided within the traditional testing pyramid and scoped based on whether there is a major release or a small hotfix release on the market.

In this section, we will highlight the key testing considerations across the previously mentioned types as they relate to modern web applications.

With web applications that are intended to run on any kind of desktop and mobile OS and device, covering all angles of the app is crucial to ensure a top-notch user experience.

Web applications are based on continuous interactions between components, UIs (the presentation layer), databases, microservices that communicate through an API gateway with other components, servers, various APIs such as payment, authentications, business workflows (the business layer), and more.

Testing these types of applications that have multiple layers of architecture, as identified earlier, is a challenging task, especially in an Agile and DevOps reality. Multiple personas take part in the software development life cycle, different code changes (that is, pull requests) are submitted many times a day, and this ought to be properly classified and tested.

Functional testing of web applications

Let's go through the key areas of the functional testing category of web applications. Bear in mind that such testing scenarios can be broken into different types of testing, including sanity, regression, smoke, integration, and usability testing by the customer. The scope of the testing suite should be determined by the phase in the **software development life cycle** (**SDLC**), the changes within the software iteration, and the defect history of your web application (that is, stability and reliability).

The following list offers a few suggested testing pillars to consider as part of your web app testing plans. Whether you validate the following scenarios through manual testing or automation, these are the fundamental pillars to ensure that your web apps work well across the entire user journey on your website:

- The website links across the entire website should work fine, including the following:

  - Navigation links

  - Social media links

  - MailTo links

- Website forms to test for relevant pages such as registration forms and order forms:

  - Form field testing (positive/negative inputs)

  - The verification of mandatory filled fields

  - The submission of forms across all platforms (mobile/desktop)

- Testing web application policies regarding cookies:

  - Cookies are deleted when the web cache is cleared

- Business flow verification of the entire user flow within the website:

  - All internal links and user journeys are working

  - UI and layout testing

  - Localization testing

  - The compatibility of the website across all screen sizes and resolutions

  - Usability and user experience testing

The non-functional testing of web applications

Complementing functional testing with non-functional testing is imperative for the quality of your web application. At the end of the day, it does not really matter if your app fails in production either because of a functional crash or due to an availability issue due to load-related defects.

Including all types of testing within **continuous integration** (**CI**) jobs makes all the difference between a high-performing Agile team and a slow one. Such testing types should include both functional and non-functional tests that are running through automation frameworks upon any code changes.

When covering non-functional testing activities, typically, teams should consider security testing (both static and dynamic), performance and load testing, and accessibility. In some practices, teams might consider accessibility as a functional testing type, but regardless of the bucket that these testing types fit, they are all important. And executing as many of them that bring value is part of the definition of a ready and high-quality web application – if they all pass of course 😊.

Security testing

Security testing involves the following:

- Ensuring authorized access to secure pages is kept
- Preventing users from downloading restricted files without appropriate access and authentication
- Terminating user inactivity sessions automatically
- Redirecting a website to encrypted SSL pages, upon the use of SSL certificates
- Adopting industry-proven tests such as OWASP Top 10, CWE, CERT, and others
- Including code quality standards such as JSLint within SAST and DAST (`https://www.jslint.com/`)

Performance and load testing

Performance and load testing involve the following:

- Measuring against benchmarks and KPI web application response times according to different network conditions (web and mobile)
- Load testing your web application to determine its behavior under normal (single-user performance) and peak loads (millions of virtual users)
- Stress testing your web app to determine its breakpoint when it is pushed to beyond normal load at peak time
- Determining how the site recovers from crashes or availability issues

Accessibility testing

Accessibility testing involves the following:

- Covering the most common accessibility rules: WCAG, ADA, 508, and, if in Canada, ACA

- Executing accessibility tests across different platforms and languages (web and mobile)

- Ensuring proper accessibility IDs (web elements) for ease of test automation

As mentioned earlier, the combination of exploratory testing and automated testing of both the functional and non-functional areas of your web application should be included in every organization's test plan. Additionally, this should be continuously maintained to adapt to recent web application changes, defects coming from production, platform changes in the market such as new OS versions or mobile devices, and changes to industry standards such as accessibility and new security rules.

Later in this book, we will cover specific examples and tools to help cover most of the testing types recommended in this section.

After covering the main testing types that are applicable for web applications, in the next section, we will focus on the main differences between using headed browsers and headless browsers throughout the development and testing phases.

Understanding headless and headed browsers within app development and testing

In the same way that web application developers and testers have choices around frameworks and languages, they also have the option to choose whether to exercise their web application against a web browser with its UI loaded (that is, headed) or its UI unloaded (that is, headless).

> **Headless Browsers**
>
> A headless browser is a normal browser that simply does not load its UI during runtime.

The decision regarding how to use the web browser depends on the goal and objectives behind the developer's and tester's actions. We will cover these methods in a bit more detail next.

Choosing between headed browsers and headless browsers

Using a headless browser could be extremely beneficial when there is no need to explore any elements or actions on the browser UI, and the main objective is to ensure that tests or other actions on the browsers are just running properly. Another scenario where headless browsers can become very cost-effective is when running a massive set of tests in parallel where there is no need to *view* the browser UI. Such execution will run much faster due to the savings on memory and other hardware resources that UI browsers typically consume, along with the environment initiation time that each browser would typically take to render the HTML pages. Additionally, you can consider the parallel-testing-at-scale use case as part of a regression build within CI after or in parallel with the UI-based cross-browser testing.

It is important to understand that developers and testers cannot only rely on headless browser testing, which is harder to debug and does not always expose the real end user experience across the different platforms. Combining headed testing with headless testing should be strategically planned and executed by the different teams. All major browser vendors including Google, Mozilla, and Microsoft offer a headless option that the end user can turn on through command-line flags or within the various test automation frameworks such as Selenium and **Puppeteer**.

Selenium offers a nice set of code samples that can be used to launch any of the supported web browsers in headed or headless mode. Here is a sample configuration within the Selenium 4 (`https://github.com/SeleniumHQ/selenium/blob/trunk/javascript/node/selenium-webdriver/chrome.js#L333`) framework that would launch the Chrome browser in headless mode:

```
let driver = new Builder()
.forBrowser('chrome')
.setChromeOptions(new chrome.Options().headless())
.build();
```

Note that, later in the book, as we dive deeper into the Selenium framework, we will learn how to use this framework in both headed and headless modes. In general, most testing frameworks such as Selenium, Playwright, and **Cypress** support the two methods of how to test a web application.

To use the various browsers from the command-line interface, developers and testers can leverage dozens of options to take screenshots, remotely debug a web application, and more.

Here is a simple command-line option that uses the headless Microsoft Edge browser that is built on Chromium to capture a screenshot of the PacktPub website home page:

```
Msedge --headless --disable-gpu -screenshot=c:\[..]\packt.png -
window-size=1280,1696 https://www.packtpub.com/
```

Prior to running the preceding command, please ensure that you have the Edge browser in the system environment path.

As you can see, in *Figure 1.5*, the browser captured the home page with the window size that was specified in the command line:

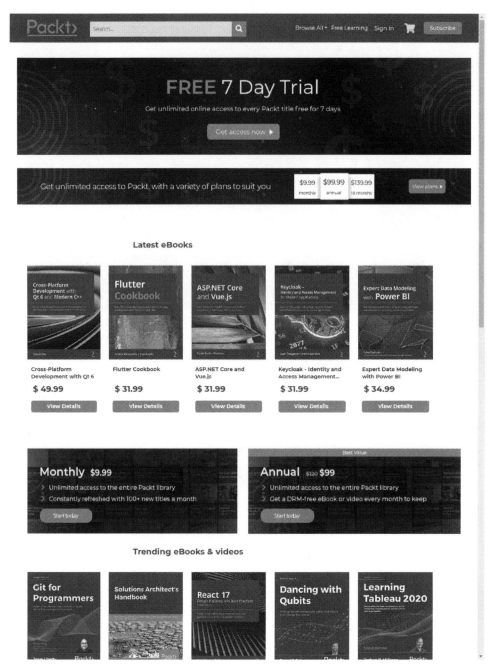

Figure 1.5 – The PacktPub website screen capture using the Edge headless browser CLI

Headless browser testing frameworks

Now that we've established the notion of a headless browser environment that is fast, cost-efficient, and quite easy to use, let's explore an automation framework that works well with the Chrome headless browser, called Puppeteer (`https://developers.google.com/web/tools/puppeteer`). This tool is a node library developed by Google and comes with a high-level API to control headless Chrome over the DevTools protocol. It has all the benefits of the Chrome browser, including form submission, user inputs, along with additional headless-specific features such as measuring the runtime performance of the web application and more.

> **Note**
>
> Microsoft is leading the development of an equivalent framework that is derived from Puppeteer, called **Playwright**. Later in the book, we will examine it in more depth.

To get started with this headless solution, please run the following `npm install` command:

```
npm install puppeteer
```

While installing the solution, developers can start scripting in JavaScript and utilize the APIs available in this framework. Using the following code snippet as an example, developers can automatically navigate to a specific website and capture a screenshot:

```
const puppeteer = require('puppeteer');
(async() => {
const browser = await puppeteer.launch({headless:false});
// default is true
const page = await browser.newPage();
await page.goto('https://www.packtpub.com');
await page.screenshot({path: 'Packt.png'});
await browser.close();
})();
```

If setting the headless flag to false, the execution of the code will launch the built-in Chrome browser.

Figure 1.6 is a screenshot of the preceding code sample that was executed:

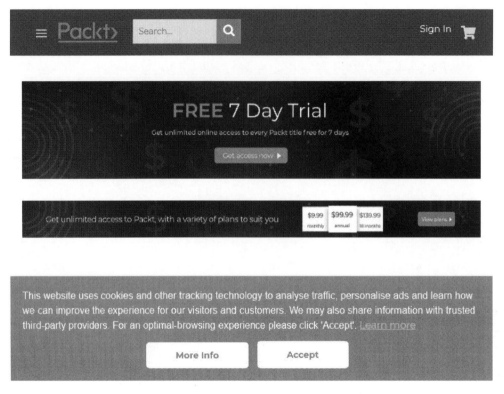

Figure 1.6 – A screenshot of the Packt home page taken through Puppeteer JavaScript
test in headless mode

The preceding example is a simple use case of Puppeteer; however, this framework can extend the DevTools protocol capabilities and generate, through automated code, an HTTP Archive file (HAR) for security, performance, and other web traffic analysis. In the recent Selenium 4 version, as well as within Cypress, developers can also leverage the **Chrome DevTools Protocol (CDP)** to benefit from some of Puppeteer's capabilities.

To generate an HAR file as part of a test automation script, developers should include the following lines of code in their test automation scenarios, after installing the puppeteer-har node module:

```
const puppeteerHar = require('puppeteer-har');
const har = new puppeteerHar(page);
await har.start({path: 'results.har'});
await page.goto('https://www.packtpub.com');
await har.stop();
```

Adding the preceding code to the screenshot example will generate a `results.har` file from the PacktPub website. Developers can use any HAR file viewer to analyze the generated resource or simply add the Google Chrome HAR viewer browser extension.

When examining the generated HAR file, developers can get insights on page load times, page statistics, website requests, and response header details:

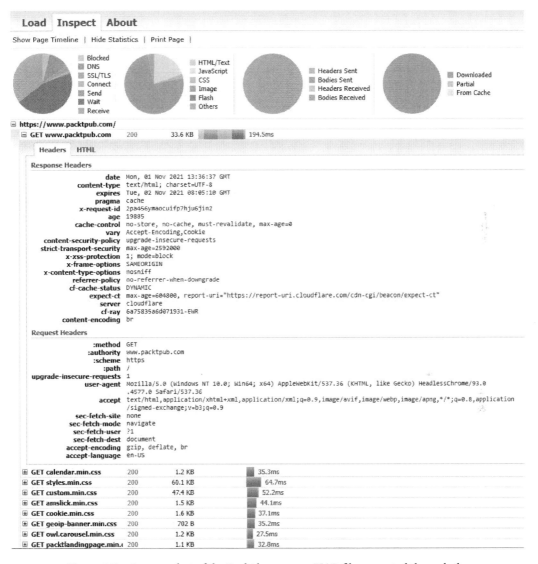

Figure 1.7 – A screenshot of the Packt home page HAR file generated through the automated Puppeteer script

Developers can then use these insights to optimize website performance, detect security vulnerabilities, and more.

As mentioned earlier, Google designed the headless browser tool to help developers test and debug their web applications. Additionally, to succeed in debugging a web application while running in headless mode, Headless browsers provide a remote debugging capability that can be used either manually from the CLI or within the automated JavaScript code:

```
--remote-debugging-port=9222 (example)
```

While running the tests with headless mode and adding this command, developers can use a headed Chrome browser to navigate to `http://localhost:9222` and inspect all the outputs coming from the execution.

Summary

Nowadays, building a winning web application is harder than ever due to the massive digital transformation in progress, and the cost of failure to the brands when something goes wrong. Utilizing all testing types earlier on in the development stages and acknowledging the different methods, tools, and browser-provided capabilities can be a great start in terms of building a quality plan for your web application. Such a plan must cover all the functional and non-functional aspects of testing. Additionally, it should consider cost and time efficiency tools such as headless browser testing, web developer tools, HAR files, and more techniques that were mentioned in this chapter.

Throughout this chapter, we have learned about the advanced web landscape and the new modern application types. We defined and provided insights into responsive web applications, PWAs, and how to properly address the quality of these types of applications. Additionally, we looked at the different testing types that are available to developers and test engineers and broke down each testing type into a web-related use case.

After covering those topics, we then discussed the concept of using headless browsers in conjunction with a headed browser as part of a development workflow to expedite feedback, address environment setup, performance, and stability, and help debug on real browsers more efficiently.

Finally, we closed the chapter with a few statements around overall cross-browser testing considerations.

That concludes this chapter! Hopefully, it will help you learn more about the web application landscape and how to build a proper testing strategy for your future web applications.

In the following chapter, we will unfold the key challenges that web application developers face and explain the reasons behind these challenges.

2
Challenges Faced by Frontend Web Application Developers

Frontend web application developers are tasked with a tough challenge: ensuring that web apps work and perform exceptionally well across all digital channels (web and mobile). In an era when a new desktop web browser version is released into the market every month, with numerous mobile smartphones and OS versions to support, this task is quite hard. Frontend web developers should address both the quality and velocity, as well as the stability of their apps, continuously.

This chapter covers the key challenges modern web application developers face and their root causes. It is specifically designed to cover the constant debate about velocity, quality, and key non-functional challenges that are a pain for developers. By the end of this chapter, you will have an understanding about the common pitfalls in web application quality assurance that covers both the functional aspects, the non-functional ones like performance, and equally important – the security level of the application being built.

This chapter will cover the following topics:

- Web application development challenges
- Coverage challenges for web application developers
- Non-functional challenges in web application development
- Compliance challenges for web applications

Web application development challenges

As highlighted in the previous chapter, the digital transformation over the years has increased the complexities in building top-notch web applications. By top-notch, we mean apps that can function properly across all web browsers, mobile devices, and operating systems, across various environment conditions, and under massive load conditions. In addition, with the rise of digitalization, security and accessibility have become key requirements for any application prior to its release.

In an insightful report (`https://insights.developer.mozilla.org/reports/mdn-browser-compatibility-report-2020.html`) published by two of the leading browser vendors, (Mozilla and Google), it was clear how complicated it is to build a web application that is *compatible* with all technologies and platforms in the market.

One of the top items found in this study was ensuring compatibility with old browsers, even with the old and end-of-life Internet Explorer 11 browser. Next on that list were layout and styling items, which consist of CSS, responsive web layout issues such as viewports, scrolling on responsive web apps, and other UI-related issues.

Layout and styling around CSS were attributed to two main CSS configurations: *Flexbox* and *Grid*.

A comparison between these two configurations can be found at `https://www.geeksforgeeks.org/comparison-between-css-grid-css-flexbox/`.

These two options help developers position UI elements within the web application in ways that can fit different screen sizes, layouts, and platforms. At the URL showing a comparison between the two configurations, there are a few examples of how the HTML code looks in both the implementation of the `<style>` code block and the trade-offs between them. While we won't dive deep into the implementation of CSS types, this item is one of the challenges developers face when building their apps. Developers find it challenging to ensure the CSS sticky and animation grids are consistent among browsers.

CSS sticky elements are used by developers to keep an element fixed on the web page while a user is scrolling throughout the page. Items such as headers and navigation bars or other core elements of the web application could be set as sticky to always be visible and accessible to the user. While this is a great usability feature for developers, this isn't always a compatible feature across browsers on web and mobile.

Other issues that were high on the list were web performance maintainability, web app quality on the Safari browser on mobile platforms, and the item previously covered in *Chapter 1, Cross-Browser Testing Methodologies*: PWAs.

In the following summary graph, for each survey respondent, the report classified their top five categories out of the 12 available. With that in mind, the following shows the top pain points averaged by all respondents that are listed; the IE browser and layout and styling emerged as top challenges.

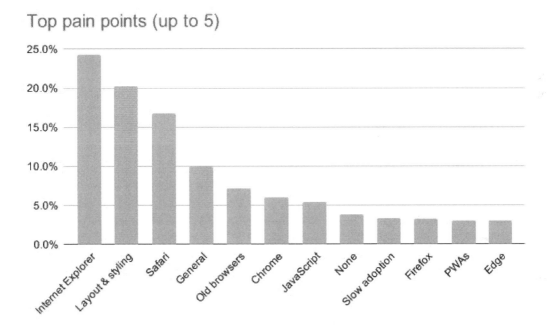

Figure 2.1 – Top pain points for web application developers (source: MDN Web Docs, Mozilla (https://insights.developer.mozilla.org/reports/mdn-browser-compatibility-report-2020.html))

JavaScript is the dominant development language for building web applications, but it is also among the pain points developers tend to highlight. In some cases, the reason is coping with different *ECMAScript* versions that are not always aligned across all browser versions, and sometimes it can be very specific language issues on a given browser version and how that version can be used in each web application scenario.

ECMAScript

ECMAScript is a standard for ensuring the interoperability of web pages across different browsers. JavaScript is, in a sense, an implementation of the original ECMAScript standard. The most recent standard version out there is the ES6 edition (`https://262.ecma-international.org/12.0/`). Web application developers should use this set of standards throughout the implementation phases.

Next, we will dive into additional challenges around market platform coverage, and later in the chapter, we will discuss non-functional related aspects such as security, performance, availability, and accessibility.

Quality vs velocity

An important debate that is agnostic to any software development project is the one that tries to balance between the velocity of the release cycles and the quality of the deliverables. To take the debate forward, practices such as Agile, DevOps, and continuous testing were defined to allow practitioners to better balance release velocity and quality while being able to continuously deliver value to customers. Velocity varies between organizations, and it depends on the application complexity, the scope of the release, and the maturity of the teams working on the release. All these considerations can impact the release frequency (velocity). On the other hand, the quality of the app is something that can be considered infinite because you cannot test each single line of code and use case; therefore, risks are taken all the time. The art of Agile software development is to properly balance the speed and release cadence with the quality criteria that are considered safe to the end users. Test automation is a key enabler for software velocity since it drives faster feedback back to the developers and allows them to gain confidence in their latest code changes as well as the overall application quality from a regression standpoint. When product management and engineering work together with the QA teams to define a software iteration cadence of, for example, every 2 weeks, the teams must plan these iterations carefully and allocate room for test automation development and execution so that quality goals match the velocity ones with minimal risks.

Coverage challenges for web application developers

An additional challenge that developers face is **coverage** across web and mobile operating systems and platforms. On a monthly basis, both Google (`https://www.chromestatus.com/features/schedule`) and Mozilla (`https://wiki.mozilla.org/Release_Management/Calendar`) release public **General Availability** (**GA**) and beta versions to the market. Such releases disrupt the web applications in many cases and require developers to ensure that the new versions are still compliant with their apps. As web traffic is higher on mobile platforms nowadays, ensuring the continuous quality of the web application across different iOS and Android devices and OS versions is key to success.

The following figure shows the browser market share month on month for the period from October 2020 to October 2021:

Figure 2.2 – Browser market share worldwide, all platforms (source: Statcounter GlobalStats)

Google Chrome is the most used browser in the market, but with a monthly release cadence, the cost of failure is high; hence, developers and testers must keep up with the newly introduced browsers and features. After the Apple Safari browser, which holds a significant market share, the bigger problem is the rest of the market share is distributed across five or six browser vendors with similar levels of adoption. This mandates proper attention to the other less popular browsers such as Opera and Samsung internet since these browsers carry similar market share as Firefox and Edge.

In the following market share snippet, also from *Statcounter* (`https://gs.statcounter.com/browser-market-share/mobile/worldwide`), we can see a different market segmentation across browsers when we only focus on mobile platforms:

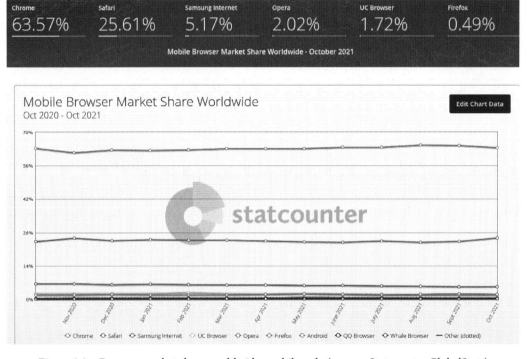

Figure 2.3 – Browser market share worldwide, mobile only (source: Statcounter GlobalStats)

In the preceding screenshot, Google Chrome on Android is leading the industry, with the second highest market adoption rate being seen for Safari WebKit, and Samsung Internet Browser.

We should now also consider on top of the above web browser compatibility challenge, the ever-growing mobile challenge with so many Android device providers globally, and the numerous iPhones and iPads on the market.

Based on the *Statcounter* market share analysis of mobile device providers (`https://gs.statcounter.com/vendor-market-share/mobile`), Apple holds around 28% of the global mobile market share, which leaves the remainder of the market to various Android providers, such as Samsung, Xiaomi, and Huawei, among others. Some of these vendors (for example, Samsung) provide their own built-in browsers, and others support Chrome, Opera, Firefox, and UC browsers running on their devices.

With the various types of web applications that were introduced in *Chapter 1, Cross-Browser Testing Methodologies*, web developers need to ensure that regardless of whether they are building a responsive web app, a PWA, or a standard web application, they should all work perfectly well across the different mobile and web platforms.

To be able to at least know where to focus the platforms testing on in this complex marketplace, it is highly recommended to periodically obtain a web traffic analytics report that can provide developers and testers visibility into the top user agents and platforms that are visiting the websites, and also, from which country or location they originate. It's known that each geography has a different mobile and web market share; therefore, knowing which users visit your website the most is key to building a proper development and testing lab.

From market analytics sources like the one in *Figure 2.4*, developers and testers can realize the breakdown of mobile platform per country and better plan their testing.

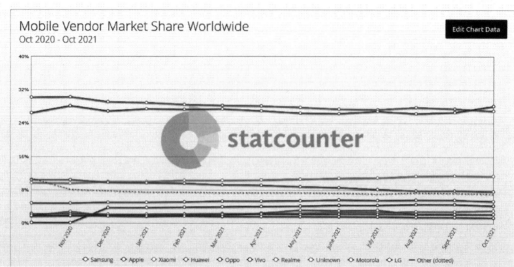

Figure 2.4 – Mobile vendor market share worldwide (source: Statcounter GlobalStats retrieved from https://gs.statcounter.com/vendor-market-share/mobile)

Note that on top of the standard web and mobile platforms, there is a new set of mobile devices called *foldables*. Such devices are unique in many ways, having two layout features (folded and unfolded) and the ability to run up to three applications in the foreground in parallel, including the browser; therefore, these devices need to be also considered as part of the web application development and testing. Another growing trend in the market is a new type of framework called Flutter, (some organizations might consider React Native as an alternative to Flutter). The challenge with such apps is that while a single code base can produce multiple binaries that run on mobile devices and desktop browsers, such apps are built with the *Dart* language and use a unique architecture developed by Google that web application developers are not yet familiar with.

Flutter

Flutter is Google's free and open source UI framework for developing cross-platform rich applications from a single code base. A Flutter application can be compiled into a mobile Android and iOS binary, as well as a desktop and Linux application. The Flutter framework consists of various reusable UI elements, such as sliders, buttons, and text inputs. Developers building mobile applications with the Flutter framework will do so using a programming language called Dart. You can read more about Flutter architecture here: `https://flutter.dev/docs/resources/architectural-overview`

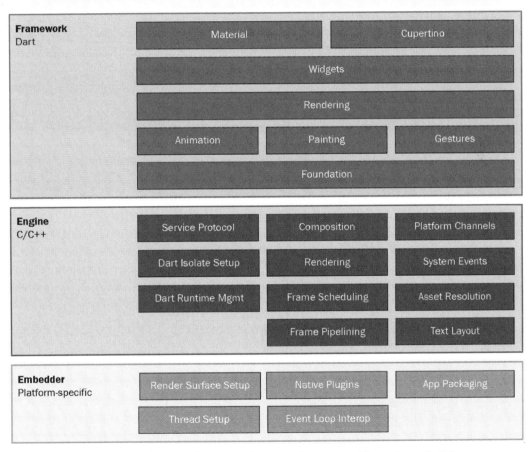

Figure 2.5 – Flutter application architecture (source: the Flutter.dev website)

With the aforementioned challenges in mind, it's also important to note the growing selection of web development frameworks as highlighted in *Chapter 1, Cross-Browser Testing Methodologies*, which includes Vue, React, and Ember. This is an additional challenge for developers who need to select a framework that will grow with their web applications for the long term. There is a lot at stake when choosing the right technology.

Let's summarize the high-level pain points that we've covered so far in this chapter:

- Compatibility with new and trending digital platforms as well as old browser support
- Coverage strategy for web and mobile platforms
- Style and layout across different browser versions and OS versions (CSS, animation grids)
- JavaScript and ECMAScript compatibility across browsers
- Complexities around new types of web applications, including PWAs and Flutter
- Choosing the right web development framework

Now that we have understood these key functional challenges, let's learn about non-functional challenges web application developers face.

Non-functional challenges in web application development

In addition to the challenges mentioned so far, web application developers are also required to continuously guarantee high-performing web applications that are always on and available, as well as an app that 100% adheres to complex accessibility requirements. In this section, we will explore performance and accessibility challenges across web applications.

Performance challenges

For many years, the industry considered a response time of more than 3 seconds for a web application to load (whether running on a desktop browser or a mobile browser) to cause a customer to move to a different website. Research conducted by *Limelight Networks*, which was featured in an online document published by Broadcom (`https://docs.broadcom.com/doc/its-all-about-the-user-experience`), shows the different time thresholds and the patience levels of end users today when using web applications. The majority of users will not be willing to wait more than 3-5 seconds for a website to load. For websites that exceed these thresholds, users will switch to an alternative website.

Ensuring high-performing web apps with the growing load and usage that is experienced nowadays is a huge challenge for developers. Developers should consider performance and availability as part of the web application design, think about ways to optimize load times across the different web pages in a web application, consider multiple platforms across geographies and network conditions, and consider peak usage versus standard usage. Businesses consider data-driven strategies to enhance the **user and customer experience** (**UX/CX**) by providing the most relevant, highly downloaded content at the top of their web applications to keep users engaged and satisfied.

Performance testing as well as load/stress testing is no longer simply a nice-to-have or an activity that can be left to the end of the software sprint; rather, it needs to be shifted to the early stages of the sprint. Identifying bottlenecks and performance issues against agreed benchmarks and **key performance indicators** (**KPIs**) late in the cycle is a very risky and expensive practice. Finding the root causes of such issues and fixing them is a highly time-consuming activity for developers; hence, this type of testing must be given equal importance among other functional testing processes.

Developers have various mature performance testing tools that perfectly integrate with the CI and **Continuous Deployment** (**CD**) tool stack that can be adopted and used regularly to ensure the continuous performance of web applications. In addition, web browser vendors, including Google, Microsoft, Mozilla, and Apple, provide built-in developer tools that can cover performance and monitoring aspects, as well as accessibility and PWA compliance.

Accessibility challenges

Organizations and practitioners might argue that accessibility is not a non-functional requirement but rather a function of the app that needs to be always covered. Regardless of the segment or testing type in which we classify accessibility testing, this type of testing, like performance testing, should be part of any software sprint and automated and shifted left as early as possible in the development cycle. Web and mobile accessibility is not an option but a key requirement that comes with massive fines and business implications when done wrong.

Based on the ADA compliance law website (`https://getadaaccessible.com/ada-compliance-law-and-penalties/`), organizations can expect fines of $55,000 for their first WCAG violation and/or 508 non-compliance, with a double fine of $110,000 for any subsequent violation.

> **WCAG**
>
> WCAG is a wide range of recommendations that can help make websites more accessible for impaired users and people with disabilities. W3C stands behind the definition of the rules, and constantly updates and maintains them. These rules are technology agnostic and are developed to ensure that people who suffer from low vision, deafness and hearing loss, cognitive limitations, and other issues can also consume website content at all times.

The WCAG (`https://www.w3.org/TR/WCAG21/`) organization has defined and continuously maintained its requirements around web accessibility to ensure that any user with any kind of disability can consume the web application content, engage with the application across any form factor, and get the same value from the web as any other user. Developers are required to keep accessibility at the front of their minds when adding any new field or element to their web application. They are required to provide accessibility IDs, tooltips, voice-over functionality for screen readers, and much more. To comply with these accessibility requirements, product managers, R&D managers, and businesses need to properly allocate time within the sprint to allow developers to properly implement their features and meet these guidelines.

At the other end, software testers must continuously test and cover the accessibility aspects of the web applications using automated software and other exploratory techniques.

There are several tools available for automatically checking for accessibility issues. Here is an example of an accessibility issue that can be easily and automatically captured through the Google Chrome built-in Lighthouse tool running against a given website, in this case, `http://msn.com`. As identified by the scan, the contrast ratio between the background and foreground colors is insufficient, which will make it hard for visually impaired users to see the images on the website:

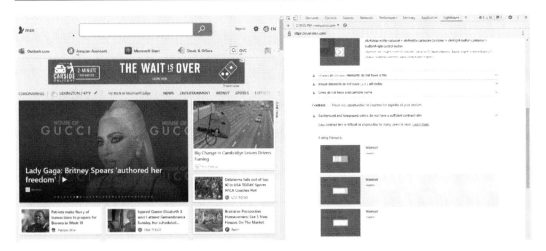

Figure 2.6 – Accessibility scan via the Google Lighthouse tool on the msn.com website

Web testing for accessibility can be done free today by using the open source **AXE** (`https://www.deque.com/axe/`) framework from Deque. Running this tool in conjunction with the W3C Selenium framework provides both functional and accessibility coverage. The AXE plugin was also added to the Cypress plugin store and allows developers and test engineers to create JavaScript test code that validates both the functionality of a web application as well as its accessibility level.

Later in the book, we will cover in more depth how Selenium and Cypress can help web application developers validate many of the challenges highlighted in this chapter.

Now that we've looked at some of the non-functional challenges faced by developers during testing, let's look at some compliance challenges.

Compliance challenges for web applications

Data privacy and cyber security have grown to become two of the biggest challenges and concerns for web and mobile application developers. Failing to protect a web application from significant data breaches and other vulnerabilities can mean the difference between a living business and a failing one. Since security and data privacy is a 24/7 risk, web application developers must build security early into the functionality of their apps, leverage **Static Application Security Testing (SAST)** and **Dynamic Application Security Testing (DAST)** tools, and maintain their code continuously.

SAST

SAST is a method for inspecting and analyzing application source code, byte code, and binaries for coding and design conditions to determine security vulnerabilities. Unlike DAST, SAST is also known as a *white box* testing approach that scans the source code of the application in a non-running state.

DAST

DAST is a method that is also known as *black box* testing. It is designed to scan the source code of a running and compiled application. It tests the application software from the outside in, unlike SAST, which tests the application code from the inside out. To run a DAST scan, developers need a running and compiled application made available to them.

There is no good or bad with SAST and DAST: both are important and provide value to developers in the different stages of the software development life cycle.

Developers are adopting static and dynamic code analysis tools more than ever and are executing security scans across their web apps to ensure high security and compliance with standards.

Google is enhancing its data privacy restrictions, and GDPR requirements are becoming stricter across Europe and North America. Developers should better understand the various risks and rules around data privacy and security across different market segments; for example, if the web application is intended for healthcare, then regulations such as **Health Insurance Portability and Accountability Act (HIPAA)** are relevant, and for financial industries and payments web applications, Payment Card Industry Data Security Standard (*PCI DSS*) is relevant.

Based on a **Forrester** report (`https://www.forrester.com/report/Using-AI-For-Evil/RES143162`), cyberattacks will soon be utilizing AI to attack businesses in more sophisticated ways, and with greater implications for the business.

Also, with the rise in 5G and IoT, more data streaming services are out there and being consumed across automotive infotainment systems, such as *Apple CarPlay, Android Auto,* and other devices. This big data and greater exposure bring higher risks to the business.

Developers and software testers should embrace coding standards and static and dynamic analysis of their source code earlier in their development cycle. There are many maintained security compliances, including Common Weakness Enumeration (CWE), **Open Web Application Security Project (OWASP** (`https://owasp.org/www-project-top-ten/`), and other market-specific compliances such as those mentioned earlier, to be executed and scanned within the CI/CD pipelines.

The following figure shows the trend summary of security vulnerabilities, revealing that there are a lot of shifts in security issues across applications over time:

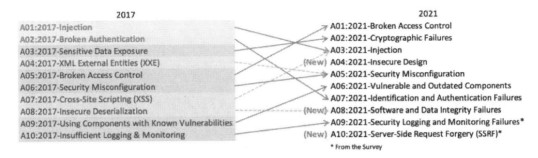

Figure 2.7 – OWASP top 10 security vulnerabilities
(source: OWASP.org - https://owasp.org/www-project-top-ten/)

As shown in the preceding figure, broken access control has shifted from being fifth on the OWASP list to first in 2021. Such shifts are attributed to the number of incidents that are being reported in the market across applications. More occurrences of such cases contribute to moving such risks higher on the list of issues. The *broken access control* vulnerability is part of the **common weakness enumerations** (**CWE**) set of security rules that applications should cover as part of their security testing. There are many areas under that rule that can cause a broken access vulnerability. Based on OWASP documentation, allowing attackers to bypass access control by modifying a URL, permitting a view or edit of someone else's account, or elevation of privilege through acting as a user without being logged in, can result in the above security issue.

Developers should in such cases enforce record ownership as part of the web application model access control or disable a web server directory listing to ensure file metadata and backup files are not present within web roots.

Security, data privacy, and compliance are huge challenges and great business risks, and as such, must be part of web developers' objectives and strategy. As identified previously, security threats are dynamic and can vary across segments; hence, it is critical to train web application developers on security topics, mitigation of such vulnerabilities, and provide them with access to online training tools around security such as *Secure Code Warrior* (`https://www.securecodewarrior.com/`) and others.

Summary

Web application developers today are not only required to be highly skilled JavaScript developers, but also trained and aware of many other considerations, to ensure that a web application is successful, high-performing, and secure.

In this chapter, we covered the various challenges that developers should not only be aware of but need to plan for, as part of their ongoing software iterations. We specifically covered the functional challenges involved in building a winning web application, such as coverage and cross-browser compatibility, as well as the layout and styling, such as CSS, of web applications. We then touched on JavaScript coding challenges before moving on to non-functional challenges. These non-functional challenges included the performance, accessibility, and security of web applications, and what web application developers should consider daily to prevent such issues.

Keep in mind that all the challenges that were covered in this chapter are relevant for a moment in time – security risks change, accessibility requirements change, and so do functional issues across new browsers and mobile platforms. Continuous coverage of the previously mentioned challenges as part of a quality strategy can ensure ongoing application functionality, performance, and security.

When building a quality plan for your web application, developers, testers, and product management must huddle together and ensure that all of the considerations covered earlier in this chapter are addressed and have dedicated owners.

In the following chapter, we will start covering the top market cross-browser test automation frameworks: Selenium, Playwright, Cypress, and Puppeteer.

3
Top Web Test Automation Frameworks

When it comes to end-to-end test automation frameworks, frontend developers have a variety of choices to pick from. The open source community continues to innovate, as well as leverage, existing technologies to enhance testing frameworks and offer more coverage and depth to practitioners.

This chapter focuses on the top four leading open source frameworks in the market and provides an intermediate tutorial on how to get started with each of these. Since web developers have so many choices around testing their application code, it is very important that they understand the architecture and fundamentals of the top frameworks out there, so they can make guided decisions.

After reading this chapter, you will know how to get started with the four leading JavaScript open source test automation frameworks and run a basic test scenario on a web browser.

This chapter is specifically designed to cover the following:

- An overview of the web testing market
- Getting started with the Selenium WebDriver framework
- Getting started with the Cypress framework
- Getting started with the Google Puppeteer framework
- Getting started with the Microsoft Playwright framework

An overview of the web testing market

The web testing market constantly changes, and newer versions of existing frameworks are being developed with brand new solutions. A great resource to learn about what's trending, what's declining, and how big the community is behind leading open source technologies is the npm trends website (`https://www.npmtrends.com/site`). When focusing on the top four frameworks available for frontend developers that support JavaScript, at the time of writing this book, Cypress emerges as the leading framework. As highlighted in an npm trends report (`https://www.npmtrends.com/cypress-vs-playwright-vs-selenium-webdriver-vs-puppeteer`), Cypress has over 3 million weekly downloads compared to **Selenium WebDriver**, which has just over 2 million downloads. Keep in mind that we are only showing in this resource the JavaScript flavor of these frameworks. For frameworks such as Selenium and Playwright that support more language bindings, the market share and downloads will probably be higher; however, here we are focusing only on JavaScript testing:

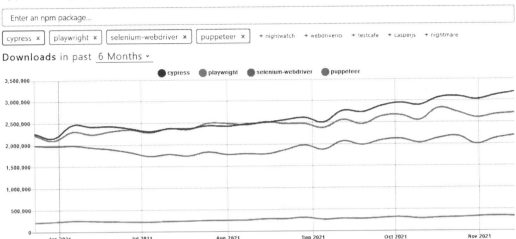

Figure 3.1 – npmtrends frameworks comparison – Cypress, Playwright, Selenium, and Puppeteer (source: `https://www.npmtrends.com/cypress-vs-playwright-vs-selenium-webdriver-vs-puppeteer`)

It is not only the number of downloads that helps determine the popularity of one framework over another, but also the number of ratings (known as stars) each repository on GitHub receives, the last change made to the framework, the number of versions, and other factors. The decision of a frontend developer to go with one framework over another is larger than just the stats behind the framework on GitHub and the number of downloads, but such stats do help us to realize whether a technology is backed by a community, and whether it's being adopted. In addition to these stats, a user would obviously need to perform proofs of concept, understand the best fit for their needs, and other requirements. In *Chapter 7, Core Capabilities of the Leading JavaScript Test Automation Frameworks*, we will dive deeper into ways to better compare frameworks and match each one based on relevant considerations.

While in the previous statistics and this book we are only focusing on the four leading open source frameworks, it's important to note that the market is flooded with dozens of additional open source frameworks, as well as many commercial tools that can be used for cross-browser testing, such as WebDriver.io, TestCafe, and NightWatch.js. These are not part of the scope of this book.

As Gleb Bahmutov classifies the four different frameworks in his blog (`https://glebbahmutov.com/blog/cypress-vs-other-test-runners/`), it is important to understand some of the fundamental differences between the four technologies.

While Selenium and its underlying frameworks are built on the **WebDriver** protocol and provide maximum cross-browser platform coverage and various language bindings, this framework is known to be flakier than Cypress, as well as slower from a test execution performance perspective. On the other hand, **Playwright** and **Puppeteer** are built on top of the **Chrome DevTools Protocol (CDP)**, which gives them the advantage of gaining deep coverage of inner features of browsers, as well as enhanced debugging abilities. Cypress is unique in its architecture since it is a JavaScript framework that runs on the browser itself, making the execution performance extremely fast, and the debugging, including the **document object model (DOM)** access, great. Cypress is also known for its test reliability and low flakiness – it is also a framework that utilizes a flakiness test filter that comes with the framework itself:

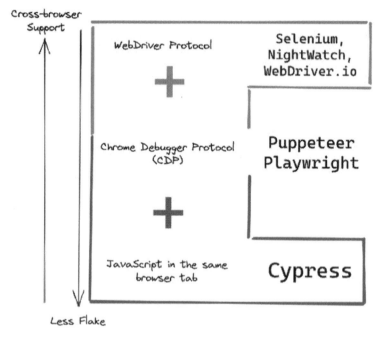

Figure 3.2 – High-level classification of cross-browser testing frameworks (sourced from Gleb Bahmutov: https://glebbahmutov.com/blog/cypress-vs-other-test-runners/)

Now that we've classified the web testing landscape at a high level and examined the high-level architecture of each framework, let's dive into the frameworks and learn how to install and get started with them.

Getting started with the Selenium WebDriver framework

To get started with Selenium, you'll need to follow a number of steps that include the installation of the framework, as well as setting up the grid for the specific browser drivers on which you would like to run your tests (Chrome, Firefox, Safari, or Edge).

Your main website to learn from and get started with Selenium is `https://www.selenium.dev/`. From this link, you will be able to download the relevant driver, see the latest release notes, obtain documentation and code samples, and more.

As you'll learn in this chapter, and even more so later in this book, the Selenium framework consists of three main components:

- **Selenium WebDriver**: This is a collection of several language bindings to drive different browsers for testing purposes, as well as the individual browsers controlling code.

- **Selenium Grid**: This is a Selenium framework component that is designed to distribute and scale test automation by running tests in parallel across different combinations of browsers/OS versions.

- **Selenium IDE**: This is a quick ramp-up solution that through recording helps generate, the first basic Selenium scripts through a browser plugin, with no lines of code needing to be written.

In this chapter, we will only cover Selenium WebDriver and Selenium Grid. Selenium IDE is a basic entry-level browser plugin that allows beginners to record their first Selenium script without writing a single line of code. Once the script is recorded, they can copy the code to their IDE and continue building on top of it using code.

Setting up Selenium WebDriver

To install the Selenium libraries, please run the following command from your desktop **command-line interface (CLI)**:

```
npm install selenium-webdriver
```

Selenium WebDriver is a recommended W3C testing technology that is intended to drive native browsers effectively and in adherence to the W3C standards. This conformance ensures that all scripts across different browsers are written in the same way and are simple to use.

As illustrated in the Selenium provided architecture (`https://www.selenium.dev/documentation/webdriver/understanding_the_components/`), a test framework that implements the WebDriver technology would drive the tests through an installed Selenium server that communicates with a specific browser driver (for example, a Chrome or Firefox driver):

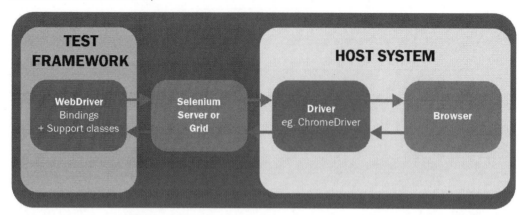

Figure 3.3 – Selenium WebDriver framework components and architecture (sourced from selenium.dev)

Now that we have installed the Selenium framework locally, let's move on to the next steps.

Download any of the WebDriver that you're interested in using locally, for example, the Chrome driver from the following URL: (`https://www.selenium.dev/documentation/getting_started/installing_browser_drivers/`). Once downloaded and installed, make sure to set the path to where the driver is placed to ease the execution from the CLI, as indicated here:

```
Setx PATH "%PATH";c:\users\ekinsbruner\WebDriver\bin"
```

Now that we've installed the Selenium package and a specific browser driver, let's run the first basic test written in JavaScript. Next, we will enhance the project to run within a grid across more than one browser.

From your CLI (Windows machine), launch the Google `chromedriver`:

```
chromedriver
```

You should see a prompt in your CLI with the following text:

```
"Started ChromeDriver (v2.0) on port 9515"
```

The version number in the output would obviously match the version you downloaded from the previous URL.

Now that `chromedriver` is running, run the following JavaScript Selenium scenario from any of your preferred environments. It can be from Visual Studio Code, Eclipse, IntelliJ Idea, or from a simple command line. Note that you would also need to have installed `node.js` on your local machine. I named the file `GoogleSelenium.js`:

```javascript
const {By,Key,Builder} = require("selenium-webdriver");
require("chromedriver");

async function example(){

    var searchString = "packt publishing";

    //To wait for browser to build and launch properly
    let driver =
      await new Builder().forBrowser("chrome").build();

    //To fetch http://google.com from the browser with
    //our code.
    await driver.get("http://google.com");

    //To send a search query by passing the value in
    //searchString.
    await driver.findElement(By.name("q")).sendKeys(
      searchString,Key.RETURN);

    //Verify the page title and print it
    var title = await driver.getTitle();
    console.log('Title is:',title);

    //It is always a safe practice to quit the browser
    //after execution
    await driver.quit();

}

example()
```

To run the preceding test that open a Chrome browser and search for Packt publishing, simply run the following command:

```
node GoogleSelenium.js
```

If there are no issues within your environment, you should see the Chrome browser launched and the preceding test running. At the end of the test, you will also get the following prompt to your CLI:

```
C:\Users\ekinsbruner\WebDriver>node GoogleSelenium.js

DevTools listening on ws://127.0.0.1:65288/devtools/browser/d36984d8-3089-4f53-989e-20d407458170
Packt | Programming Books, eBooks & Videos for Developers
```

Figure 3.4 – First Selenium test execution example in JavaScript

Note that all the previous scenarios could have been similarly executed against *Mozilla geckodriver* upon installation of the driver.

Node.js

Based on the Wikipedia definition (`https://en.wikipedia.org/wiki/Node.js`), Node.js is an open source, cross-platform, backend JavaScript runtime environment that executes JavaScript code outside of a web browser. In the previous example, we used the `node` command to run the Selenium script from a CLI outside of the browser.

Selenium Grid

Let's scale the previous execution example to run using Selenium Grid's capabilities

The Grid option can be set up as standalone or as a hub with nodes. We will look at the standalone option. On a simple setup of a Selenium local Grid, the Selenium server will listen by default at `http://localhost:4444` and detect any installed drivers that the developer downloaded and added to their machine `PATH`.

After downloading the `selenium-server` JAR file from the Selenium website, simply run the following command to launch the server:

```
java -jar WebDriver\bin\selenium-server-4.1.0.jar standalone
```

Do make sure prior to running the command, that the relevant drivers you wish to run against are launched in the background (for example, Chrome, Gecko, or Edge). Please also ensure you have Java installed on your machine prior to running the preceding command.

You should see the following prompt in your CLI:

```
C:\Users\ekinsbruner>java -jar WebDriver\bin\selenium-server-4.1.0.jar standalone
11:51:32.906 INFO [LoggingOptions.configureLogEncoding] - Using the system default encoding
11:51:32.909 INFO [OpenTelemetryTracer.createTracer] - Using OpenTelemetry for tracing
11:51:34.116 INFO [NodeOptions.getSessionFactories] - Detected 12 available processors
11:51:34.147 INFO [NodeOptions.discoverDrivers] - Discovered 2 driver(s)
11:51:34.162 INFO [NodeOptions.report] - Adding Chrome for {"browserName": "chrome"} 12 times
11:51:34.163 INFO [NodeOptions.report] - Adding Firefox for {"browserName": "firefox"} 12 times
11:51:34.306 INFO [Node.<init>] - Binding additional locator mechanisms: name, id, relative
11:51:34.317 INFO [LocalDistributor.add] - Added node 2d300760-7c2a-4f6a-8cf2-c530e49290ef at http://192.168.1.157:4444. Health check every 120s
11:51:34.317 INFO [GridModel.setAvailability] - Switching node 2d300760-7c2a-4f6a-8cf2-c530e49290ef (uri: http://192.168.1.157:4444) from DOWN to UP
11:51:34.801 INFO [Standalone.execute] - Started Selenium Standalone 4.1.0 (revision 87802e897b): http://192.168.1.157:4444
```

Figure 3.5 – Launching output of Selenium Grid command-line execution

Once the Grid command has been executed and assuming all local drivers were installed and launched successfully, you should be able to see the following output on your browser when navigating to `localhost:4444`:

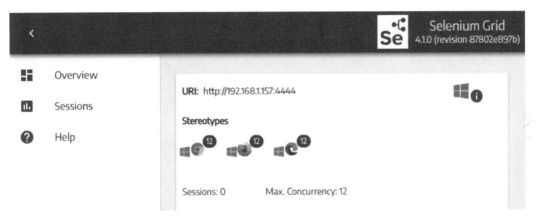

Figure 3.6 – Local Selenium Grid output within a browser

To run a code sample against a *Grid* of browsers, you will need to modify your code and point the WebdDriver URL to the local host Selenium grid:

```
let driver = await new webdriver.builder()
    .forBrowser(' chrome')
    .usingServer('http://localhost:4444/wd/hub')
    .build();
```

When running the new project when the grid is set as the target driver, the test would run against the browsers that are registered in that grid, as shown in *Figure 3.6*.

Lastly, developers can easily configure their desired capabilities when using larger grids and trying to run their Selenium tests in parallel using the supported W3C capabilities (https://w3c.github.io/webdriver/). Selenium supports a wide range of capabilities that allow the test to run across different and complex configurations. To learn about the supported driver capabilities, please visit https://www.selenium.dev/documentation/webdriver/capabilities/driver_specific_capabilities/.

In the below subset table taken from the W3C documentation (https://w3c.github.io/webdriver/#capabilities), you can see some of the common WebDriver capability that a Selenium test would need to use in order to launch a specific browser with a specific version:

Capability	Key	Value Type	Description
Browser name	"browserName"	string	Identifies the user agent.
Browser version	"browserVersion"	string	Identifies the version of the user agent.
Platform name	"platformName"	string	Identifies the operating system of the endpoint node.
Accept insecure TLS certificates	"acceptInsecureCerts"	boolean	Indicates whether untrusted and self-signed TLS certificates are implicitly trusted on navigation for the duration of the session.
Page load strategy	"pageLoadStrategy"	string	Defines the current session's page load strategy.
Proxy configuration	"proxy"	JSON Object	Defines the current session's proxy configuration.
Window dimensioning/positioning	"setWindowRect"	boolean	Indicates whether the remote end supports all of the resizing and repositioning commands.
Session timeouts	"timeouts"	JSON Object	Describes the timeouts imposed on certain session operations.
Strict file interactability	"strictFileInteractability"	boolean	Defines the current session's strict file interactability.
Unhandled prompt behavior	"unhandledPromptBehavior"	string	Describes the current session's user prompt handler. Defaults to the dismiss and notify state.

Figure 3.7 – W3C WebDriver supported capabilities (sourced from W3C - https://w3c.github.io/webdriver/#capabilities)

Selenium is a rich framework and while we are focusing on JavaScript in this chapter (and book), the framework fully supports multiple language bindings, including C#, Python, Ruby, and Java. It also supports all the different browsers that are out there.

To better develop Selenium code, developers should leverage best practices including the **page object model** (**POM**), the use of relative locators that were introduced in Selenium 4, the use of reliable locators out of the eight types that are supported by Selenium, and more. Later in the book, we will cover advanced practices with Selenium, and I expand on these items.

Selenium-Supported Element Locators

Selenium supports the use of finding elements across the following element types:

ID, name, tagName, className, linkText, partialLinkText, xpath, and cssSelector

For example, to search for an element on the website under test, a developer would use the following command:

driver.find_elements(By.XPATH, //button)

Now that we've gone through the basics of Selenium WebDriver and Selenium Grid, let's continue with an introduction to the Cypress framework.

Getting started with the Cypress framework

As noted earlier in the chapter, Cypress (https://www.cypress.io/) is by far the fastest and most adopted cross-browser frontend JavaScript testing framework. It is a developer-friendly, fast execution solution by design, and runs on the browser. In this section, we will learn how to install, set up, and run the first Cypress test in JavaScript. Note that Cypress also supports **TypeScript** and can be configured to run with the Cucumber BDD framework as well.

To get started with Cypress, please run the following command to install the node package on your machine:

```
npm install cypress --save-dev
```

Similar to Selenium and JavaScript, Cypress also requires Node.js to be installed on the local machine to run the Cypress tests. If you do not have Node.js installed, please make sure that, in addition to the installation of Cypress, you install it as a dependency as well.

Once the Cypress framework is installed, users can drive the tests either through an IDE such as IntelliJ or Visual Studio Code or through the CLI/Jenkins.

From the CLI, users can launch the GUI version of Cypress and launch any tests that are available in the testing directory or connect the Cypress framework with the online Cypress web dashboard.

We can launch the Cypress GUI by using the following command:

```
npx cypress open
```

Upon execution of this command, the Cypress GUI will launch as follows:

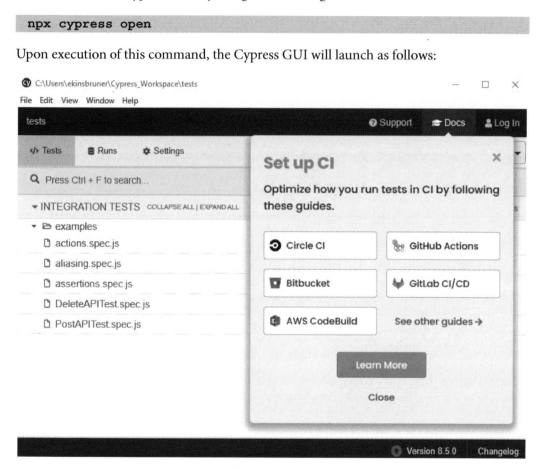

Figure 3.8 – Cypress GUI interface when launched from the CLI

When a user clicks on any of the available JavaScript tests on the left panel under **INTEGRATION TESTS,** the execution will immediately start on a local browser. Users who have multiple browsers installed locally can define which of these will be used for the target executions.

The following is a screenshot of a live execution on a local browser using Cypress:

Figure 3.9 – Cypress live execution of a JavaScript test scenario on a local browser

To run the exact same test spec, you can also use the following command line:

```
Cypress run --spec .\cypress\tests\cypress\integration\
examples\actions.spec.js
```

If you want to get started with a basic test spec that you can use with Cypress, the basic installation comes with a set of pre-defined scenarios. Many of them use the `https://example.cypress.io` website as a target to learn and ramp up with the frameworks and their APIs. Here is basic test code that you can use:

```
describe('My First Test', () => {
    it('Gets, types and asserts', () => {
        cy.visit('https://example.cypress.io')


        cy.contains('type').click()


        // Should be on a new URL which includes
        // '/commands/actions'
        cy.url().should('include', '/commands/actions')


        // Get an input, type into it and verify that the value
```

```
// has been updated
cy.get('.action-email')
    .type('fake@email.com')
    .should('have.value', 'fake@email.com')
})
})
```

To learn more about the basic steps that you can do with Cypress, visit (https://docs. cypress.io/guides/getting-started/writing-your-first-test#Add-a-test-file).

Now that we've covered the basics of Cypress, let's briefly explore some additional capabilities of this framework. Later in the book, we will dive much deeper into using the advanced features of the Cypress framework.

Important features of Cypress

A unique and very powerful feature that Cypress offers developers as part of the debugging and real-time feedback from the web application is *Time Travel*.

Time travel allows developers to hover their mouse over commands on the left panel of the test runner and view in real time what happened on the web application, including DOM snapshots and other debugging insights. Such a capability allows developers to debug their web applications step by step and fix issues in real time. The following is a screenshot of a mouse hover action on a test step in the left panel of the test runner, with synchronized action visibility on the right side, as it occurred on the web application under test:

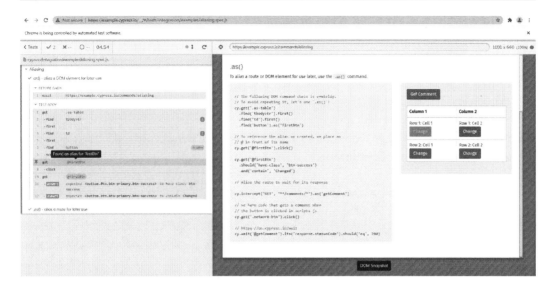

Figure 3.10 – Cypress time travel example (mouse hover action in sync with web DOM tree)

Developers who wish to expand the abilities of Cypress and run tests in parallel, examine flaky tests, and track test execution history, can easily connect their Cypress framework to the web-based Cypress dashboard, and more. From the Cypress UI test runner, developers would sign in with email or GitHub credentials and be able to get started. Cypress offers through its web portal multiple types of reporting dashboards that are add-ons and require a paid license as opposed to the free open source framework covered earlier.

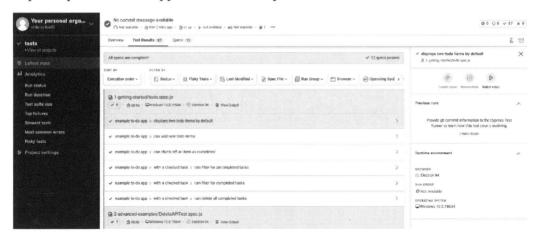

Figure 3.11 – Cypress dashboard user interface and capabilities

Now that we've covered the basics of Cypress, let's briefly explore some of the additional capabilities of this framework.

Cypress offers developers the ability to create component test scenarios (`https://docs.cypress.io/guides/component-testing/introduction#Getting-Started`). Such tests are the middle layer between unit and integration tests that allows us to test the quality of a single component within a web application. The capability of component testing is still being built by Cypress, but developers can already start using it by running Cypress with the relevant command-line option, as follows:

```
npx cypress open-ct
```

Do note, that prior to running the preceding command, a project needs to be set up according to the Cypress guidelines. The following image shows the Cypress component testing screen that you can access after running the preceding command:

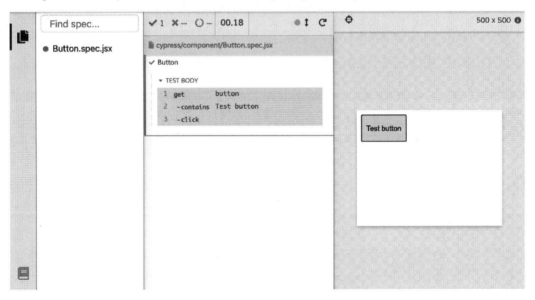

Figure 3.12 – Cypress component testing screen

As mentioned previously, the Selenium framework comes with a basic Selenium IDE recorder to help users get started with their first Selenium scripts. Similarly, Cypress is developing its own version of such a recorder under the name of *Cypress Studio* (`https://docs.cypress.io/guides/core-concepts/cypress-studio`). This solution will allow new users of the technology to record Cypress scripts through a GUI tool. The recorded tests will generate a JavaScript test code that can then be modified and enhanced. In addition, there is also a good list of browser extensions, such as this Chrome Cypress recorder: `https://chrome.google.com/webstore/detail/cypress-recorder/glcapdcacdfkokcmicllhcjigeodacab`, that are worth exploring.

Later in this book, when we cover the advanced capabilities of Cypress, we will touch upon the mocking and network control abilities of Cypress, using various plugins with Cypress, automating Cypress for react native applications, and more.

Now that we have covered the basic abilities of Cypress, let's proceed to Google Puppeteer.

Getting started with the Google Puppeteer framework

Puppeteer is an open source node library and a framework developed by Google that is based on the **CDP**. It allows web application developers to control headless or headed chrome browsers through high-level APIs over the above mentioned CDP or DevTools protocol (`https://chromedevtools.github.io/devtools-protocol/`). As described earlier in this chapter, Puppeteer and Playwright share the same architecture and CDP to create and run tests.

Unlike Selenium and Cypress, Puppeteer only supports Chrome and Chromium-based browsers, which means that testing end-to-end across all other browsers, such as WebKit Safari and Mozilla Firefox, isn't supported.

Among the core capabilities of Puppeteer is the generation of screenshots and PDFs of websites' pages, crawling a single-page application, and generating pre-rendered content, automating form submission, UI testing, and user gestures such as keyboard inputs. With the support of the CDP, developers can test Chrome extensions, as well as capture a timeline trace of the site for performance monitoring.

To get started with Google Puppeteer, you should obviously have Node.js installed on your local machine, and then run the `install` command as follows:

```
npm install puppeteer
```

Keep in mind that Google provides two versions of Puppeteer: a standard installation, which is done using the preceding command, and a puppeteer-core version that by default does not download any of the Chrome browsers to your local machine. The standard installation downloads the latest Chrome browser to the local machine and uses it as the target browser for testing. Puppeteer supports both the headed and headless execution modes. Scripting with Puppeteer is done with JavaScript, which makes the framework very appealing for frontend web application developers. As seen in *Chapter 2*, *Challenges Faced by FrontEnd Web Application Developers*, a developer can easily create a Puppeteer script that takes a full website screenshot, monitors performance, or even validates the accessibility of a website that is under development.

A website **HTTP archive** (**HAR**) file can be easily generated using Puppeteer. Using a generated HAR file, developers can review the entire traffic within their website and get performance and security insights for each of the transactions.

The following code snippet will navigate to the Packt website and generate a HAR file for review (for that, you need to install the npm package puppeteer-har):

```
const puppeteer = require('puppeteer');
const PuppeteerHar = require('puppeteer-har');
(async () => {
  const browser = await puppeteer.launch();
  const page = await browser.newPage();
  const har = new PuppeteerHar(page);
  await har.start({ path: 'book_demo.har' });
  await page.goto('https://www.packtpub.com/');
  await har.stop();
  await browser.close();
})();
```

On running the preceding test code, a new HAR file under the name book_demo.har will be generated:

```
node [filename.js] //depends on the JavaScript file name given
above
```

Opening the generated HAR file with the Google HAR analyzer web tool will show the following output that can be examined by the frontend developers for web traffic issues, performance issues, and more.

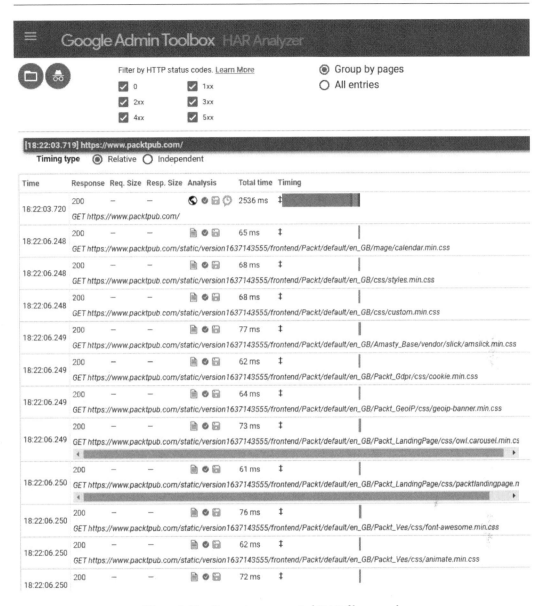

Figure 3.13 – Puppeteer-generated HAR file example

To get more examples, it's highly recommended to bookmark the Google GitHub repository for Puppeteer (`https://github.com/puppeteer/puppeteer`).

Later in the book, we will cover more advanced features of the Puppeteer framework.

Now that we have covered the basics of Puppeteer, let's proceed with Microsoft's Playwright framework.

Getting started with the Microsoft Playwright framework

Playwright is one of the newest but fastest-growing cross-browser test automation frameworks. Built by the same team that built Puppeteer, Playwright is also a CDP-based framework. As opposed to Google's Puppeteer, Playwright supports multiple languages and most leading browsers. With Playwright, developers can script in JavaScript, TypeScript, Python, Java, and .NET, and execute across most leading browsers including Chrome, Firefox, Edge, and WebKit Safari. The Playwright framework can be executed in headed or headless mode and can also support mobile viewport emulation (`https://playwright.dev/docs/emulation#devices`) with various user agents, as opposed to Cypress, for example.

From an architecture perspective, Playwright uses the CDP to interact with the browsers, drive actions such as browsers' pages inputs, scan for security, monitor network processes, and much more. A thorough architectural review is presented by Microsoft in this online session: `https://www.youtube.com/watch?v=PXTspGn1im0`.

To get started with Playwright, simply install the Node.js package through the following commands:

```
npm i -D @playwright/test
npx playwright install
```

Note that Playwright automatically downloads the Chromium, WebKit, and Firefox browsers to a local folder on your machine. You can learn more about the installation of the framework here: `https://playwright.dev/docs/intro#installation`.

Once installed, simply create a basic JavaScript test file, save it with the extension of `*.spec.js`, and place it in the `tests` folder:

```
const { test, expect } = require('@playwright/test');
test('basic test', async ({ page }) => {
await page.goto('https://github.com/login/');
await page.fill('input[name="login"]', ' [user name]');
await page.fill('input[name="password"]', '[password]');
await page.click('text=Sign in');
});
```

The preceding code snippet will navigate to the GitHub website and perform a simple sign-in.

To run the test with the browser in a headed mode, run the following command:

```
npx playwright test --headed
```

If the preceding command is not specified, the execution will run in headless mode.

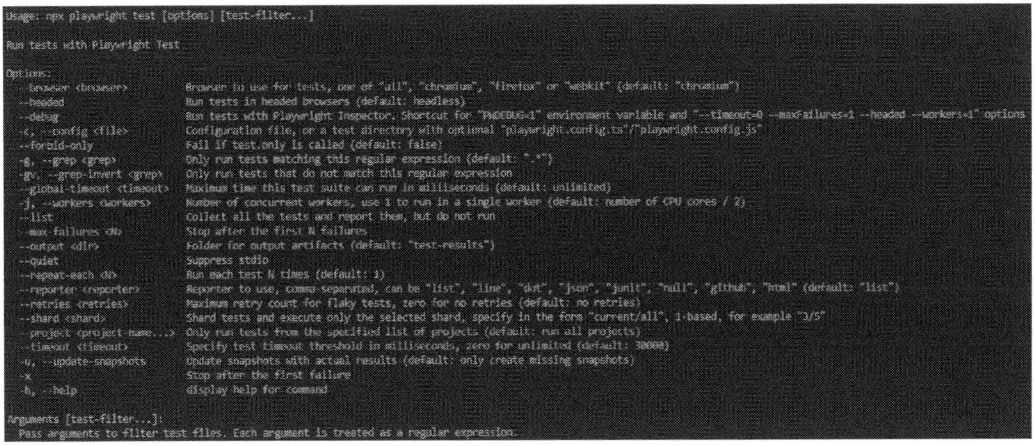

Figure 3.14 – Playwright command-line options

If you wish to run the previous test on a specific browser, you'd need to use `"--browser=webkit"` as an example.

When using Playwright, unlike using Cypress, developers cannot utilize the time travel functionality for immediate debugging; however, Playwright does support some very valuable features including geolocation testing, mocking, file handling, using parameters, and iFrames, which are specifically unsupported by Cypress at the time of writing this book.

> **iFrame**
> An iFrame is an HTML document that is embedded inside another document on a website. It is typically used to insert content taken from another source or website.

While for most of the frameworks that we cover in this book, there is available integration with cloud vendors such as Perfecto, Sauce Labs, and BrowserStack, Playwright offers built-in parallelization and sharding to drive the tests faster and at scale.

Playwright uses the term `worker` to run tests in parallel. From a practitioner standpoint, there are two methods to run tests in parallel.

The first one is through an additional command-line option that should be added to the execution:

```
npx playwright test --headed --workers 4
```

The second option is to edit the `playwright.config.js` file that comes with the framework installation, and add the following line:

```
Const config = {
Workers: process.env.CI ? 4: undefined,};
Module.exports = config;
```

There are additional useful features within Playwright, such as stopping the entire test execution upon a certain amount of test failures. For example, if within a large test execution of a suite, the failure number (using `--max-failures=10`) reached 10 failures, the entire test run will stop at that point to avoid running the full suite.

Playwright can also help perform visual validations, monitor network traffic, and help test complex scenarios. We will discuss some of these capabilities later in the book.

Lastly, Playwright integrates with most of the continuous integration tools, as well as with Docker, and other third-party test runners, such as Jest and Mocha.

Summary

As highlighted in this chapter, web application developers have a wide range of technology selections when it comes to their frontend web application testing. There are some commonalities between the frameworks; however, there are also some material differences between them. Selecting what makes the most sense for the short term, as well as for the long term, is a tough challenge that we will cover later in this book.

In this chapter, we covered the fundamentals of the top four JavaScript test automation frameworks for web developers.

We provided an overview of the core benefits of the frameworks together with some getting started instructions, so that developers can get a sense of what it takes to use these frameworks for a new project.

As we move forward in the book, we will provide a deeper dive into the advanced capabilities of each framework, as well as some recommendations on when it's best to use one framework over another.

In the following chapter, we will cover tips and recommendations to help developers and other testing personas within the project better match the test framework to their objectives and use cases.

4

Matching Personas and Use Cases to Testing Frameworks

Choosing a test automation framework is a fundamental aspect of the software development life cycle. A test automation framework serves so many different objectives and, as such, must be suited to cover different needs of both developers as well as test engineers. Specifically, in web application testing, the variety of frameworks that are available is huge; hence, there needs to be a prescriptive methodology that considers all the relevant pillars, as well as meeting the current and future-looking needs of users. Within a typical web application software release, there are a couple of personas that contribute to the overall quality of the product, including frontend developers and test automation engineers (also known as **SDETs – software developer engineers in testing**). A test automation framework and, in many cases, a combination of more than a single framework ought to match these personas' needs, skill sets, and expected velocity around scale and feedback loops.

In this chapter, we will provide a set of considerations to help these two main personas to choose the best test automation framework for their needs and suggest an innovative Venn diagram that illustrates these requirements and differences between the personas, their use cases, and the top-four test automation frameworks (Selenium, Cypress, Puppeteer, and Playwright).

The chapter is designed to cover the following:

- Introduction to the key personas within a web application development project
- Specifying the various use cases and considerations that need to be top of the mind when picking a test framework
- The test automation frameworks evaluation matrix – a table comparing the features across leading test frameworks

Upon completion of the chapter, you will understand the differences between each persona, the main objectives of various persona within a web application development project, and the differences in each test automation framework by category.

Technical requirements

The code files for this chapter can be found here: `https://github.com/PacktPublishing/A-Frontend-Web-Developers-Guide-to-Testing`.

Web testing personas overview

As already stated earlier in this book, it takes a village to build high-quality web applications, and specifically, testing such advanced apps is quite a challenge.

To cover all the testing types, including functional and non-functional, in a short amount of time, feature teams or squads consist of both developers and SDETs. Such high-skilled and technical resources are tasked with creating new test code upon any new product requirements, as well as maintaining older regression testing suites.

The frontend developer usually cares about the following objectives:

- Ease of creation of test code.
- High-scale and parallel testing to expedite feedback from their test runs.
- The creation of unit and API tests are typically top of mind.
- Having a framework with debugging and mocking abilities

- Integration with CI/CD tools, such as Jenkins and Azure DevOps.

- Integration with defect management and task management tools, such as Jira.

Since the developer persona commits multiple code changes a day, they need to develop very specific test code to cover these changes. In addition, developers unfortunately also create defects; hence, having the ability to properly reproduce bugs, analyze logs and network traffic, and monitor APIs is key for fast resolution of these defects (**MTTR – mean time to resolution**).

Some of the test automation frameworks cover the preceding objectives more than others, as we will specify later in this chapter. However, these are some of the top-of-mind objectives developers care about when evaluating different test automation frameworks. As *Indeed*, which is a hiring website, defines, a frontend web application developer is a developer that is responsible for all user-/client-side web application creations, from UI elements, buttons, and menus to compatibility across web and mobile platforms, high-quality code creation, and much more (`https://www.indeed.com/hire/job-description/front-end-developer`).

For frontend developers to be successful in what they create, they get tremendous help and support from **SDETs**.

SDETs are responsible for complementing the quality objectives that the developer doesn't. This includes higher coverage of testing types, multiple-platform testing, performance, accessibility, and different functionality testing that isn't in the scope of the developer to cover.

The SDET usually cares about the following objectives:

- Test automation scenario coverage (including the most advanced user flows within the app)

- Cross-platform support (web and mobile)

- Support and documentation within the community

- Support for multiple testing methodologies (functional, non-functional)

- Ease of use and ramping up

- Reporting and debugging abilities

- Integration with CI/CD tools, such as Jenkins

- Integration with defect management and task management tools, such as Jira

As identified, there are a few commonalities between the two persona types of objectives, which makes sense. Test code is code like any other software development project; hence, it needs to be managed, maintained, and used like production code.

Now that we've listed, at a very high level, some of the persona types and their objectives, let's identify what constitutes a solid test automation framework.

Use cases and considerations for picking a solid test automation framework

When considering the long list of activities that both developers and SDETs are responsible for, considering the tool stack that's available for them to accomplish these activities is imperative for success.

The following diagram presents a set of very important considerations that should be part of any proof of concept when choosing a web application testing framework:

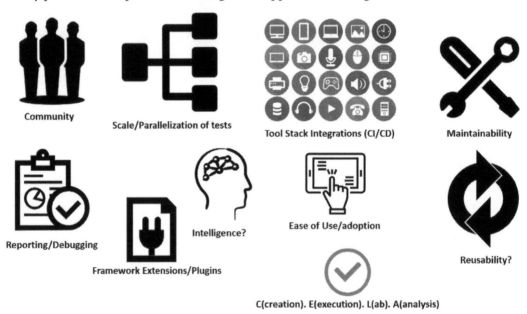

Figure 4.1 – Key pillars of a high-value test automation framework

When starting to investigate a web application test automation framework, looking at the previously illustrated pillars is imperative. Let's look at each of them in the following sections. We will not address C.E.L.A as a standalone section since this refers to the overall capabilities together and it sums the software testing life cycle from test creation through its report at the end of execution.

Community considerations

Having a strong community behind the test automation framework is a key requirement for many reasons. Getting ongoing support, innovation, best practices, online discussions, code samples, and more are just a subset of the benefits a strong community can bring to any technology. A small community, an inactive community, and lack of contributions to an open source technology can be a negative sign that this solution is not really ramping up and adopted, and it can suggest that developers should look into other alternatives.

Scale testing capabilities

Building web applications these days with the ever-growing prevalence of digital transformation isn't just about covering a large range of desktop browsers and OS versions; it is also about mobile devices and OS versions. A test automation framework that can support high-scale parallel testing across these platforms is obviously important. Among the various test automation frameworks, there are a few frameworks that do not support all browsers, including mobile devices, which poses a limitation for developers and SDETs. Setting a coverage platform matrix during the test automation framework evaluation phase can help surface such limitations.

Tool stack integrations and plugins

Both developers and SDETs work with a wide range of technologies and tools when building their applications. Such tools include CI/CD tools, such as Jenkins and TeamCity, as well as defect management and user story management tools, such as Jira. In addition, these personas also work with **Source Control Management (SCM)** tools, such as GitHub, and other tools, such as Perforce's Helix Core, API management tools, security scanning tools, and network analysis tools. Test automation frameworks that can create and execute various testing types should also integrate properly with the existing tools within squad teams to ensure a fluent process as well as continuous productivity. In addition, such personas also rely on different plugins for accessibility, visual testing, code coverage analysis, and more; hence, working nicely with these plugins is a great advantage to consider and evaluate.

Ease of use and adoption

Getting started with any technology can make the difference between the successful evaluation and adoption of a tool and a failure. To get started quickly and have a positive experience, a test automation framework should have an easy-to-use guide with basic code samples and environment setup and dependency instructions, as well as documentation and examples of more advanced capabilities. Since the personas that are evaluating these frameworks have very technical knowledge and skills but are also short on time, it's important to inform them upfront what the unsupported features and limitations are so they do not waste time chasing something that is simply unavailable. A good example that I found was from Cypress. The Cypress documentation clearly states what's never going to be supported by the tool, as well as providing a dynamic web page with its upcoming roadmap items (`https://docs.cypress.io/guides/references/roadmap`).

For example, the iFrames testing capability is not supported at the time of writing this book (`https://docs.cypress.io/api/commands/clock#iframes`), which is clearly stated in the documentation, but appears as a future roadmap item.

Reusability and maintainability

Both developers and SDETs do not try to reinvent the wheel when it's not required. Since their time is short within the software sprints, they love to use framework capabilities that enable them to optimize their workloads and be more efficient.

Things such as test reusability, page object model support, and working with advanced framework capabilities (for example, the new **Selenium 4** introduced one called **Relative Locators**) are great examples of productivity features developers would appreciate.

When evaluating a test automation framework, it's important to look for things that can optimize our workload and make our daily tasks more efficient. Also, thinking about maintaining the test code over time is very important, since the product and the web landscape evolve over time and the tests should also be resilient to these changes.

Reporting, test analysis, and intelligence

Test execution cycles happen multiple times a day, and this results in huge volumes of test data across different environments and from target web and mobile platforms. Having the ability to analyze test reports properly, either through intelligence (AI/ML) or built-in capabilities, is key for agility. When evaluating test automation frameworks, developers and SDETs should investigate the reporting layer and see what they can get out of the box from the framework, and if it's not directly built into the framework, whether there can be solid integrations with reporting frameworks such as Allure (`https://github.com/allure-framework/allure-js`) or the Perfecto cloud solution reporting SDK (`https://help.perfecto.io/perfecto-help/content/perfecto/test-analysis/test_analysis_with_smart_reporting.htm`).

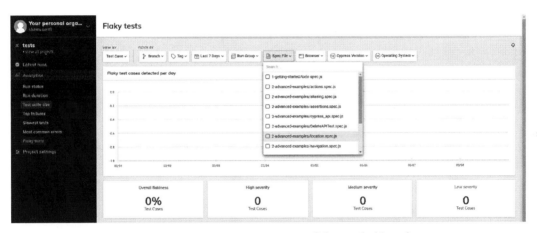

Figure 4.2 – Cypress test automation flakiness dashboard

A nice example of a reporting feature Cypress provides within its dashboard is the automated classification of flaky and inconsistent testing scenarios (`https://docs.cypress.io/guides/dashboard/flaky-test-management#Flaky-Test-Analytics`). With such an ability, frontend developers can filter out noise and keep their testing pipeline more stable and reliable.

Now that we've looked at some of the core pillars and considerations of a test automation framework that both developers and SDETs should care about, let's look at a methodology that can help to connect all these dots and serve as a tool to evaluate the different frameworks continuously.

Testing automation evaluation matrix

To realize continuous value from your selected test automation framework, you need to get support for the core elements that you need, as highlighted previously. From language support through to community, advanced testing scenarios support, and testing types of support, those in charge must have a clear picture that they can analyze prior to, as well as during, the adoption and usage of these technologies. The continuous part here is very important, since, for example, as described previously, Cypress currently does not cover iFrames and cannot test WebKit Safari browsers, but these are on their roadmap, so that soon might change. Note that picking your tool stack is good for a given time frame, hopefully long enough, up until you need to re-evaluate your choices and either keep on using what you have or make changes.

In the following table, we will look at the differences and commonalities across the four leading test automation frameworks. This tool can help us visualize the benefits and disadvantages of each.

Other resources and comparisons between the frameworks are constantly being done by individuals, and such comparisons might change over time. A nice resource I was able to find was from BlazeMeter (`https://www.blazemeter.com/blog/selenium-vs-cypress-a-complete-comparison-between-the-two-testing-frameworks?utm_content=180888216&utm_medium=social&utm_source=linkedin&hss_channel=lcp-2364558`), which is worth reading.

Any given web application project has unique requirements, and these requirements should be compared across the available tools. While not supporting iFrames can seem like a limitation of Cypress, if this is not something that your app uses, it's not really a relevant limitation.

The following is a categorized table that breaks down each of the test automation frameworks according to the core capabilities test engineers would mostly care about. As you will observe, there are a few capabilities that are supported by more than a single framework; however, when considering the wider range of capabilities and matching them to the persona requirements, the decision around which framework to use becomes easier:

Capabilities	Cypress	Playwright	Puppeteer	Selenium
Supported languages	JavaScript TypeScript	Java JavaScript TypeScript Python .NET	JavaScript	Java JavaScript Ruby Python C# Kotlin
Supported browsers	Chrome Edge Firefox	Chrome Edge Firefox Safari WebKit	Chrome only	Chrome Edge Firefox Safari WebKit Opera Internet Explorer (legacy)
Accessibility testing support	Through AXE plugin	Through AXE plugin and a built-in method `https://playwright.dev/docs/api/class-accessibility/`	Can utilize Lighthouse and devtools, as well as the Puppetaria library for an accessibility snapshot of a website `https://developer.chrome.com/blog/puppetaria/`	Through the AXE plugin
API testing support	Supported `http://cypress.io`	Supported `https://playwright.dev/docs/test-api-testing/`	Unsupported	Unsupported Can be extended with Rest-Assured integration

Visual testing support	Percy, Happo, and Applitools plugins (commercial) Storybook (open source)	Visual assertions against baseline screenshots built in. Commercial integration with Applitools and Percy	Basic screenshots built into the framework. Integration with Percy (`https://docs.percy.io/docs/puppeteer`)	Through integrations with Storybook, Galen, Percy, and Applitools
Low code testing	Cypress Studio	Playwright codegen autogenerator	Unsupported	Selenium IDE
Cloud integrations for scaled testing	Perfecto Sauce Labs BrowserStack	Immature	Immature	Perfecto Sauce Labs BrowserStack
Unique features	Flaky tests identification DOM snapshot/time travel Component testing Code coverage plugin Spy, stub, and clock support for server response control Autoawaits UI elements Network control Cypress Dashboard	iFrame Network control CDP tools and Lighthouse UI element automated awaits Testing Safari WebKit on Windows Built-in reporter including Allure Playwright Inspector for authoring and debugging Advanced retry mechanism Network monitoring APIs Parallel testing through workers	Headless browser CDP native integration Chromium built-in browser (local) Crawl web page and generate prerendered content **Server-Side Rendering (SSR)** Capture timeline trace for debugging and performance diagnostics Testing Chrome extensions	Multitab support Relative locators Page object model W3C-compliant Selenium Grid Self-healing (**Healenium**)

Headed and headless support	Not a core strength	Supported	Supported	Not a core strength
Continuous integration support	CircleCI GitHub Actions GitLab Bitbucket AWS CodeBuild	Jenkins CircleCI Bitbucket Docker Azure Pipelines Travis CI GitHub Actions GitLab	GitHub Actions CircleCI Docker	Jenkins GitHub Actions CircleCI GitLab Azure DevOps Bitbucket
Performance testing	Through Google Lighthouse	Supported via web performance APIs	Lighthouse/ devtools and web performance APIs `https:// github.com/ addyosmani/ puppeteer- webperf`	Possible through BlazeMeter JMeter `http:// jmeter. apache.org`
Community engagement	Very high	Low	Medium and growing	Very high
Supported test runners	Mocha	Mocha Jest Jasmine	Jest	Mocha Jest Jasmine Protractor WebdriverIO PyUnit JUnit TestNG
Mobile device testing	Support for viewport changing and user-agent specification	Supported through viewport simulation (playwright. devices())	Supported through simulation (emulate() function)	Supported via Appium

While the preceding table is not a complete deep dive and does not go through, API by API, everything that is supported by the various frameworks, it can be used to understand some of the core commonalities as well as unique strengths of each.

In many projects, a combination of more than one framework might prove to be the best approach since all the preceding have JavaScript support as a common entry point with similar test runners driving the test creations (Mocha, Jest, and so on). In addition, specific frameworks offer built-in unique features that frontend developers and SDETs would benefit a lot from.

Test coverage across web and mobile platforms is also among the strong requirements of each web application; hence, Selenium in such cases is the most mature framework to support real and virtual device testing either through its parallel Appium framework or its integration with mobile cloud vendors such as Perfecto (`http://perfecto.io`).

The preceding table should help frontend developers to better look at the different frameworks. In *Chapter 7, Consideration Matrix between JavaScript Test Automation Frameworks*, we will dive deeper and provide a breakdown of the key use cases mentioned previously.

It is important that frontend developers consider that as part of a single pipeline, there are various quality-check activities to perform, ranging from API testing, visual testing, accessibility testing, and performance testing to network control, functional testing, and other types of integration testing. As we will learn later, while almost every capability can be implemented by developers, there are some capabilities that are built into some frameworks that need to be integrated by others.

As an example, visual testing could be advanced through built-in capabilities within the Playwright framework, while for other frameworks, frontend developers will need to rely on third-party integrations.

Summary

In this chapter, we went deeper into the high-level considerations frontend web application developers have when it comes to selecting a test automation framework.

As outlined in the chapter, there are a few generic considerations, such as ease of use and reporting, but also some specific requirements around test coverage, API and mock testing abilities, visual testing, and others that would vary from one project to another.

We provided a useful table that can be used as a baseline for a comparison of the various test automation frameworks.

Later in the book, in chapters 9-12, we will look into each of the capabilities (supported languages, community engagement, and so on) represented in the table, and provide a deep-dive analysis and comparison of each of these categories.

That concludes this chapter!

In the following chapter, we will advance the preceding test consideration matrix and provide a way to match each test automation framework with a testing methodology, such as API testing, performance testing, and functional and accessibility testing.

5

Introducing the Leading Frontend Web Development Frameworks

In previous chapters, we looked at the four leading frontend web test automation frameworks (Playwright, Puppeteer, Selenium, and Cypress), and outlined the key testing types, which include functional, non-functional, API, and accessibility. We also looked at some of the key testing objectives that developers and **SDETs** (**software developer engineer in testing**) consider when choosing a test automation framework.

In this chapter, we will look at the test frameworks from the web development and application perspectives and provide guidelines on how to ensure that your test framework best fits the application type as well as the web development frameworks.

The chapter is designed to cover the following:

- Charting the leading web development frameworks by their types
- Guidelines for picking the most advanced JavaScript web development technology

The goal of this chapter is to familiarize you with the most used web development frameworks on the market. As a test engineer, knowing these leading technologies, their advantages, and core features, as well as getting references to sample web applications built using these frameworks, can help with test planning activities.

Technical requirements

The code files for this chapter can be found here: `https://github.com/PacktPublishing/A-Frontend-Web-Developers-Guide-to-Testing`.

Introduction to the leading web development frameworks

We've already established a good level of understanding about the advancements in web testing frameworks and reviewed some of the differences and unique capabilities of each. The four leading test automation frameworks that we are covering in this book are challenged daily by the technology that frontend web application developers use to build their software.

After looking at the State of JavaScript survey for the past few years, specifically for 2020 (`https://2020.stateofjs.com/en-US/`), as well as researching dozens of blogs and online resources, we can see that there are 5-7 web development technologies that are leading the industry and have become the preferred choices for frontend developers.

The following are the most used frameworks:

- Vue.js (`https://vuejs.org/`)
- ReactJS (`https://reactjs.org/`)
- AngularJS (`https://angularjs.org/`)
- Ember.js (`https://guides.emberjs.com/release/tutorial/part-1/`)
- Svelte (`https://svelte.dev/`)

These frameworks are the ones that are used for most web applications; however, with the rise of more modern digital apps, we also see frameworks such as React Native, which is an older technology but very rich and popular for mobile-friendly app development, and Flutter (`https://flutter.dev/`), which is considered for newly built applications to create a single code base that can run on both mobile and desktop platforms. Since the landscape is so rich and dynamic, we will only focus on the preceding five frameworks. However, it is worth mentioning that other frameworks, such as the following, also received positive feedback from developers across surveys: *Preact* (`https://preactjs.com/`), *Backbone.js* (`https://backbonejs.org/`), *jQuery* (`https://jquery.com/`), *Flutter,* and *Semantic UI* (`https://semantic-ui.com/`).

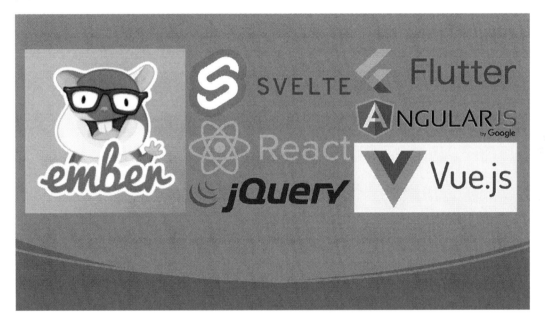

Figure 5.1 – Leading web development frameworks' logos

Now that we've identified the most commonly used web development frameworks, we are going to dive deeper into each and every one of these frameworks and learn their key strengths and characteristics, as well as how to get started using them.

Guidelines for picking a web development framework

When picking a web development framework, frontend developers must consider the following:

- Features and differentiating abilities of the framework against the user stories at hand

- Rapid development abilities with fewer coding requirements

- Vast community support (open source benefits)

- Simplified debugging

- Learning curve

- Consistent performance

- Reusability of application components

- Built-in security features of the framework

- Misc: Built-in dev tools (DOM snapshots), plugin-friendly, app layout design, support for the TypeScript language, accessibility support

The previously mentioned development frameworks vary by their age, features, community, and suitability for the application types that are being built. It is nice to see how these frameworks have trended throughout the years based on Stack Overflow questions (`https://insights.stackoverflow.com/trends?tags=angular%2Creactjs%2Cjquery%2Cvue.js%2Cember.js%2Csvelte`).

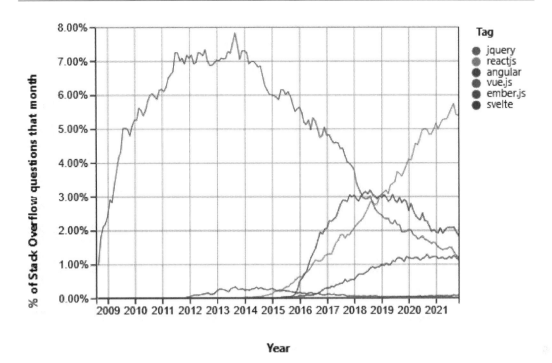

Figure 5.2 – Stack Overflow trends for JavaScript web development frameworks (source: Stack Overflow)

Let's compare, at a high level, the top web development frameworks and understand some of the pros and cons of each.

ReactJS

ReactJS is an open source framework developed and created by Facebook. With over 179,000 stars on GitHub, 36.500 forks, and 110 branches, it is by far the most adopted web development framework.

Among the main benefits of ReactJS are the use of a virtual DOM for efficient web page loading and server-side rendering, which does most of the page rendering on the server side and contributes to the high performance of the web application. In addition, ReactJS uses **JSX**, which is a **JavaScript extension** that looks like an XML file and can be mixed with the JavaScript website code to set up tree structures and other complex blocks within the code by using opening and closing XML tags.

Some sample and very well-known websites that are built using ReactJS are **Pinterest**, **Netflix**, and **Dropbox**.

Many frontend web application developers would agree that ReactJS offers great reusability of components and high-performing applications across high-traffic websites due to its built-in capabilities, being easy to learn and ramp up, its rich dev tools for building and debugging web apps, and the strong community behind the open source framework.

However, while JSX is aimed at helping developers cope with challenging DOM trees, the community argues that it's hard to understand and use this JavaScript syntax extension.

To get started with building a new web application with ReactJS, run this set of commands:

```
npx create-react-app packt-app
cd packt-app
npm start
```

The preceding commands will create a basic web application for a developer to start editing and building upon.

Once the preceding commands are executed, the developer will need to edit the App.js file that was created under the new folder (in our case, under packt-app), as well as the index.html and the related JSX files as and if needed.

The following is a basic welcome page for a newly created web application using ReactJS that frontend developers can use as a baseline for their new application:

Figure 5.3 – Sample main website application page built using ReactJS

> **Virtual DOM**
>
> **Virtual DOM** is a very efficient capability of ReactJS. It is a tree based on JavaScript objects created with ReactJS that mimics the web page DOM tree. Every time a developer changes something in the DOM, ReactJS employs a different algorithm that only refreshes and renders the changed DOM nodes. This contributes to the performance and loading of the DOM, which enhances the end user experience when visiting ReactJS-based websites across desktop and especially mobile devices.

This chapter and book are not aimed at guiding you on how to develop different web applications but rather how to test them. But to understand how to test such apps, it is beneficial to understand how these frameworks are built and how they differ from each other, since the framework of choice impacts the testing activities and framework that will be picked, also because not every test automation framework is suited to test every type of web application. As highlighted in *Chapter 4, Matching Personas and Use Cases to Testing Frameworks*, Playwright and Puppeteer support the Jest test runner, and Jest is among the frameworks that are suited to test ReactJS applications (`https://jestjs.io/docs/tutorial-react`), since it gets shipped and installed when you run the preceding ReactJS setup commands.

To use Jest with Playwright, you will need to install the Jest dependency on top of your Playwright and Node.js environment:

```
npm install -D jest jest-playwright-preset playwright
```

In addition, you will need to add a file instruction to the `jest.config.js` so it knows to use the previously installed preset:

```
module.exports = {
    preset: "jest-playwright-preset"
}
```

To learn more about how to test ReactJS apps using Playwright and Jest, please refer to this great online resource: `https://playwright.tech/blog/using-jest-with-playwright`. Since Playwright is a rich testing framework that covers more than just functional testing, it is recommended to build the test strategy around a higher-level and broader technology than just Jest.

Like Playwright, Google's Puppeteer framework is also built with support for the Jest test runner. Hence, it can also be used to test ReactJS applications; however, as highlighted in *Chapter 4, Matching Personas and Use Cases to Testing Frameworks*, Puppeteer is limited to only Chromium browsers and has limited testing abilities, such as unsupported API testing and smaller community support. To get started with setting up a Puppeteer test environment with Jest for ReactJS application testing, you can refer to this nice guide: `https://rexben.medium.com/end-to-end-testing-in-react-with-puppeteer-and-jest-6a0b1b8cff6b`.

Since Selenium is the most mature and commonly used framework on the market and supports the Jest test runner, it can also be used for the **end-to-end** (**E2E**) testing of ReactJS applications. It has JavaScript language binding and can be used to test such apps at scale and in the cloud using vendors such as **Perfecto**, **Sauce Labs**, and **BrowserStack**. Since the Selenium WebDriver technology is React-agnostic, it may be a bit complex to handle element locators, deal with waits, and more.

Lastly, the Cypress framework also offers a modern way to test ReactJS applications through its new component-based testing methodology (`https://www.cypress.io/blog/2021/04/06/cypress-component-testing-react/`), as well as through standard JavaScript and TypeScript testing specs.

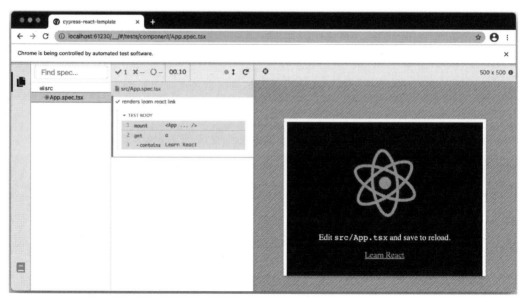

Figure 5.4 – Main testing screen for testing a React web application with Cypress
(source: Cypress documentation)

Now that we've introduced the ReactJS web development framework, let's move on to the next leading framework, which is AngularJS.

AngularJS

AngularJS is among the leading frontend web application development frameworks. Originally established by Google in 2016, AngularJS allows developers to use HTML as their template language and then extend it through four different directives: **ng-app** and **ng-init**, **ng-bind**, and **ng-model**. One of the benefits of the AngularJS framework is that it requires less coding to build a web application through the use of data binding and dependency injection. Based on the main website of AngularJS (`https://docs.angularjs.org/guide/introduction`), this framework was built with **create, read, update, and delete** (**CRUD**) in mind, allowing developers to build efficient websites using a high level of abstraction. With that in mind, the Angular community itself states that complex GUI or gaming websites might not be the sweet spot for AngularJS.

From a community standpoint, AngularJS has over 78,000 stars and 20,500 forks on GitHub, and it is actively maintained by contributors (`https://github.com/angular/angular`).

Figure 5.5 – Basic AngularJS web application code snippet (source: https://www.w3schools.com/angular/tryit.asp?filename=try_ng_intro)

As highlighted in the preceding code snippet, the application code is a sample HTML template with added directives, such as **ng-bind**, which equals **name**.

Among the key benefits of AngularJS, frontend developers consistently list low coding effort, the reusability of code components, the usage of dependency injection, and HTML extensions using declaratives, as well as the vast community standing behind this technology. In addition, the use of a **two-way data binding** architecture is considered a huge benefit to AngularJS developers. Two-way data binding enables real-time synchronization between the view and the model of the application. This capability can be quite powerful in cases where a user changes the order within a drop-down menu on the website, as AngularJS will cause the view of the menu on the page to automatically update with no need to manipulate any of the DOM code.

Some of the challenges that come up with AngularJS are dealing with complex websites with dynamic content, such as games websites, as well as coping with large-scale web applications from a code structure perspective.

AngularJS is powerful when building frontend web applications, as well as **progressive web apps** (**PWAs**), and it is considered a high-performing web application development framework.

When it comes to testing AngularJS applications, there are multiple test automation framework choices. In the past, Protractor was a great choice; however, over the years, it has become obsolete and the support for it has seized. So, as of the time of writing, frontend web application developers who build AngularJS applications can use the dedicated framework built by the AngularJS team called **Karma** (`http://karma-runner.github.io/latest/index.html`). Karma can be used with a test runner such as **Mocha** or **QUnit**, or with **Jasmine**, which is more of a **behavior-driven development** (**BDD**) JavaScript test framework.

To install Karma for your AngularJS web application testing, simply run the following commands:

```
npm install karma karma-chrome-launcher karma-jasmine
npm install karma-cli
```

Leading frameworks such as **Selenium** can test AngularJS applications; however, you need to be aware of the asynchronous nature of AngularJS applications and the use of implicit and explicit waits, as well as dedicated libraries such as `JavaScriptExecutor`, which can help better and more reliably identify web page elements and handle complex testing scenarios.

Cypress is also able to test AngularJS applications (`https://github.com/bahmutov/cypress-angular-unit-test`) through a dedicated library that is added to the framework.

To add AngularJS testing support to your Cypress framework, run the following command:

```
npm install -D cypress cypress-angular-unit-test
```

The next step is to add the preceding dependency to the Cypress `index.js` file:

```
require('cypress-angular-unit-test/support');
```

Lastly, Playwright also has the ability to test AngularJS applications through its built-in APIs (`https://stackoverflow.com/questions/69891101/how-to-run-e2e-angular-tests-with-playwright/69891102`), as well as Google's Puppeteer, which can be configured within the outdated Protractor configuration file to be used as the test runner (`https://stackoverflow.com/questions/51536244/how-to-use-puppeteer-in-an-angular-application`).

It is important to note that the top-four leading frameworks featured in this book can cope agnostically with any web application development framework; however, as we see in this case with AngularJS, there are some unique frameworks that were built as part of the development life cycle of these technologies, such as Karma, that should also be heavily considered.

Vue.js

Vue.js (`https://vuejs.org/`) is definitely one of the most widely adopted technologies by frontend developers. It is a very strong open source framework backed by a large number of contributors, with over 191,000 stars, 30,000 forks, and 72 branches on GitHub (`https://github.com/vuejs/vue#readme`). The Vue.js framework is designed to enable frontend web application developers to build rich UI websites. With a core, focused library dedicated to the view layer, Vue.js is designed to be flexible in building single- page applications (**SPA**), full stack applications, and even apps that target both desktop and mobile.

To install Vue.js on your local environment, run the following command:

```
npm install vue
```

The preceding installation of Vue.js will install different builds of this framework, including full, runtime-only, full (production), and runtime-only (production). Typically, you would use the **full** build so you can use both the compiler and the runtime capabilities of the framework.

One of the great capabilities of Vue.js is the DevTools extension (`https://devtools.vuejs.org/`), which offers advanced debugging abilities of web applications. Developers can add this extension as a plugin to their Chrome or Firefox browsers.

Alternatively, developers can install it as a command- line interface through the following command:

```
npm install -g @vue/devtools
```

Once the DevTools extension is installed, frontend developers will find the tool quite powerful for the real-time debugging of their web applications, analyzing the elements of a page, and measuring other aspects of their web application, such as performance and accessibility.

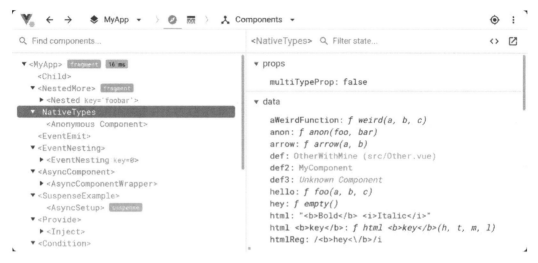

Figure 5.6 – Screenshot of Vue.js DevTools (source: https://github.com/vuejs/devtools)

Frontend web application developers state that Vue.js is powerful due to its extensive and detailed documentation, vast community, contributions to the open source project, simple syntax that allows getting started quickly with the framework, and flexibility from a website design perspective.

Like with AngularJS, Vue.js also employs two-way data binding and supports both modern web application development as well as complex PWAs.

Vue.js is so successful due to its simplicity, flexibility, and advanced DevTools extension, as well as its ability to support most web application types.

The Vue.js community recommends using a mix of tools to test web applications. The community splits the frameworks based on the following testing types:

- Unit testing
- Component testing
- E2E testing

For **unit testing**, Mocha (`https://mochajs.org/`) and Jest (`https://jestjs.io/`) are the recommended frameworks. To cover **component testing**, the testing framework should ensure that the component under test is mounted to the DOM for assertion purposes. Vue.js offers a built-in component testing library (`https://testing-library.com/docs/vue-testing-library/intro/`); however, we also learned that Cypress has its own ability to perform component-based testing in *Chapter 4*, *Matching Personas and Use Cases to Testing Frameworks*.

To get started with component testing using the built-in Vue.js library, you should install the dedicated testing library using the following command:

```
npm install –save-dev @testing-library/vue
```

Lastly, for E2E testing, the Vue.js community recommends the Cypress and Puppeteer frameworks as the most capable ones. For Cypress, there is even a dedicated Vue CLI plugin (`https://cli.vuejs.org/core-plugins/e2e-cypress.html#injected-commands`).

Ember.js

Ember.js (`https://emberjs.com/`) is also one of the top JavaScript web development frameworks, founded in 2011. With over 22,000 stars, 4,300 forks, and 45 branches on GitHub (`https://github.com/emberjs/ember.js`), the framework is very well known and adopted by frontend web developers. Among the key benefits that Ember.js promises developers are stability and security of the code together with most modern JavaScript features (`https://guides.emberjs.com/release/upgrading/current-edition/`), including **autotracking** and advanced app configuration capabilities that support feature flags (`https://guides.emberjs.com/release/configuring-ember/feature-flags/`) and environment type settings (test, production, and so on).

Ember.js Autotracking

One of the features of the Ember.js framework is autotracking. It is defined as a reactive model that automatically decides which elements of the web application need to be rerendered and when. As an example, when there is a component within the website that might change, a developer will mark it as `@tracked`, and when there is a change to that element (for example, to the language), the website will autorender only the impacted areas of the page (for example, the relevant text in the relevant language).

Obviously, such advanced capabilities as autotracking should be properly tested using unit tests and so on to ensure that the autorendering works as expected.

Some very well-known websites are built on top of Ember.js, including **LinkedIn**, **Netflix**, and **Microsoft**.

Among the most loved features that Ember.js has are the speed and performance that the framework provides, the two-way data binding features, which was also listed as an advantage of some of the preceding frameworks (such as AngularJS), solid documentation, and the previously highlighted features: autotracking and zero-config for apps.

Compared to the other frameworks, the community behind Ember.js is relatively small and there is a steep learning curve.

The Ember.js community recommends testing web applications through three types of testing methods:

- Unit tests

- Rendering (integration) tests

- Application (acceptance) tests

For unit tests, the community refers to QUnit (`https://qunitjs.com/`) and Mocha as recommended tools, as well as the built-in Ember.js CLI tools (`https://cli.emberjs.com/release/advanced-use/blueprints/`). To create rendering tests, which can also be considered component tests, you can use the preceding CLI tools to create such testing scenarios. A great guide to get started with the preceding testing types for an Ember.js application is available here: `https://medium.com/@sarbbottam/the-ember-js-testing-guide-i-made-for-myself-c9a073a0c718`.

```
tests/integration/components/simple-button-test.js                              JS

1   import { click, render } from '@ember/test-helpers';
2   import { setupRenderingTest } from 'ember-qunit';
3   import { hbs } from 'ember-cli-htmlbars';
4   import { module, test } from 'qunit';
5
6   module('Integration | Component | simple-button', function(hooks) {
7     setupRenderingTest(hooks);
8
9     test('should keep track of clicks', async function(assert) {
10       await render(hbs`<SimpleButton />`);
11       assert.dom('[data-test-label]').hasText('0 clicks');
12
13       await click('[data-test-button]');
14       assert.dom('[data-test-label]').hasText('1 click');
15
16       await click('[data-test-button]');
17       assert.dom('[data-test-label]').hasText('2 clicks');
18     });
19   });
```

Figure 5.7 – Sample rendering testing-type code snippet for Ember.js (source: https://guides.emberjs. com/release/testing/test-types/)

Based on community discussions, while leading frameworks, such as Selenium, Cypress, Playwright, and Puppeteer, can automate any type of web application, Ember.js apps can be quite challenging to test using them. A set of recent posts on Stack Overflow shows some of the challenges in dealing with dynamic objects generated within Ember.js apps across Selenium and Cypress:

```
https://stackoverflow.com/questions/37026817/automate-ember-
js-application-using-selenium-when-object-properties-are-
changed
```

```
https://stackoverflow.com/questions/53422339/ember-cypress-
integration-test-failing-likely-due-to-lack-of-store-context
```

Svelte

Svelte (`https://svelte.dev/`) is considered a transformational web development framework.

To quote the home page of the Svelte framework:

> *Svelte is a radical new approach to building user interfaces. Whereas traditional frameworks like React and Vue do the bulk of their work in the browser, Svelte shifts that work into a compile step that happens when you build your app.*
>
> *Instead of using techniques like virtual DOM diffing, Svelte writes code that surgically updates the DOM when the state of your app changes.*

With over 53,600 stars on GitHub (`https://github.com/sveltejs/svelte#README`), Svelte is becoming very well known and adopted by the frontend developer community. The framework was downloaded ~250,00 times over the second half of 2021 (`https://www.npmtrends.com/svelte`).

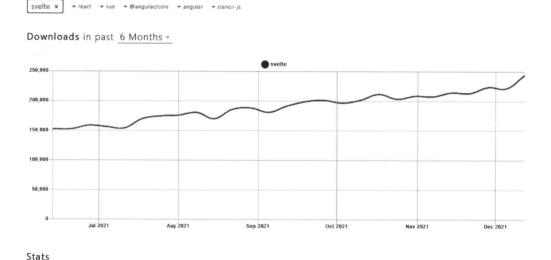

Figure 5.8 – Download and community trends for the Svelte framework
(source: npmtrends `https://insights.stackoverflow.com/trends?tags=angular%2Creactjs%2Cjquery%2Cvue.js%2Cember.js%2Csvelte`)

To get started with building websites using Svelte, please use the following commands:

```
npx degit sveltejs/template my-first-project
cd my-first-project
npm install
npm run dev
```

Svelte also provides a quick ramp-up for building a web application online from their main website.

Among the core benefits of the Svelte framework, frontend developers list the better reactivity of web apps, faster performance compared to AngularJS and React apps, and it being more lightweight than others. Among the disadvantages, developers list the community size, which is relatively small, and the lack of tooling and support for the framework. Websites such as **eBay** and **Pixar** are built using Svelte technology.

From a testing perspective, since Svelte considers itself a compiler rather than a library (`https://svelte.dev/faq`), it has different approaches to testing. Svelte comes with its own testing library (`https://svelte-recipes.netlify.app/testing/`), as well as Jest, like other app types covered previously.

To use the integrated testing library, you will need to install the dedicated component through this command:

```
npm install @testing-library/svelte --D
```

To get started with the library, you can refer to this basic tutorial: `https://timdeschryver.dev/blog/how-to-test-svelte-components#writing-a-test`.

The community recommends Cypress as the leading test framework for apps built on top of Svelte (`https://www.thisdot.co/blog/svelte-component-testing-with-cypress-vite`) and states that a test engineer would need to create a testing bundle for each component of the web application prior to testing it using Playwright, Puppeteer, Selenium (`https://medium.com/@oyetoketoby80/automating-your-front-end-application-testing-with-selenium-8e9d51f0f73c`), and Cypress.

Summary

In this chapter, we looked into the leading and most used web development frameworks. We provided a high-level overview of their main features, information to get started, as well as pros and cons of each.

We specifically looked at, for each of the web development frameworks, some of the testing tools that cover a wide range of testing types.

What is important to take away from this chapter is that while the variety of web development frameworks is rich, there are material differences in the development workflow and the core features and abilities of each web framework, and these differences have implications on the testing tools that should and can be used.

We have learned some core terms that are common across the different web development frameworks, including **virtual DOM** and **two-way data binding**.

That concludes this chapter!

In the following chapter, which opens *part 2* of this book, we will look into the key pillars of building a continuous testing strategy for a web application and how to measure the success of the strategy over time.

Part 2 – Continuous Testing Strategy for Web Application Developers

Ensuring web application quality isn't a one-and-done activity but, rather, a continuous process that should be built upon a solid strategy, involve multiple personas, and be properly measured through metrics and **Key Performance Indicators (KPIs)**. In this part of the book, you will learn how to build a proper testing strategy for any of the web application types, and maintain and modify the strategy over time based on changes to objectives, roadmaps, market events, and so on.

In this part, we will cover the following chapters:

- *Chapter 6, Map the Pillars of a Dev Testing Strategy for Web Applications*
- *Chapter 7, Core Capabilities of the Leading JavaScript Test Automation Frameworks*
- *Chapter 8, Measuring Test Coverage of the Web Application*

6

Map the Pillars of a Dev Testing Strategy for Web Applications

This chapter opens the second part of the book and is aimed at addressing the testing strategy aspects of a web application development project, from the requirements and objectives stages up until the measurements of success.

Building a testing strategy for a given web application depends on the product requirements, the quality acceptance criteria, the available skills and resources within the team, and the target markets (end users) for which the application is intended. In this chapter, you will learn how to combine the relevant considerations into a testing strategy that covers all quality aspects and continuously meets the end user experience. In addition, you will learn about some key metrics that can be used to monitor and measure the success of a strategy.

The chapter is designed to cover the following topics:

- The key pillars of a web application testing plan and strategy
- Measuring the success of your continuous testing strategy
- A case study – a real-life web application testing strategy

The key pillars of a web application testing plan and strategy

In the first part of the book, we covered both the leading frontend test automation frameworks available for web developers, as well as the leading web application development frameworks. We learned that each development or testing framework comes with pros and cons. Knowing this upfront is an advantage, but this alone does not make up the main element within a testing strategy. These frameworks are the tools and, most likely, the enablers to drive a solid test plan from A to Z.

How and which tool to use needs to be driven by the testing plan and strategy itself, and to build such a plan, software leaders must rely on the core fundamentals of the testing pyramid matched to the product business requirements.

Let's start with the types of testing that any web application needs to undergo prior to being released to production. In *Chapter 1*, *Cross-Browser Testing Methodologies*, we covered the main web application testing types, which consist of functional, non-functional (performance, security, accessibility, and so on), APIs, visual, and so on. Illustrated at a high level in *Figure 6.1* is the basic testing pyramid:

Figure 6.1 – The basic software testing pyramid (source – "The test automation pyramid.png" uploaded by Croncal, licensed under the CC BY-SA 4.0 license (https://creativecommons.org/licenses/by-sa/4.0/deed.en) at https://commons.wikimedia.org/wiki/File:The_test_automation_pyramid.png)

When you build a web application, you ought to consider each aspect of the product from an end user experience perspective. The end user cares about the look and feel of a website, how fast it performs, whether the site is available across all digital platforms (mobile and web), and how the services and third parties that the app uses work for them.

It's a recommended practice to spread all testing types throughout the pipeline. When doing so and providing frontend developers with a proper feedback loop, it allows them to fix issues faster and reduce the number of escaped defects that seep through to production.

In addition, partnering with the SDETs within the agile teams early in the requirements phase is imperative to allow them to develop test automation scenarios in time for the **End-to-End (E2E)** testing cycles.

In this section, we are going to discuss six pillars or considerations for building a reliable and robust web application. But all development must start with recognizing and defining the target users of the application.

Know your target users

When releasing a web application version to the public, knowing more about your end user traits can serve as a huge advantage from both development and testing perspectives. If the release is a brand-new application that doesn't carry any user analytics history, it is important to get clear targets from the product managers and business units so that a tester knows which mobile and web platforms, including versions and geographies, the application supports. If the release is a follow-up on top of an existing web application, web traffic analytics can be leveraged to figure out user journeys, the most used mobile and web platforms, regression defects from previous releases, and so on. This process can help to tailor the scoping of the testing plan and allow a timely release, optimize testing activities, and reduce risk.

When you consider your audience, of course, it should also be very industry- and vertical-specific. End users across verticals differ in many ways: age, expectations, the mobile and web platforms used, accessibility focus, the languages known, compliance requirements, and so on. So, knowing about all these traits pertaining to target users is essential to build a proper test plan.

Building a test plan

By knowing your target audience and understanding the product requirements for an upcoming release, test managers and developers can realize the scope of testing that needs to be part of the release definition of done.

Such a test plan needs to properly cover all the website workflows and end user journeys, as well as consider every dependency on the web application that can be an issue from a quality perspective. The test plan must cover all the relevant testing types and the most critical mobile and web configurations. Test data and test environments for both the development stages and testing stages must be part of the plan and become available prior to initiating the testing process.

We won't define again what each testing type means, since we did a lot of this in *Chapter 1, Cross-Browser Testing Methodologies*; however, as a reminder, we covered testing all internal and external links, the functionalities of each web page and user flow, usability and accessibility, localization and internationalization, coverage of the legacy, the latest and beta versions of web and mobile, layouts and views, and so on.

Make sure that you outline the preceding and check all boxes from a testing type perspective as part of the plan. As already highlighted in previous chapters, it takes a village to build and test a modern web application, so, ensuring that there are sufficient resources and tools and acquiring licenses for the project are other key requirements to address upfront.

Prep your tool stack and environments

Test development and execution do not happen in a void and require solid and up-to-date environments for both the creation, maintenance, and execution of each of the aforementioned testing types. Ensure as part of your plan that each resource from your team has valid access to the tools and environments that they need to accomplish their goals. In many cases, these practitioners will need a mocking services environment and pre-production test datasets to create and validate their testing. Development and testing leaders should be responsible for the tools and environments that their team members will use throughout the pipeline.

Set quality criteria and objectives

This is a crucial part of the test plan and requires handshakes between testing, development, product, and business owners. To know with confidence that a release is ready from a quality perspective, it needs to adhere to key metrics such as test coverage, defects opened with severity/priority in the system, platform coverage, functional and non-functional quality criteria, performance and availability measures, proper product release notes, available documentation, and so on.

Build a timeline and a schedule

Based on the available resources, tools, environments, and testing requirements, there needs to be an agreed-upon timeline that illustrates the different phases of the development life cycle, a definition and criteria that allows movement from one stage to another, and of course, a target release date with quality criteria and metrics to measure the release readiness. Orchestrating the release pipeline across the different practitioners is an art and requires communication and discipline across the different parties. Bear in mind that times and schedules have their own external and internal dependencies; hence, ensure that you put buffers (some would recommend +25% extra time added to the original estimates) into the planning to accommodate the unexpected.

Execute, monitor, measure, and document

This might be among the most critical and challenging phases of a plan, since it involves different personas, different objectives, and different goals that need to be tracked, monitored, and measured to provide decision-makers with the right data to make a go/no-go release decision.

The execution upon the agreed timeline and schedule together with the evidence of quality metrics and criteria are the ingredients of a successful release. Confidence is derived from data and test analysis, which needs to be present prior to the release date.

Making all the six pillars come together is dependent on the three well-known agile components – people, process, and technology:

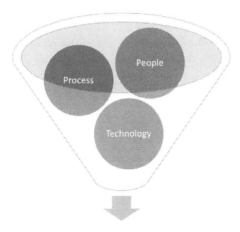

Figure 6.2 – People, process, and technology enable release success

It is important to consider all the preceding aspects as part of your development of the testing plan as well as measuring the test deliverables coming from the different personas. Note that some of the preceding items need to be maintained over time as the product changes, the market evolves, and the end user's behavior changes.

Now that we've covered the building blocks of a solid test plan, including the technology stack, customer profiles, and processes within the software development life cycle, let's understand how to measure the preceding plan and determine whether a software release is on track and meets the criteria of success or not.

Measuring the success of your continuous testing strategy

Now that we've defined at a high level the steps and scoping for a generic test plan, let's look at some common and important metrics and KPIs that can help assess the level of quality of your web application. These KPIs should be part of the **Definition of Done** (**DOD**) (to learn more about DOD, see `https://www.scruminc.com/definition-of-done/`) for a scoped software release. In addition, quality metrics should be part of the quality criteria section within any test plan document.

Success, like quality, is a moment in time; therefore, it needs to be well monitored and structured in a way that decision-makers can analyze on demand.

There are various types of metrics that can be used, based on product requirements, the market vertical that is being served, historical data, and any other category of metrics that is relevant to the business.

The following are 27 suggested metrics by categories that can be adopted by web application teams and used as a basis to add more specific organizational metrics.

I decided to break these metrics into three categories:

- **Speed**
- **Quality**
- **Cost**:

TOP 27 METRICS TO MEASURE IN A CONTINUOUS TESTING PROCESS

Figure 6.3 – The recommended continuous quality metrics for agile teams

As you can see in the preceding figure, each category focuses on a challenge or an objective and offers only a few items for measurement. Teams can pick all of them or a subset, as well as add to these, but successful projects are the ones that cover all three aspects over time.

To highlight a few of the preceding metrics, starting with *quality*, we can focus on the **Mean Time to Detect** (**MTTD**). The MTTD refers to the time it takes to identify a defect in the code based on the total test execution time. Obviously, the shorter it takes to uncover a defect and then resolve it, the better. It also reflects on the effectiveness of the test code. Another example from the preceding metric is the defect distribution by different considerations – priority, severity, functionality, and so on. Knowing the volume of defects and the priority attributed to each testing type and web application area helps to determine the current quality plans, as well as the future testing scope. From a *speed* and *velocity* perspective, knowing within the testing suites the percentage of false-positive and blocked tests provides visibility into the value of your testing suite and can eliminate waste within the pipeline. From a *cost* perspective, looking at the cost of test execution can provide insights to decision-makers regarding tools and testing lab utilization, how well parallel testing is being implemented within the teams, and so on.

Make sure that you use the preceding set of metrics and include the relevant ones within your testing plan and strategy, as well as leveraging the preceding metrics as part of your evaluation process for tools that you have within your DevOps stack.

As a last tip from a measurement and continuous improvement perspective, it is always a great idea to benchmark your own web application and compare it to previous historical industry incidents, such as security issues, functionality, performance, and other quality-related pitfalls.

There is a useful list of common performance defects published on the *iLabquality* website (`https://www.ilabquality.com/the-10-most-common-web-app-performance-problems/`), highlighting things such as unoptimized databases, poorly written code that does not follow best practices, poor load distribution, and troublesome third-party services as common root causes for performance problems in web applications. From a functional standpoint, common bugs that keep coming up across web applications involve poor site navigation, poor mobile device optimizations, inconsistent user experience across platforms, navigating back and forward within a website, negative input into textboxes, and so on.

Functionality and performance are only a subset of an entire test plan and strategy, so learning from others' mistakes around different types of defects can save a great amount of time, resources, and money throughout the life cycle of your project.

The preceding guidelines should help frontend developers and test engineers to properly define metrics to measure their success in a given software release. Now that we have provided in the preceding two categories of functional and non-functional quality both a structured way of building a test plan and measuring its success, let's take a real-time web application and design a test plan that covers the aforementioned building blocks.

A case study – a real-life web application testing strategy

Let's take a specific website and design a testing strategy that will fit end user expectations. For this exercise, I used the Miro tool to create a mind map of the E2E website application flows and scoping of the tests.

The following illustration is based on the *Barclays* website application, serving mainly the UK. I placed the major testing types with some real-life navigation options that are available for the customers of this bank from any mobile device or desktop OS:

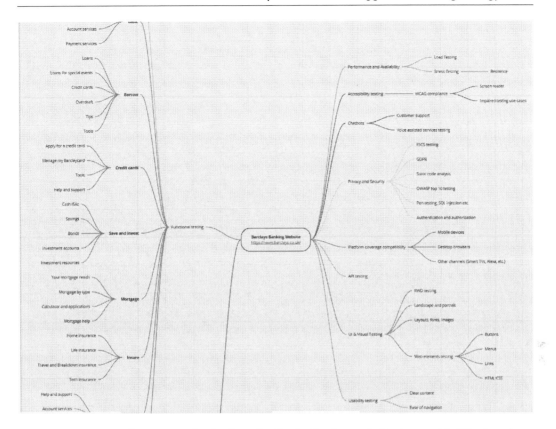

Figure 6.4– A mind map example of web testing for the Barclays website, drawn with Miro boards

As you can see from the preceding mind map, the website testing plan covers all types of test categories to ensure the high quality and performance of the web application. The mind map focuses on tests such as API testing, functional testing broken by the navigation flows within the website, the usability of the web application, performance, and availability. In addition, it covers more advanced aspects of the web application, including accessibility and chatbots, and considers full platform coverage for the types of mobile and desktop systems that will be used within the testing lab. Lastly, the mind map covers production testing for both performance and availability of the web application, as well as service monitoring.

The preceding mind map is not complete; it is just a subset, since each branch continues to an inner link or page, which includes usability, accessibility, performance, security, and many other testing items that fall into the testing plan. However, the mind map provides an understanding of what a real-life testing plan and scoping exercise should look like, and how many complex considerations ought to be planned throughout the teams.

Since agile and DevOps teams are issuing daily to weekly releases, the mind map and testing activities must be part of a strategy that does some level of incremental and differential analysis of the changes between the previous and current version of the web application so that teams can better optimize and scope the entire testing throughout the pipeline, within and outside of the CI process. In addition, even if there is no change to the website, as we learned earlier in the book, every few weeks a new web platform or a mobile platform is introduced and needs to be fully covered and supported, and that is what continuous testing is all about – automating and running continuously tested subsets to ensure high-quality production websites.

Summary

This chapter offered an experience-driven testing plan and strategy so that developers and test managers can scope properly their web application projects from one release to the next.

We then unfolded the scoping of a test plan into three categories of metrics and KPIs to help decision-makers better assess, using data, the quality of a given application. We focused on quality, speed, and cost to categorize these metrics.

Lastly, we took a real-life production website from the financial industry and created a thorough mind map that scopes most testing types across the different testing types: functional, performance, security, APIs, usability, and so on.

We clarified that scoping and planning is always a moment in time, especially for agile and DevOps teams; hence, they need to be always validated and modified to be relevant at the right production moments.

That concludes this chapter! In the following chapter, we will provide a deeper consideration matrix between the top four JavaScript test automation frameworks.

7

Core Capabilities of the Leading JavaScript Test Automation Frameworks

Earlier in the book in *Chapter 4, Matching Personas and Use Cases to Testing Frameworks*, we provided a table that broke down all the critical capabilities across the top four test automation frameworks – Selenium, Cypress, Playwright, and Puppeteer. In this chapter, we will connect these capabilities and provide per each capability the recommended test framework to go with it. When combining multiple capabilities with the recommended frameworks, frontend developers can use this chapter to make a data-driven decision.

The chapter is designed to offer the following:

- An overview of the core capabilities of the leading test automation frameworks

- A compelling events list that can suggest a re-assessment of the test automation framework currently in use

After reading this chapter, you should be able to better evaluate a web test automation framework while considering its core capabilities, as well as understand the differences between built-in capabilities and capabilities obtained through plugin installation.

Comparing the test automation framework capabilities

As illustrated by the core capabilities in *Chapter 4, Matching Personas and Use Cases to Testing Frameworks*, each aspect of a web application needs to be tested; however, there are strengths and weaknesses across the top four testing frameworks, which need to be known upfront.

In the following section, we will dive deeper into the core categories of a web application testing plan and provide some recommendations for a framework that can get the highest coverage of testing per category or use case. The order of the following use cases and categories is random and not based on any kind of priority.

Visual testing

A successfully built web application obviously needs to function properly and perform at high speed; however, the look and feel from a UI standpoint is also a key factor within testing, since the range of screen sizes, resolutions, and devices that the web app will run on is huge.

This is where visual testing comes into play. The visual testing of a responsible **Progressive Web App** (**PWA**) or standard web application can be either done within a core capability of a test framework that the developers are using or through a third-party library that is imported as part of the framework dependencies.

In many cases, having visual testing as a core capability of the framework that we use is a great advantage, since we do not need to continuously maintain and import updates to the dependent library. However, sometimes, there will be exceptions where the third-party solution (such as Happo) provides unique capabilities that are not built into the framework out of the box.

Let's look at visual testing across the different frameworks, starting with Cypress.

Cypress visual testing

For the Cypress framework, visual testing elements that are built into the framework are limited to taking a screenshot of the web application screens that are under test using the `cy.screenshot()` APIs (`https://docs.cypress.io/api/commands/screenshot`), as well as taking screenshots upon a validation failure using the `cy.OnRunFailure()` APIs. Also, as part of the Cypress APIs, a test developer can leverage the CSS assertion functions via `have.css`, but as the Cypress framework suggests, this might become hard to maintain, especially when a web application has many CSS styles.

The main Cypress screenshots commands are listed as follows and can be used within the JavaScript test code:

```
cy.screenshot()
cy.screenshot(fileName)
cy.screenshot(options)
cy.screenshot(fileName, options)
```

To extend visual testing on top of the aforementioned capabilities, Cypress relies on third-party plugins such as **Applitools** (`https://applitools.com/tutorials/cypress.html`), **Percy** (`https://docs.percy.io/docs/cypress`), **Happo** (`https://github.com/happo/happo-cypress`), and the **snapshots** plugin (`https://github.com/meinaart/cypress-plugin-snapshots`).

Keep in mind that all the aforementioned tools, including Applitools, Happo, and Percy, are commercial add-ons to Cypress that you'd need to obtain a license to use. To a limited level, some of these tools such as Happo can be used for free through the open source library.

There is also an existing integration between Cypress and Storybook that can be used for free for visual testing (`https://github.com/storybookjs/storybook/tree/next/cypress`).

Playwright visual testing

Playwright offers a nice out-of-the-box way of creating visual test assertions against a baseline of images that are captured upon the first test run (`https://playwright.dev/docs/test-snapshots`). From the second run and beyond, each screenshot or visual assertion is compared with the stored baseline, and any inconsistencies are reported to the tester for evaluation and decision making.

To make the aforementioned clearer, when running the following sample code for the first time, what Playwright will do is create a new visual baseline image called `landing.png` that will be compared and validated from the next run.

The concept of baselines in visual testing isn't new, and that's the main methodology behind many of the aforementioned commercial tools. Some would add AI as a method of analyzing these screenshots, such as Applitools, but that's an added benefit, of course:

```
// snapshot.spec.js
const { test, expect } = require('@playwright/test');
test('example test', async ({ page }) => {
    await page.goto('https://www.packtpub.com');
    expect(await
        page.screenshot()).toMatchSnapshot('landing.png');
});
```

Playwright visual comparisons can compare images and also text on these screens. It uses a library called `pixelmatch` (`https://github.com/mapbox/pixelmatch`) to perform its visual analysis.

If you need to extend the aforementioned visual testing built-in capabilities and perform at a higher scale and more intelligent visual testing, you can use the available integration Playwright has with Applitools through this tutorial (`https://applitools.com/tutorials/playwright.html`) and/or with Percy (`https://docs.percy.io/docs/playwright`).

Puppeteer visual testing

Google's Puppeteer framework has built-in capabilities to take basic web page screenshots, which are not that useful from a complete visual testing perspective. There is a more solid integration between Puppeteer and Percy (`https://docs.percy.io/docs/puppeteer`) that developers can use to perform visual analysis comparisons with the baseline concept and higher scale and assertions.

To easily get started with Percy and Puppeteer, you will need to install the dependency, and since it is commercial, you'll need to obtain a license and a security token to use it:

```
npm install --save-dev @percy/cli @percy/puppeteer
```

For each JavaScript file that you have and want to use Percy for visual testing, you would need to add this dependency requirement:

```
const percySnapshot = require('@percy/puppeteer')
```

Once the preceding dependencies are set, you can start using the Percy APIs such as `percySnapshot()`.

Selenium visual testing

Selenium is one of the oldest and most mature frameworks in the industry, which integrates with a variety of commercial visual testing tools and works nicely with the open source platform called **Storybook** (`https://storybook.js.org/tutorials/design-systems-for-developers/react/en/test/`) and **Galen** (`http://galenframework.com/docs/reference-javascript-tests-guide/`).

Unlike Playwright, which has some built-in APIs for visual testing, with Selenium, a developer would need to learn the methodologies of Galen, Storybook, and Applitools to integrate them into their source code. It is, of course, doable, and fully supported and maintained by both communities and vendors, so adding visual testing to Selenium is a matter of choice and budget if you choose to go with the commercial vendors (Applitools, Percy – `https://docs.percy.io/docs/selenium-for-javascript`).

Adding such code to a Selenium JavaScript test scenario would perform the visual validation and check the page layout. Galen with Selenium is very strong for responsive web application testing (responsive web design):

```
test("Home page", function() {
var driver = createDriver("http://galenframework.com",
                          "1024x768");
checkLayout(driver, "homePage.gspec", ["all", "desktop"]);
});
```

So far, we have seen that visual testing can be accomplished across all four test automation frameworks; however, **Playwright** is the only framework that has such capabilities built into its core APIs, while the others require third-party integrations with either open source frameworks such as Galen and Storybook, or commercial ones such as Percy and Applitools.

API testing

In the traditional testing pyramid, it's clear that lower-level automated testing is API testing. However, it is powerful, fast, very reliable, and stable. Most testing projects use API testing as part of their test plan scoping; however, when it comes to API testing within the four leading frameworks, not all of them offer this ability as a built-in capability.

Cypress API testing

Cypress offers built-in support for API testing. With the Cypress testing framework, developers and test engineers can create any kind of API testing across all different types of methods (GET, POST, DELETE, PATCH, and PUT).

Cypress performs most of its API tests via the `cy.request()` method, which serves as a GET command to the web server being tested.

In the following examples, we will be using a free website (`http://jsonplaceholder.typicode.com/`) that is available for API testing activities. On the website, there are several resources that can be used for testing purposes and training, such as 200 to-do list items, thousands of photos, 10 usernames, and many other options.

With the Cypress API testing abilities, you can perform various validations on the aforementioned sample website.

When a user installs Cypress locally, they can learn from a built-in code sample how to test different network requests.

In the following snippet, Cypress uses the `request` method to retrieve the first user ID from the user's website and then adds a new entry with the ID `'Cypress Test Runner'`:

```
it('cy.request() - pass result to the second request', () => {
    // first, let's find out the userId of the first user
    // we have
    cy.request(
        'https://jsonplaceholder.cypress.io/users?_limit=1')
        .its('body') // yields the response object
        .its('0') // yields the first element of the returned
                  // list
        // the above two commands its('body').its('0')
        // can be written as its('body.0')
```

```
    // if you do not care about TypeScript checks
  .then((user) => {
    expect(user).property('id').to.be.a('number')
    // make a new post on behalf of the user
    cy.request('POST',
      'https://jsonplaceholder.cypress.io/posts', {
      userId: user.id,
      title: 'Cypress Test Runner',
      body: 'Fast, easy and reliable testing for
              anything that runs in a browser.',

    })
  })
  // note that the value here is the returned value of
  // the 2nd request which is the new post object
  .then((response) => {
    // new entity created
    expect(response).property('status').to.equal(201)
    expect(response).property('body').to.contain({.
      title: 'Cypress Test Runner',
    })
})
```

It is very clear from an API testing standpoint that Cypress can check the box of a supported capability. While it is not as thorough as dedicated solutions such as Postman, REST-Assured, and others, it does provide an easy user experience to add to the functional testing layer API tests and the creation of network request scenarios.

Playwright API testing

Similar to Cypress, the Playwright framework also provides a set of capabilities to create API test scenarios (`https://playwright.dev/docs/test-api-testing`). With Playwright's methods under `appiRequestContext` (`get`, `post`, `fetch`, `put`, `delete`, `patch`, `dispose`, `head`, and `storageState`), developers can perform a wide range of API test validations. `apiResponse` (body, status, headers, and so on) methods will return the responses returned by the `apiRequestContext` methods:

apiRequestContext.get(url[, options])

- `url` <string> Target URL.
- `options` <Object>
  - `failOnStatusCode` <boolean> Whether to throw on response codes other than 2xx and 3xx. By default response object is returned for all status codes.
  - `headers` <Object<string, string>> Allows to set HTTP headers.
  - `ignoreHTTPSErrors` <boolean> Whether to ignore HTTPS errors when sending network requests. Defaults to `false`.
  - `params` <Object<string, string|number|boolean>> Query parameters to be sent with the URL.
  - `timeout` <number> Request timeout in milliseconds. Defaults to `30000` (30 seconds). Pass `0` to disable timeout.
- returns: <Promise<APIResponse>>

Sends HTTP(S) GET request and returns its response. The method will populate request cookies from the context and update context cookies from the response. The method will automatically follow redirects.

Figure 7.1 – An apiRequestContext syntax example (source – Playwright documentation `https://playwright.dev/docs/api/class-apirequestcontext#api-request-context-get`)

At the time of writing, Playwright supports API testing only using JavaScript and Python languages, with Java and .NET coming later in the roadmap.

Selenium API testing

This is a short section since Selenium cannot automate API testing as a built-in capability, only through integrations with third-party API testing frameworks such as REST-Assured (`https://rest-assured.io/`).

Puppeteer API testing

This is a short section since Google Puppeteer cannot automate API testing as a built-in capability.

Supported development languages

While this book is 100% focused on JavaScript test automation development, some of the four leading frameworks that we're covering can support other language bindings.

To give a brief comparison of the supported languages, here is a snippet from *Chapter 4, Matching Personas and Use Cases to Testing Frameworks*, that should make it clear and easy to understand the differences between the test frameworks:

Capabilities	Cypress	Playwright	Puppeteer	Selenium
Supported languages	JavaScript	Java	JavaScript	Java
	TypeScript	JavaScript		JavaScript
		TypeScript		Ruby
		Python		Python
		.NET		C#
				Kotlin

Knowing the supported languages of each framework lets test and development managers know that for some frameworks, they can have more flexibility around test creation. If among the developers there are individuals that, for example, are stronger in **Java** or **Python**, **Selenium** and **Playwright** are strong options to consider. As shown in the preceding table, languages such as **C#**, **Ruby**, and **Kotlin** are only supported by **Selenium**.

Mobile device testing

It is a fact that websites are used more nowadays on mobile devices than on desktop machines. With that in mind, developers and test engineers must include mobile device testing as part of their test plan. This core capability can be a bit complicated across analyzed test automation frameworks, since testing on simulated viewports or emulators/simulators is only good to some extent. To ensure real-world user experience, performance, and quality on mobile devices, testing must be also done on real devices.

Cypress mobile device testing

Cypress can use the `cy.viewport()` APIs to mimic the width and height of a mobile phone screen's viewport for the website under test; however, this will only give you a basic look and feel for your web application across specified screen sizes. In addition, Cypress offers the use of `userAgent` as part of the simulation of a real mobile device property (`https://docs.cypress.io/guides/references/configuration#Browser`). A developer can either specify the use of a specific mobile platform `userAgent` string within the `cypress.json` file or embed it in the test code itself within the `onBeforeLoad()` method. The **Mozilla Developer Network (MDN)** web docs by Mozilla provide very useful documentation on how to use and specify `userAgent` (`https://developer.mozilla.org/en-US/docs/Web/HTTP/Headers/User-Agent`).

As an example, to test a Cypress web application scenario on a Google Pixel 6 device running on Android 12 on a Chrome 96 browser version, you can use the following declaration in your test code with the `value: [userAgent]` attribute, as specified in the following:

```
value: Mozilla/5.0 (Linux; Android 12; Pixel 6 Pro)
AppleWebKit/537.36 (KHTML, like Gecko) Chrome/96.0.4664.92
Mobile Safari/537.36
```

> **userAgent**
>
> `userAgent` is a characteristic string that lets servers and network peers identify the properties of an application, type of operating system, vendor, and the OS version of the requesting platform. W3C defines it at a high level as *"software that retrieves, renders and facilitates end user interaction with Web content, or whose user interface is implemented using Web technologies."* (`https://www.w3.org/WAI/UA/work/wiki/Definition_of_User_Agent`).

With the preceding two methods in mind (`userAgent` and using a viewport), this is still considered a very limited set of capabilities from a mobile testing perspective.

Playwright mobile device testing

Similar to how Cypress offers testing different viewports as part of its extended mobile testing abilities, Playwright also offers the use of the `playwright.devices()` API (`https://playwright.dev/docs/api/class-playwright#playwright-devices`), which allows frontend developers and SDETs to specify device characteristics.

The preceding capability is used by adding to your test code the following specific lines (in the following, we are using iPhone 12 characteristics to test the *Packt* website):

```
const { webkit, devices } = require('playwright');
const iPhone = devices['iPhone 12'];
(async () => {
const browser = await webkit.launch();
const context = await browser.newContext( {
...iPhone
})
const page = await context.newPage();
await page.goto('http://packtpub.com');
await browser.close();
})();
```

As clarified in the previous Cypress section, Playwright does not offer any advanced mobile testing ability here.

Puppeteer mobile device testing

Google's Puppeteer framework also offers a simulation capability through the `emulate()` method. Basically, the previous code snippet is very close to the Puppeteer syntax with minor adjustments, as shown in the official Google documentation (`https://pptr.dev/#?product=Puppeteer&version=v12.0.1&show=api-pageemulateoptions`). As with Cypress, Puppeteer can also specify `userAgent` and viewports through the `page.setUserAgent(userAgent)` and `page.setViewport(viewport)` methods. If you're planning to juggle multiple devices, using the Puppeteer-supported device descriptors option can be very useful.

Selenium mobile device testing

Selenium is the most advanced testing framework when it comes to mobile and web application testing. The Appium framework (`https://appium.io/`) is derived from the Selenium WebDriver implementation, but it's fully aimed at testing mobile web, hybrid, and mobile-native applications across most language bindings, including JavaScript. If you wish to extend your web testing to mobile devices at scale, using Appium might be a good option, and it leverages the same core APIs with new and specific ones that are relevant to the mobile landscape.

Performance testing

The user experience and performance of a web application are equally important as functionality. Ensuring that the response time of any web application transaction is reasonable across mobile and web platforms, including when the load on the backend servers is growing, should be part of any web application testing plan. There are leading performance-testing frameworks on the market, such as JMeter (open source) with its supported load testing product BlazeMeter (`https://www.blazemeter.com/`) and NeoLoad from Tricentis. From the perspective of the four main JavaScript testing frameworks covered in this book, most can offer measurements of transaction timing or, through browser developer tools (such as the CDP), utilize the Lighthouse tool to perform some advanced measurements of such transactions. Keep in mind that none of these frameworks comes with built-in load testing capabilities.

Cypress performance testing

As we will see, in most of the test automation frameworks that we're evaluating in this book, **Google Lighthouse** can be utilized to measure the following top six key performance indicators:

- **First Contentful Paint (FCP)**
- **Large Contentful Paint (LCP)**
- Speed index
- **Time To Interactive (TTI)**
- Total blocking time
- **Cumulative Layout Shift (CLS):**

Figure 7.2 – The Google Lighthouse performance output on the Packt website

In addition to embedding Lighthouse in the Cypress test code, frontend developers can also measure specific web application transactions using the two following methods:

```
win.performance.mark("start-loading");
performance.mark("end-loading");
performance.measure("pageLoad", "start-loading",
                    "end-loading");
```

The preceding commands will measure a given page load time from the start of the load until the end-load command. This code can measure any given components that are being loaded on the page in between the start and endpoints.

Playwright and Puppeteer performance testing

Since both frameworks were developed by the same team, we can see that there are many similarities in the APIs offered by Playwright and Puppeteer. Specifically for performance testing, both Playwright and Puppeteer provide navigation timing (`https://www.w3.org/TR/navigation-timing/`) and resource timing APIs (`https://www.w3.org/TR/resource-timing-1/`) that frontend developers can embed in their test code to measure timestamps for a given web application load. A short simple code snippet that assesses basic performance metrics for a web application can be obtained from this GitHub repository (`https://github.com/PacktPublishing/A-Frontend-Web-Developers-Guide-to-Testing/blob/master/perfTest.js`). Download and execute it using the following:

```
node perfTest.js
```

When running the test, you should observe the following output in your console:

```
PS C:\Users\ekinsbruner\Playwright_code> node .\perfTest.js
{
    connectStart: 1646060494675,
    navigationStart: 1646060494668,
    loadEventEnd: 1646060500267,
    domLoading: 1646060494832,
    secureConnectionStart: 1646060494688,
    fetchStart: 1646060494669,
    domContentLoadedEventStart: 1646060495878,
    responseStart: 1646060494829,
    responseEnd: 1646060494834,
    domInteractive: 1646060495445,
    domainLookupEnd: 1646060494675,
    redirectStart: 0,
    requestStart: 1646060494760,
    unloadEventEnd: 0,
    unloadEventStart: 0,
    domComplete: 1646060500236,
    domainLookupStart: 1646060494673,
    loadEventStart: 1646060500236,
    domContentLoadedEventEnd: 1646060495878,
    redirectEnd: 0,
    connectEnd: 1646060494760
}
```

Figure 7.3 – Performance test execution output on the Packt website

The preceding output consists of the most common performance metrics such as domLoading and domInteractive. Note that the test was executed locally without applying any kind of load on the backend. To analyze the web application under high user volume, it is recommended to use a load testing tool that applies a significant load on the backend while running this test.

The preceding code snippet uses the performance timing APIs to measure the timestamp of the Packt page load time.

For the Puppeteer framework, there are also external libraries such as the Web Perf measurement library, which was developed by the community and can be used to perform web page KPI measurements using Chrome DevTools (https://github.com/addyosmani/puppeteer-webperf).

Obviously, since both frameworks are based on the CDP, they can use the developer tools from the Chromium and Edge browsers, as well as the Lighthouse tool to perform single-user performance testing on their web applications.

Selenium performance testing

Selenium is a very thorough test automation framework; however, even the Selenium documentation states that using Selenium for performance testing is not advised (`https://www.selenium.dev/documentation/test_practices/ discouraged/performance_testing/`), since it's not optimized to measure user experience. Selenium is built on the WebDriver protocol, which may add a payload to the measurements of page load time and other testing transactions. Therefore, it is recommended to use a neutral tool for such testing activities. Selenium refers users to JMeter for performance testing, which can then be extended using BlazeMeter, as previously mentioned.

Accessibility testing

Each website these days must adhere to the strict accessibility requirements defined by WCAG and other bodies. Enabling people with various disabilities to consume data on websites and perform all available transactions is a mandatory requirement. Hence, designing a web application for accessibility and testing for it is a key requirement for each software iteration. For web accessibility testing, Deque has developed the widely adopted axe open source framework (`https://www.deque.com/axe/`), which most test automation frameworks today support through APIs and plugins.

Cypress accessibility testing

As mentioned, most frameworks utilize the axe framework for checking website accessibility issues.

To validate your website accessibility, install the axe plugin on top of your local Cypress installation folder by running the following command:

```
npm install --save-dev cypress-axe
npm install --save-dev cypress axe-core
```

After both libraries are installed, add the import line to the `index.js` file in your `cypress/support` folder:

```
import 'cypress-axe'
```

The axe library will provide you with the following useful methods:

- `cy.injectAxe()`
- `cy.configureAxe()`
- `cy.checkA11Y()`

Running your test code in JavaScript or TypeScript with the axe plugin will generate a detailed A11Y accessibility test report, which will be available on both the Cypress GUI dashboard as well as within the local test report. Frontend developers should then analyze and resolve all violations.

Puppeteer accessibility testing

Google Puppeteer can also leverage the axe framework to run accessibility tests on web applications.

A dedicated plugin can be installed above the local Puppeteer folder through this command:

```
npm install axe-puppeteer
```

This plugin will add the `AxePuppeteer(page).analyze()` method, which can be used to run a scan on a given page and report back the results. A dedicated document was created by the Deque team to help get started with the solution (`https://www.deque.com/blog/axe-and-attest-integration-puppeteer/`).

Playwright accessibility testing

As with Puppeteer, axe is the preferred and recommended plugin to use with Playwright to test for web application accessibility. To get started with the plugin and to add its supported APIs to your Playwright test code, run the following command:

```
npm i -D axe-playwright
```

A complete guide of how to use the plugin with Playwright was created by Deque and can be obtained here: `https://www.deque.com/blog/new-axe-devtools-integration-playwright/`. In contrast to Puppeteer, with Playwright, the method to use within the test code to analyze the accessibility of a specific page is `AxeBuilder({page}).analyze()`.

Selenium accessibility testing

To use Selenium WebDriver with the axe plugin, visit the Deque GitHub repository (`https://github.com/dequelabs/axe-webdriverjs`).

As with the preceding framework, you will need to install the node library. To do so, run the following command:

```
npm i axe-webdriverjs
```

Once you have the library installed and added to your local Selenium environment, you can start using it to analyze your web application pages. Since axe is constantly updating its rules, frontend developers can specify and pass the `axe-core` source file as a parameter and use a specific rules version out of the many that axe provides.

Network control testing and mock services

Testing web applications is not just about the functionality of an app; it's also about all the services that build the app and that the app relies on. Some of the problems when testing web apps pre-production are that not all the services are ready to be used during the development stage, or that these services and test data are dynamically changing, and developers and testers have no control over the data.

Test automation frameworks can utilize mock services as well as use network control capabilities, such as changing the clock time, to assess web application output based on triggered events.

Cypress network control and mocking

Cypress has a great set of network controls and mocking capabilities that can solve problems around a lack of control over test or production data and thereby add more reliability to the testing cycles.

`cy.intercept()` and `cy.clock()` are two of the strong capabilities of Cypress for controlling and testing some services of a web application. An additional use case of `cy.intercept()` is **stubbing**. Using the method testers can stub a response and control the body, status, and headers and even delay them. It is a way of manipulating an application by cutting off parts of the application to send a controlled response and validate the application behavior.

The use of `cy.clock()` and `cy.tick()` help to override native global functions related to time and allow them to be controlled synchronously. You can set timeouts and much more and, thereby, perform time-based assertions on a dynamic page where elements appear or change when you want. Lastly, when using Cypress with mock data, testers can utilize the `fixtures` folder and place in it mock data files in a JSON format. Such test data can be any relevant data that your web app should be tested against, such as items in a cart prior to purchasing, notes, and a list of items. Using the test data under that folder is done by calling `cy.fixture()` with the path to the JSON test data file. To learn more about Cypress network control as well as get some code samples, refer to the Cypress documentation (`https://docs.cypress.io/guides/guides/network-requests`).

Playwright network control and mocking

Playwright has its own APIs that can be used to monitor and modify the network traffic for a web application under test. All the supported APIs are documented here (`https://playwright.dev/docs/network`) and include capabilities around authentication, and handling and modifying network requests. There is a great use case that combines Playwright's `context.route()` method and the *CodeceptJS* testing framework to perform mocking of network requests (`https://codecept.io/playwright/#accessing-playwright-api`).

You can learn more about network mocking APIs with Playwright here: `https://playwright.dev/docs/test-configuration#network-mocking`.

Puppeteer network control and mocking

Google Puppeteer, as mentioned previously in this book, is at the core of Playwright and comes with built-in network control capabilities, including mocking services. To perform network interception within your test code, you should utilize the `page.setRequestInterception(true)` APIs. The following insightful blog provides a great example of how, by using the preceding method, testers can block unnecessary elements such as images from loading to expedite page load time and test faster: `https://www.checklyhq.com/learn/headless/request-interception/`.

In addition to the preceding, the Puppeteer framework also has a way of emulating cellular network conditions (3G, 4G, and so on) by using the `page.emulateNetworkConditions(networkConditions)` method (`https://pptr.dev/#?product=Puppeteer&version=v13.0.1&show=api-pageemulatenetworkconditionsnetworkconditions`).

Lastly, there is a useful library called `puppeteer-mock` that can be used as a bridge between the Puppeteer framework and an open source mocking library (`https://www.npmjs.com/package/puppeteer-mock`). To install it on top of your local Puppeteer framework, run the following command:

```
npm install --save-dev puppeteer-mock
```

The preceding library has three main functions – `activate()`, `deactivate()`, and `isActive()`.

Selenium network control and mocking

Selenium 4 brought advanced capabilities around network control and mocking APIs. The added support for CDP (`https://chromedevtools.github.io/devtools-protocol/`) opened the door for Selenium to use the DevTools package and perform network requests among other things. Prior to Selenium 4, this was quite difficult and, in many cases, required additional third-party plugins and libraries, or setting servers such as WireMock (`http://wiremock.org/docs/getting-started/`).

With Selenium 4 and the CDP DevTools, testers can use the `devTool.send()` API and other APIs to block CSS from loading, intercept network requests, ignore security certificates, and so on.

To learn more about the aforementioned CDP in Selenium 4, refer to the Selenium official documentation (`https://www.selenium.dev/blog/2020/what-is-coming-in-selenium-4-new-tricks/`).

Working with elements

At the core of test automation scenarios are element locators. Without properly identifying web application elements, the test automation code will not be able to run properly, since it can't find the elements on the web pages and perform actions on them. Obviously, all the four leading test automation frameworks work perfectly well with the elements within the website DOM tree. Some of the frameworks even make element identification and maintenance easier through object spies, page object model support, and even test automation recording.

Cypress working with elements

Unlike Selenium, Cypress queries the DOM and works only on **CSS selectors** (`https://www.w3schools.com/cssref/css_selectors.asp`), which include ID, class, and attribute. To use XPATH within the Cypress test code, you will need to install the **cypress-xpath** (`https://www.npmjs.com/package/cypress-xpath`) plugin. Cypress can also use `.contains()` to select an element that contains, for example, some text. Cypress can also find elements by their position in a list by using the `.first()`, `.last()`, or `.eq()` methods:

```
cy
  .get('list')
  .first(); // "select first item in the list "
cy
  .get('list')
```

```
    .last(); // "select last item in the list "
cy
    .get('list')
    .eq(2); // "select 2nd item in the list
"
```

There are various methods to locate elements in Cypress. You can use the DevTools utilities from the browsers themselves and inspect specific pages and elements, or you can use the Cypress GUI element selector and identify the target elements that you want to perform an automated action on. Another method that can be used is the SelectorsHub Google Chrome extension utility (https://chrome. google.com/webstore/detail/selectorshub-xpath-plugin/ ndgimibanhlabgdgjcpbbndiehljcpfh):

Figure 7.4 – The Cypress CSS selector playground within the Cypress GUI used to identify web page elements

Playwright working with elements

Unlike Cypress, Playwright performs all of its actions on the .page() class (https:// playwright.dev/docs/api/class-page). It has unique methods that are used to click on elements, enter text, navigate, and so on. The most common methods that are used to perform actions on elements within web applications are .page.fill("some text"), .page.press("button"), .page.dblclick("selector,options"), and assertThat(page.locator(".'selector')).hasText("some text"), which is used to find text in a given element on the website.

In addition to the page APIs that are quite efficient in performing actions on the elements, Playwright also supports and recommends the implementation of a **Page Object Model (POM)** as part of its best practices (`https://playwright.dev/docs/pom`). A POM is a great way to maintain elements across test code and simplify test code creation.

As with Cypress, Playwright also offers a built-in inspector tool (`https://playwright.dev/docs/inspector`) that can help with element identification, as well as test code debugging:

Figure 7.5 – The Playwright Inspector tool (source – https://playwright.dev/docs/inspector)

Puppeteer working with elements

Google's Puppeteer frameworks inevitably allow frontend developers and testers to use Chrome DevTools and a built-in browser inspector to identify elements on web applications.

Great documentation can be found at `https://devdocs.io/puppeteer/` on how to work with Puppeteer across the different layers of a web application, including the page, the frames within the page, and the application context. Since Puppeteer drives the test through the DevTools protocol from the browser through the page, that's how you would design the test as well. The following code snippet shows how you would first launch Puppeteer and then create a new Incognito browser context before opening a new page on the Packt website:

```
(async () => {
    const browser = await puppeteer.launch();
    // Create a new incognito browser context.
    const context =
        await browser.createIncognitoBrowserContext();
    // Create a new page in a pristine context.
    const page = await context.newPage();
    // Do stuff
    await page.goto('https://www.packtpub.com');
})();
```

Puppeteer also uses the CSS selector syntax and specifically provides the `querySelectorAll(selectors)` APIs to search through the list of elements on the page (`https://devdocs.io/dom/element/queryselectorall`), as you can see in the following screenshot:

Figure 7.6 – Google's DevTools console used to perform an element query

Selenium working with elements

Earlier in the book in *Chapter 3, Top Web Test Automation Frameworks*, we covered the eight supported element locators by Selenium. The Selenium framework offers, like Playwright, the use of a POM, and through the Selenium IDE, it allows the recording of test scripts that can automatically identify the elements of a web application. Being the oldest framework on the market, Selenium already has very structured methods of working with elements through findElement(By. [supported locators]). As with the other testing frameworks, users can also leverage the browser DevTools inspector to identify elements and use them within their test code:

Figure 7.7 – Selenium-supported web element locators

It is the test engineer's responsibility to properly use the most robust and reliable element locator to ensure test stability over time. With the most recent release of Selenium 4, the community introduced the use of relative locators to better identify complex elements, based on their relationship with other elements on a page. Users can choose from the following relative locator-supported methods – preceding(), below(), toLeftof(), toRightof(), and near(). I strongly recommend reading *Angie Jones's* blog on relative locators in Selenium 4 (https://angiejones.tech/selenium-4-relative-locators/) to better understand the syntax and value of this feature.

CI/CD integration

Lastly, to meet the strict timelines within a software iteration, developers and testers run their test automation scenarios within **Continuous Integration** (**CI**). All the test automation frameworks support running tests in CI as well as in CI through cloud vendors such as **Perfecto**, **SauceLabs**, and **BrowserStack**.

As already identified in *Chapter 4, Matching Personas and Use Cases to Testing Frameworks*, these test frameworks somewhat differ from the CI servers that they best work with. It is up to developers to choose whether they prefer one framework over another, based on the following supported tools:

Continuous Integration Support	Cypress	Playwright	Puppeteer	Selenium
	Circle CI	Jenkins	GitHub Actions	Jenkins
	GitHub Actions	Circle CI	CircleCI	GitHub Actions
	GitLab	Bitbucket	Docker	CircleCI
	Bitbucket	Docker		GitLab
	AWS CodeBuild	Azure Pipelines		Azure DevOps
	Docker (Cypress even provides ready-made images)	Travis CI		Bitbucket
		GitHub Actions		
		GitLab		

With the preceding CI tools overview, we conclude the full coverage of the different test automation framework capabilities.

In this section, we provided an overview of the most important capabilities across the leading test automation frameworks, including working with elements, performing visual testing, accessibility testing, network control, API testing, integrating into a CI/CD tool stack, performance testing, mobile testing, and more.

In the following section, we will provide the key compelling events that may cause a change to the existing test automation framework that is in use by your teams.

A re-evaluation of test automation frameworks due to compelling events

Comparing all the preceding capabilities is a great way to perform due diligence across the leading test automation frameworks on the market; however, such a comparison is a timely activity that must be done multiple times.

The market and the web application project life cycle often trigger a need to change the framework that's being used by frontend developers and SDETs. The following are a few examples of such compelling events:

- **A new web application developed from scratch**: Within a web project life cycle, the product management team or the business as a whole may decide that it's time for a full refresh of a website. With such a refresh, developers might pick a new development framework, as well as decide that the web application will be of the PWA type. A new project has a new UI, new requirements, new business flows, and so on. That's a valid trigger to re-assess the test automation framework that a team has been using and decide on a different one, based on the project requirements.

- **Instability and flakiness within the testing pipeline**: Even though a team has been using a solid test automation framework for an existing web application project, there are cases where the test automation percentage as well as the pass rate are too low, due to a mismatch of the framework to the testing scenarios, a skillset within the team, or simply the limitations of the framework. This is also a great moment to reassess and make changes to the tool stack. In many cases, bringing a secondary framework to complement the existing one can prove a great strategy to fix these instabilities and increase the test scenario coverage.

- **Organizational-related changes**: In this category, the change can involve offshoring the testing activities to a remote team that uses a different test framework and has different skillset levels, or within the development team there is a re-organization, and new leadership is brought in that has better experience with different tools. In such cases, a reassessment of the test frameworks might happen to better fit the technology with the current test developers' skills and needs.

- **Market tool stack evolution**: Lastly, as software development projects evolve, so do test automation frameworks. In this chapter, we gave some examples of the modifications made to the Selenium 4 framework, and such changes are constantly being made to other leading frameworks. Closing gaps in test frameworks by adding new features and the evolution of frameworks are great examples, providing an "excuse" to re-evaluate an existing test framework selection and either bring in a second one or replace the existing one with another.

Summary

In this chapter, we explored the different but important capabilities of a test automation framework and dived deeper into how each of the four leading test automation frameworks supports and works to address these capabilities. There is no clear-cut choice of framework, since a web application project is very complex and has different requirements and testing criteria.

This chapter gave some guidance in terms of each capability about whether a test framework can accomplish more, or if it's easier to use one compared to another. We have seen examples of capabilities that are built into the test frameworks as opposed to those that require an external plugin to be installed (such as XPath support).

As a frontend developer and/or SDET, you can use this chapter to create your own tailored consideration matrix that will fit your project. If your project requires more in-depth visual testing, performance testing, and network control, you can clearly see which of the four frameworks supports these requirements and to what extent, making your decision easier.

We also listed a few of the top compelling events that might cause a team to re-evaluate and change an existing framework for another.

This concludes this chapter! In the following chapter, we will focus on measuring test coverage across the four test automation frameworks and offer guidance on tools and practices to succeed in this objective.

8

Measuring Test Coverage of the Web Application

How do you know that you've tested your web application enough? There are many metrics and measures for code quality, including defect density, user stories covered, and other "black-box" measurements. However, there is also a complementary metric that has been on the market for a long while and is more of a "white-box" metric, which is code coverage. In this chapter, you will learn how to complement the quality assessment of your web application with code coverage across the various test automation frameworks featured in this book (**Selenium**, **Cypress**, **Playwright**, and **Puppeteer**).

The chapter is designed to cover the following:

- Understand the differences between code coverage and test coverage and when to use them.

- Learn about the recommended tool(s) for JavaScript code coverage measurements.

- Understand how to complement code coverage measurements with test coverage capabilities (for example, production data, platform coverage, and analytics).

The goal of this chapter is to help frontend developers and SDETs build code coverage into their software development life cycles and recommend the right tools to use with the leading test automation frameworks.

Introduction to code coverage and test coverage

When assessing code quality, there are various metrics and methods to do so. However, when referring to quality and coverage metrics, there is often confusion between code coverage and test coverage. In this section, we will define and clarify what each of them means and focus on the definition and value of code coverage to frontend web application developers.

Test coverage

Test coverage refers to the level of testing against requirements that you cover via all types of testing (functional, non-functional, API, security, accessibility, and more). Within test coverage, you can also identify the platform coverage metric, which includes the required permutations of browser/OS and mobile/OS platforms. Within the tool stack landscape, there are **application life cycle management** (**ALM**) solutions as well as other test management tools that can measure and provide high-level metrics around test coverage.

Typically, the QA manager would build a test plan that specifies all the testing efforts that are planned for the software version under test. As part of the plan, the QA manager will also provide test coverage goals and criteria.

Running all testing types that are required based on the test plan should ensure not only the high quality of the release but also a decent test coverage percentage. Based on the pass/fail ratio, decision-makers will know whether the product is ready to be released or whether it has quality risks.

In many practices, test coverage encapsulates the following pillars:

- **Product features coverage** – how well we are covering all business flows, website screens, and navigation flows within the application, and how they work from a quality perspective.

- **Product requirements coverage** – this pillar refers to all the product user stories and capabilities that were supposed to be part of the product. The fact that we've tested, as identified previously, all available features does not mean that all the features that were supported to be included in the version are implemented.

- **Boundary values coverage** – this aspect ensures that the application works fine in all types of user inputs, whether they are appropriate or unappropriate. This can be testing all types of input fields and forms, entering different characters, mixing languages, and more.

- **Compatibility coverage** – as mentioned previously, this type of category refers to the level of platforms that are covered within all types of testing. For web applications, we typically refer to the most relevant configurations of web and mobile platforms against supported OS versions.

- **Risk coverage** – in specific market verticals, this type of pillar is even greater than others. However, measuring and addressing product risks within the test plan and the test coverage analysis is critical to ensure safe and high-quality software. An example of risk coverage is ensuring that dependencies for the web application are properly monitored and that there is a fallback plan (for example, third-party services or databases).

The bottom line is, test coverage looks at the software from a higher level and from a product requirement testing perspective.

Code coverage

Unlike test coverage, code coverage is very much technical and goes down to the code level to measure and assess how many lines of code are exercised and "touched" by different types of tests. In many cases and practices, unit tests would be the highest-priority testing type to attach to code coverage since the method of measuring code coverage requires high development skills, instrumentation of the code, and understanding of the code coverage outputs. With that in mind, this does not state that code coverage cannot be measured by running functional and other types of testing, as we will learn later in this chapter.

In a more scientific manner, code coverage aims to indicate the percentage of the code that is covered by different types of test cases. The output of a code coverage report typically consists of the following pillars of categories:

- **Branch coverage** – this metric ensures that every possible branch used in a decision-making process is executed. A good example is if within the code for your web application there is a conditional scenario based on user input, you are properly covering all possible cases.

- **Function coverage** – this metric measures whether all available functions within the web application code are executed.

- **Statement coverage** – this metric, which is part of most common code coverage tools, will show that every executable statement in the code is executed at least once.

- **Loop coverage** – as in statement coverage, loop coverage refers to the measurement of loops within the source code of the application under test being executed at least once.

To perform code coverage properly, frontend web application developers need to perform code instrumentation to add the coverage measurements to the code under test.

```
------------------|----------|----------|----------|----------|----------------|
File              | % Stmts  | % Branch | % Funcs  | % Lines  |Uncovered Lines |
------------------|----------|----------|----------|----------|----------------|
All files         |   98.92  |   94.36  |   99.49  |    100   |                |
 yargs            |   99.17  |   93.95  |    100   |    100   |                |
  index.js        |    100   |    100   |    100   |    100   |                |
  yargs.js        |   99.15  |   93.86  |    100   |    100   |                |
 yargs/lib        |    98.7  |   94.72  |   99.07  |    100   |                |
  command.js      |    99.1  |   98.51  |    100   |    100   |                |
  completion.js   |    100   |   95.83  |    100   |    100   |                |
  obj-filter.js   |    87.5  |   83.33  |   66.67  |    100   |                |
  usage.js        |   97.89  |   92.59  |    100   |    100   |                |
  validation.js   |    100   |   95.56  |    100   |    100   |                |
------------------|----------|----------|----------|----------|----------------|
```

Figure 8.1 – Sample code coverage output from the Istanbul JavaScript code coverage tool (source: https://istanbul.js.org/)

Now that we have clarified the differences between code and test coverage, let's see how one of the leading coverage tools can work with the leading test automation frameworks on the market.

JavaScript code coverage tools for web application developers

As identified in the previous section, to measure code coverage, frontend web application developers should use tools that can measure the depth of testing done by the testing types during the test execution phase. To do so, frontend developers use tools that instrument their website source code by adding different counters and analyzers that in return report back the percentage of lines of code covered by testing and the percentage of statements and branches, and with that, they can assess the overall coverage and quality of their product.

For the JavaScript development language, the most used tool is **Istanbul**, which also uses the **Babel** plugin. Most leading test automation frameworks have a plugin for **Istanbul**, making it the most recommended tool for measuring code coverage.

The **Cypress Istanbul** plugin can be obtained here: `https://www.npmjs.com/package/cypress-istanbul`. If you're using Jest, it comes with a built-in coverage capability (`https://jestjs.io/`) that allows measuring coverage by simply adding the `--coverage` flag to your testing command line. There are many other guides for using Istanbul with Selenium (`https://stackoverflow.com/questions/67913176/how-to-implement-istanbul-coverage-with-selenium-and-mocha`) that can be used, as well as similar guides for using Istanbul with Playwright (`https://github.com/mxschmitt/playwright-test-coverage`; `https://medium.com/@novyludek/code-coverage-of-e2e-tests-with-playwright-6f8b4c0b56e1`). Lastly, to accomplish the same for your web application in JavaScript with Google Puppeteer and Istanbul, here are two useful guides: `https://github.com/istanbuljs/puppeteer-to-istanbul` and `https://github.com/puppeteer/puppeteer/blob/main/docs/api.md#class-coverage`.

Since in theory measuring code coverage across all the preceding test automation frameworks is done using Istanbul and the Babel plugin, we will pick Cypress as a reference framework and explain how to set up, instrument, and measure code coverage of a sample web application.

Measuring JavaScript code coverage using Istanbul and Cypress

Assuming you already have a working environment for Cypress locally installed, we will now focus on setting up Istanbul and Babel.

The first step would be to install the code coverage libraries and dependencies on the Cypress local installation folder. Here, we install two main plugins – the Istanbul plugin and the code-coverage plugin from Cypress:

```
npm install -D babel-plugin-istanbul
```
```
npm install -D @cypress/code-coverage
```

The preceding plugin installation will not only enable you to measure the code coverage of your application but also allow you to perform the source code instrumentation using the **nyc** module (`https://github.com/istanbuljs/nyc`). The use of the preceding plugins on JavaScript code will transform the source code into code that is measured through **counters** of functions, statements, branches, and lines of code.

Another step that is required is to add the following import statement to the `Cypress/support/index.js` file:

```
import '@cypress/code-coverage/support';
```

After that, you need to register your code-coverage plugin into the Cypress test by adding the following block to `Cypress/plugins/index.js`:

```
module.exports = (on,config) => {
    require('@cypress/code-coverage/task')(on, config);
    return config;
}
```

The next step in the setup is to perform source code instrumentation for your application. By just installing the plugins, your code is not yet instrumented and ready to be measured. To do so, you need to either run the following command that operates on the application's `src` folder (this will be the main source folder of your application under test):

```
npx nyc instrument -compact=false src instrumented
```

Alternatively, to instrument your code on the fly, you need to add the Istanbul plugin to the `.babelrc` file.

Lastly, in the `cypress.json` file under your local installation, you should set the `coverage` parameter to `true` (replacing `true` with `false` will disable the coverage measurements) by placing the following lines in the file:

```
{
    "env": {
            "coverage": "true"}
}
```

Now, when I run the Cypress GUI tool and execute any of my tests under the Cypress installation, they will run by default with the coverage capabilities on.

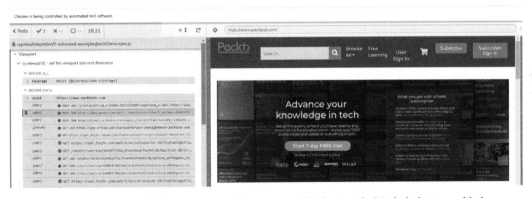

Figure 8.2 – Example for executing a Cypress test with the Istanbul/Babel plugin enabled for code coverage

For well-instrumented code using Istanbul and Babel, you will get the following output for test coverage both in the GUI as well as within the `coverage/lcov-report` folder under your Cypress local folder. As a code coverage practitioner, you need access to the source code of the web application, as well as having a clear understanding of the application architecture, so you can understand and act upon the results of this tool.

Figure 8.3 – Example of code coverage output when running Cypress with the Istanbul/Babel plugin
(source: https://github.com/cypress-io/code-coverage)

To summarize the code coverage section with Istanbul and Cypress, it is important to follow the few simple steps given previously, which include the plugin installation, setting up the configuration files, and then instrumenting your website JavaScript source code prior to running your end-to-end or unit tests.

The setting-up guides might vary between the various frameworks; however, the result is similar – the reports that will be generated will provide you with percentage coverage of the core pillars of your app (statements, branches, functions, and lines).

The percentage for each of the pillars should not just be a number for developers and QA managers, but rather guidance and actionable insight for future testing that might be required. For areas that have lower than **65-70%** coverage, it is recommended to add more test cases (unit, functional, APIs, and so on) so there are no quality risks that escape to production. In general, having a source code average coverage below 70% is not a good sign (`https://www.bullseye.com/minimum.html#:~:text=Summary,higher%20than%20for%20system%20testing`). Hence, measuring and continuously adjusting the code coverage toward 80% and above is highly recommended.

In a great code coverage measurement article that explains how to set up Cypress with Istanbul and the Babel plugin, written by Marie Drake (`https://www.mariedrake.com/post/generating-code-coverage-report-for-cypress`), you can see at the end of it a sample code coverage report that was captured by testing the Zoopla UK website.

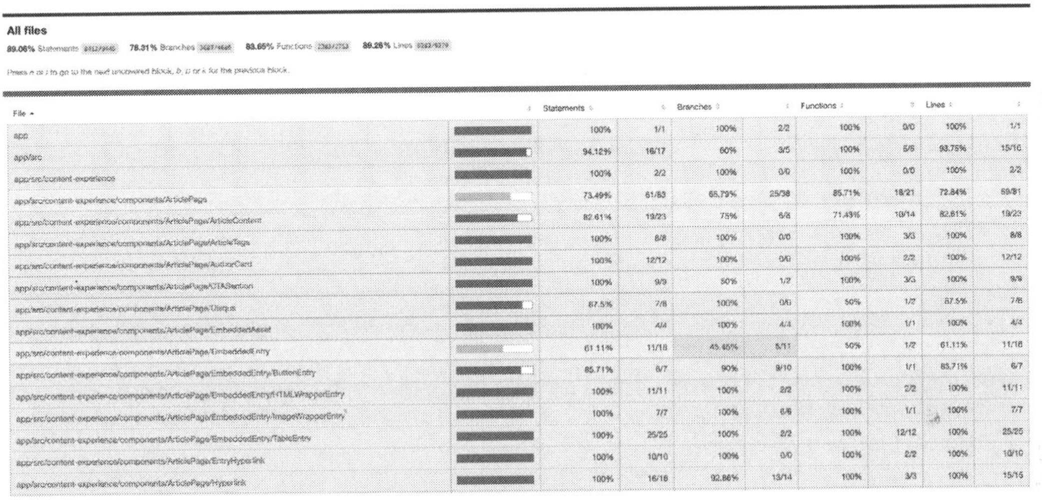

Figure 8.4 – Code coverage report for the Zoopla website using Cypress and the Istanbul plugin (source: https://www.mariedrake.com/post/generating-code-coverage-report-for-cypress)

The overall **lines of code (LOC)** coverage, as well as the branches, functions, and statements, are quite decent across most of the source code, except for the **EmbeddedEntry** and **ArticlePage** files, which are marked in yellow to highlight a potential code coverage risk. As a frontend developer and SDET, I would try and focus in the future on complementing the coverage for these two files and functional areas to enhance the coverage and raise the percentage toward 80% and above.

In this section, we covered the use of **Istanbul** and **Babel** and their role within code coverage measurements within the leading test automation frameworks. We specifically featured Istanbul within the Cypress test framework and provided a guide on how to enable this capability for any JavaScript test spec. We also provided a nice real-life report example of a code coverage measurement to explain how to read such a report and what to focus on from a coverage percentage perspective. Next, we'll see how to complement code coverage with test coverage.

Complementing code coverage with test coverage

As we explained in the previous section, measuring code coverage is critical to assessing the depth of code that is being executed and covered via testing. However, such code-level analysis alone is not sufficient and requires the combination of test coverage analysis as well. When trying to ensure the high quality of your web application, there are various factors that play a critical role in that. Code coverage guarantees that the application is tested at runtime across multiple scenarios and that most of the code is being exercised. The outcomes of the code coverage report guide managers on which areas to invest in further to reduce risks and enhance overall application quality.

Test coverage as a superset of the quality plan looks at other aspects of the application quality, such as user experience, security, accessibility, compatibility, and boundary testing. Together, code and test coverage make a great set of metrics and analysis of the entire application. It is important to understand that both code coverage and test coverage are dynamic measurements since both the landscape and platforms keep on changing, as well as the application source code changing from one iteration to the next. It is imperative to continuously test the app and report the metrics back to management, so the quality bar remains high.

Summary

In this chapter, we explored the two confusing terms of code and test coverage. We properly defined them and clarified the differences between them.

We then focused on code coverage for JavaScript web applications through the leading open source tool called Istanbul with its supporting Babel plugin.

Lastly, we gave as a reference and an example a guide for integrating the Istanbul/Babel tools into Cypress for measuring code coverage through end-to-end functional testing.

That concludes this chapter!

In the following chapter, which opens the last part of this book (*Part 3*), we will start diving deeper into the most advanced features of the leading test automation frameworks. The following chapter will start with the advanced features of **Selenium**.

Part 3 – Frontend JavaScript Web Test Automation Framework Guides

In this part, you will learn about the main features of the top test automation frameworks on the market. Each chapter in this part will feature a specific framework, with guides on how to use the framework, examples, recommended practices, and pointers to become a professional with these technologies. You will be able to use what you have learned from this part to implement various test automation suites using one or more of the featured frameworks.

In this part, we will cover the following chapters:

- *Chapter 9, Working with the Selenium Framework*
- *Chapter 10, Working with the Cypress Framework*
- *Chapter 11, Working with the Playwright Framework*
- *Chapter 12, Working with the Puppeteer Framework*
- *Chapter 13, Complementing Code-Based Testing with Low-Code Test Automation*
- *Chapter 14, Wrapping Up*

9

Working with the Selenium Framework

As highlighted in *Chapter 3, Top Web Test Automation Frameworks*, **Selenium** is one of the oldest test automation frameworks on the market. The framework is open source and supports many language bindings (Java, JavaScript, Python, and so on), and it is the base for many other leading frameworks in the marketplace such as *WebdriverIO*. Being W3C-compliant and based on the WebDriver protocol, this client-server framework allows developers to build test automation across all available browsers (desktop and mobile) and through its Grid tool, run in parallel and at scale. In this chapter, the reader will get a deep technical overview of the framework with a focus on its advanced capabilities, including support for CDP, relative locators, visual testing, cloud testing, support for **Behavior-Driven Development** (**BDD**) testing, and self-healing add-ons. The goal of the chapter is to help frontend developers enrich their test automation coverage with the more advanced capabilities of the framework, whether these are built-in features or plugins.

The chapter is designed to cover the following:

- Understanding the Selenium framework and its components
- The future of the Selenium framework

Technical requirements

The code files for this chapter can be found here: `https://github.com/PacktPublishing/A-Frontend-Web-Developers-Guide-to-Testing`.

Understanding the Selenium framework and its components

As explained in *Chapter 3*, *Top Web Test Automation Frameworks*, the Selenium framework (available at `https://www.selenium.dev/`) consists of three core pillars – **Selenium WebDriver**, **Selenium IDE**, and **Selenium Grid** (you can read more about the pillars here: `https://www.selenium.dev/documentation/grid/getting_started/`). In this chapter, we will only focus on the WebDriver protocol with JavaScript language binding and Grid, and leave Selenium IDE for *Chapter 13*, *Complementing Code-Based Testing With Low-Code Test Automation*.

Selenium WebDriver

With the release of Selenium 4, the latest release at the time of writing, the framework became fully W3C-compliant (`https://www.w3.org/TR/webdriver1/`). The richness of the WebDriver protocol enables developers to drive any possible action on a web application, running on all types of browsers.

To get started with Selenium WebDriver, simply install the node package through the following command:

```
npm install selenium-webdriver
```

Next, you need to install your relevant browser drivers (*Chrome*, *Firefox*, *Safari*, and so on) by following the Selenium documentation (`https://www.selenium.dev/documentation/webdriver/getting_started/install_drivers/`).

To start from your JavaScript code on an Edge browser, for example, you add the following lines of code (for Firefox, simply replace `edge` in the following code with `firefox`):

```
const {Builder} = require('selenium-webdriver');
var driver = new Builder().forBrowser('edge').build();
```

Since we are looking to cover the more advanced capabilities of Selenium, let's start the Selenium Grid component. This step assumes that you have downloaded Grid from the Selenium website (`https://www.selenium.dev/downloads/`).

To start Selenium Grid, simply run this command:

```
java -jar .\selenium-server-4.1.1.jar standalone
```

The preceding command refers to the version of Grid that you've downloaded and the path to it.

At this stage, you have successfully installed Selenium for the JavaScript WebDriver package and Selenium Grid and run the Grid command. If everything is okay, when navigating from your local browser to `http://localhost:4444`, you should see something like the following screenshot:

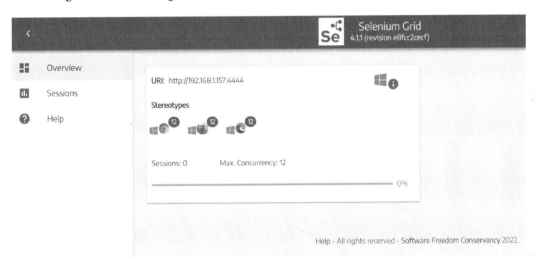

Figure 9.1 – The local Selenium Grid home page within the local browser

What we will do now is run a simple JavaScript code that navigates to the Packt website and searches for a specific book called `UI Testing with Puppeteer`, and then validate that the book home page opens successfully:

```
const {Builder, By, Key, until} =
   require('selenium-webdriver');
const by = require('selenium-webdriver/lib/by');
```

```
(async function helloSelenium() {
    let driver = await new Builder().forBrowser(
        'MicrosoftEdge').usingServer(
        'http://localhost:4444/wd/hub').build();
    await driver.get('https://www.packtpub.com');
    await driver.getTitle(); // => "Packt"

    let searchBox = await driver.findElement(By.name('q'));
    let searchButton = await driver.findElement(
        By.className('magnifying-glass'));
    await searchBox.click();
    await searchBox.sendKeys('UI Testing with Puppeteer');
    await searchButton.click();
    await driver.getTitle().then(function(title) {
        console.log("The title is: " + title)
});
    console.log
    await driver.quit();
})();
```

To better understand the preceding code, here are some of the main steps:

1. Request within the local Selenium Grid (`'http://localhost:4444/wd/hub'`) to open a WebDriver connection in an Edge browser (`'MicrosoftEdge'`).

2. Specify the website URL to navigate to. In our case, we are navigating to the Packt website home page.

3. Define two key element locators (objects) for the test to interact with on the web page. In this case, we are defining the Packt website `searchBox` object and the `searchButton` object to click. Note that we are identifying the objects by ID and `className`.

4. Input a book title in the search box (in our case, we selected `'UI Testing with Puppeteer'`), and then click on the search button to navigate to that book's home page.

5. Lastly, output to the console the page title so that you can see that you've successfully reached the preceding book's home page.

To run the preceding code from an IDE such as Visual Studio Code, simply use the following command:

```
node .\tests\test1.js
```

In this case, I named the JavaScript Selenium test `test1.js`, which resides in a subfolder called `tests`.

Assuming there are no environment issues, when running the preceding command, you will get a local Edge browser to launch and run the preceding steps in headed (with the browser UI) mode, and the following output will be shown in the IDE console:

```
PS C:\Users\ekinsbruner\Selenium_Demo> node .\tests\test1.js
The title is: Search results for: 'UI Testing with Puppeteer'
```

Figure 9.2 – The IDE console output of the page title assertion from the preceding code sample

In the preceding example, we used Grid with only one browser; however, we could have run Grid with the role of `hub`. When running Grid with such an option, Grid *listens* on port `4444` and can operate in parallel with all the subscribed nodes. To scale multiple nodes for multiple browser versions when you run the preceding `test1.js`, you can use a JSON file that will hold these configurations:

```
java -Dwebdriver.chrome.driver=chromedriver.exe -jar selenium-
server-standalone.jar -role node -nodeConfig node1Config.json
```

To learn more about configuring JSON-based Selenium Grid nodes, please refer to the following documentation: `https://www.selenium.dev/documentation/legacy/grid_3/setting_up_your_own_grid/`.

Now that we have set up Selenium locally, launched Selenium Grid, and run a nice JavaScript Selenium test, let's highlight the most useful and advanced features of Selenium 4.

The advanced features of Selenium

Selenium, as mentioned throughout this book, is a powerful and mature test automation framework, and as we learned in the preceding test code, with very little programming effort, you can perform many actions on a frontend web application. Modern websites are written with powerful web application frameworks, as described in *Chapter 5, Introducing the Leading Frontend Web Development Frameworks*, which enable developers to enrich their websites and add complex logic and components to their pages. Realizing the power of a test automation framework such as Selenium can help to automate and test with wide coverage these advanced components.

Let's start covering a newly added feature of Selenium 4 called relative locators.

Selenium relative locators

In previous versions of Selenium, it was quite challenging to identify an element on a web page, especially if there were other elements that are similar or when the web page was too crowded with UI elements. For that purpose, the Selenium community implemented a new feature that allows test developers to clearly specify an element location and a name relative to other elements on that page.

If we look at the **Packt** website under test that we covered in the previous test code, we will see that there are three buttons on the upper viewport of that page. While each of these elements has unique text that describes them, all three buttons have the same `className` identifier (`'subscribe_cta'`). With Selenium 4, we can be very accurate in identifying each of them by utilizing relative locators:

Figure 9.3 – A Packt home page screenshot used for an example of multiple close elements

To identify the middle button in the preceding screenshot with the **Essential Bundles** text, we will specify the following code that specifies that this button is to the right of the **Enter the SALE** button, as follows:

```
let enterSale = driver.findElement(By.className(
    subscribe_cta));
let essentialBundles = await driver.findElement(
    locateWith(By.className('subscribe_cta')).toRightof(
    enterSale));
```

Selenium 4 provides five relative locator options:

- `above`
- `below`
- `toLeftOf`

- `toRightof`

- `near`

Documentation on all of these locators is available here: `https://www.selenium.dev/documentation/webdriver/elements/locators/#relative-locators`.

The Selenium Chrome debugging protocol

While we mentioned CDP in the context of the Playwright and Puppeteer frameworks, for Selenium, this is a new feature that was introduced with Selenium 4. With Selenium 4, frontend web application developers can utilize the DevTools interface (you can learn more here: `https://www.selenium.dev/documentation/webdriver/bidirectional/chrome_devtools/`) to connect with the CDP and use features such as network control, geolocation emulation, performance, accessibility, a profiler, and an application cache.

Through the newly added CDP connection option (`driver.createCDPConnection(page');`), the preceding capabilities can be used.

We will not expand on all of the CDP's available APIs but will give a simple example from the Selenium community of using the CDP to set a specific geographical location through a test.

In the following code snippet, we navigate to a free geolocation website (`https://my-location.org`) that is offered as a reference to identify, via latitude and longitude coordinates, the exact location:

```
await driver.get("https://my-location.org/");
    const pageCdpConnection =
    await driver.createCDPConnection('page');
    //Latitude and longitude of Tokyo, Japan
    const coordinates = {
        latitude: 35.689487,
        longitude: 139.691706,
        accuracy: 100,
    };
        await pageCdpConnection.execute(
        "Emulation.setGeolocationOverride",
        1,
```

```
        coordinates
    );
```

Within the preceding code sample, we navigate to the website as if we were based in Tokyo, Japan, by providing the geo-coordinates and executing the command through the CDP connection. Such a testing capability is important, since many websites are location-aware by design. Hence, based on the end user location, a specific output will be displayed and, sometimes, even with a language relevant to that location.

The CDP within Selenium 4 is a powerful capability with many features and is very important to know about and use within the testing suites.

Selenium multi windows and tab management

Selenium 4 also enriches the testing of complex websites with multiple tabs and windows (you can learn more here: `https://www.selenium.dev/documentation/ webdriver/browser/windows/`). Within any traditional website, there are various menus that open new windows and tabs that should be tested in an automated fashion. Unlike frameworks such as Cypress, Selenium provides a good method of testing multiple tabs, including new windows. To perform tests on a web application when you need to switch between windows or tabs, Selenium provides APIs, including `getWindowHandle();`, `getAllWindowHandles();`, and `driver.switchTo(). newWindows('tab')`, to open a new window, switch to a new tab, close an active window or a tab, and so on.

Selenium Actions APIs – support for mouse and keyboard events

With Selenium, frontend developers can utilize mouse and keyboard events to perform actions (`https://www.selenium.dev/documentation/webdriver/ actions_api/`) on given web pages within the web application under test. The ability to send text strings to a web element such as a textbox as well as perform an *Enter* key press on a keyboard through Selenium isn't new but very useful:

```
await driver.findElement(By.name('q')).sendKeys(
    'webdriver', Key.ENTER);
```

In addition, Selenium also offers a wide range of mouse events such as `clickAndHold`, `doubleClick`, and `dragAndDrop`. In the following line of code, Selenium performs a mouse action that performs a drag from the source element (`sourceEle`) and a drop onto the target element (`targetEle`):

```
await actions.dragAndDrop(sourceEle, targetEle).perform();
```

Self-healing scripts

While this section won't look at **Artificial Intelligence (AI)**, **Machine Learning (ML)**, or low code within testing, the community has built a very interesting framework on top of Selenium to stabilize test code and, whenever possible, fix the test executions to reduce the level of brittleness. This project is called **Healenium** (`https://healenium.io/`), and its value proposition is to improve Selenium test cases' stability and better handle dynamic changes to web elements. With a nice set of documentation (available at `https://github.com/healenium/healenium-example-maven`), code samples, and IDE plugins (such as for IntelliJ IDEA), this framework is a great add-on to any Selenium project. The following is an example of how Healenium works:

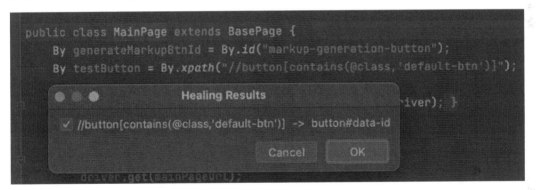

Figure 9.4 – An example of how Healenium updates broken locators within IntelliJ IDEA (source – https://github.com/healenium/healenium-example-maven/blob/master/img_4.png)

Selenium Grid in the cloud

While this is not unique to the Selenium project, teams can leverage cloud providers and run their Selenium test code in the cloud at scale and in parallel without worrying about setting up and maintaining a local Grid.

Sauce Labs, **Perfecto**, and **BrowserStack** offer a robust cloud-based Selenium Grid that covers all different browser/OS combinations across geographies, so frontend developers and testers can scale up their test executions and reduce the amount of time a test cycle takes compared to when running it locally:

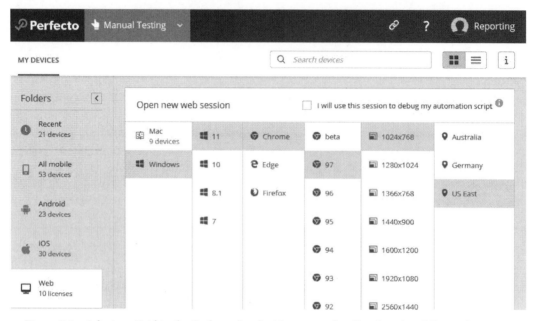

Figure 9.5 – Selenium Grid in the Perfecto cloud with support for all web and mobile combinations

Various testing methods with Selenium

In this section, we are going to cover a few testing types that are supported by the Selenium framework. We will cover testing that includes BDD with **Cucumber**, accessibility testing, and visual testing.

BDD testing with Selenium

In this section, we will not provide a thorough deep dive into BDD. However, it is important to understand that BDD can be used with Selenium easily. In the context of agile testing practices, developers who are building software through the BDD method create the test scenarios in **Gherkin**, which follows the built-in keyword-driven syntax based on GIVEN, WHEN, and THEN. In the following screenshot, we can see an example of a Cucumber test scenario in Gherkin:

```
                                                          public class GoogleStepDefs {

                                                              GooglePage googlePage = new GooglePage();
@WebDD
Scenario Outline: Search Keyword Inline Data              @Given("^I am on Google Search Page$")
    Given I am on Google Search Page                      public void I_am_on_Google_Search_Page() throws Throwable {
    When I search for "<searchKey>"                           new WebDriverTestBase().getDriver().get("http://www.google.com/");
    Then it should have "<searchResult>" in search results   }

    Examples:                                            @When("^I search for \"([^\"]*)\"$")
    | recId | recDescription | searchKey              | searchResult    |   public void I_search_for(String searchKey) throws Throwable {
    | 1     | First Data Set | quantum perfecto       | Quantum Framework |       googlePage.search(searchKey);
    | 2     | Second Data Set |perfecto quantum starter kit | GitHub |   }

                                                         @Then("^it should have \"([^\"]*)\" in search results$")
                                                         public void it_should_have_in_search_results(String result) throws Throwable {
                                                             googlePage.verifyResult(result);
                                                         }
                                                         }
```

Figure 9.6 – A Cucumber test scenario in Gherkin with a Selenium-based step definition methods

In the preceding screenshot, we can see a full Gherkin-based test scenario with the annotation name of WebDD. The scenario simply navigates to a Google search page to find two search keys that are provided within a table (a data-driven test). A data-driven test within Cucumber is defined using the Examples keyword. Previously, we created two types of data input for the test under the Examples block.

On the right side of the preceding screenshot, there is a simple Selenium code, in Java, that through the WebDriver protocol navigates to the Google home page and clicks on the search button on the page. Basically, with Selenium and BDD (Cucumber), frontend developers and testers can build all possible testing scenarios and run them through Grid or the cloud providers.

Creating test scenarios with the underlying step definitions in Selenium and JavaScript is a great way to create test automation. BDD is all about putting developers, testers, and business-facing staff on the same page through clear product scenarios that are written in the form of a user story, with a functional test that validates it. A few years ago, I delivered a deep workshop on testing with BDD, and you can find some interesting insights in the guide I created: https://www.slideshare.net/ek121268/mastering-bdd-eran-kinsbruner-workshop-quest-2018.

Visual testing with Selenium

As highlighted briefly in *Chapter 7, Core Capabilities of the Leading JavaScript Test Automation Frameworks*, practitioners can grab screenshots for basic visual assertions with Selenium's built-in functions, as well as utilize some of the tools and frameworks out there, which include *Storybook*, *Galen*, and *Percy*. To conduct advanced visual testing with Selenium, leverage AI and ML capabilities, and increase testing scale, it is also possible to integrate the *Applitools Eyes SDK* into Selenium across its language bindings, generate baselines, and perform visual assertions at a much higher quality. *Figure 9.1* shows an Applitools visual test result, which we can further analyze:

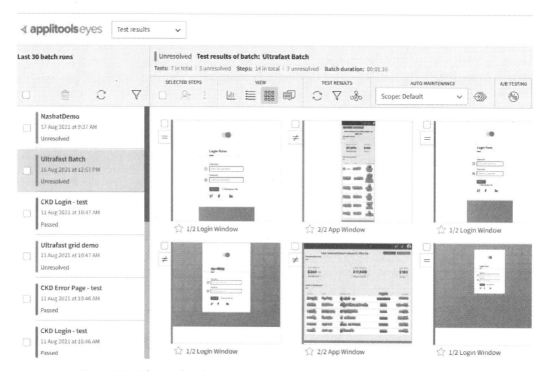

Figure 9.7 – The Applitools visual test results within their web-based dashboard

From the preceding visual, if we focus on the **Unresolved** test case titled **2/2 App Window**, the solution will be able to spot visual differences between that screen and the saved baseline.

Figure 9.8 shows the analysis of the differences, which allows a practitioner to either waive these differences as not an issue or report them as a regression bug:

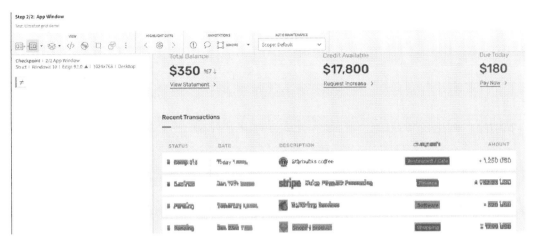

Figure 9.8 – A deep analysis of an unresolved test case with the differences highlighted in pink

To get started with Applitools and Selenium with JavaScript language binding, follow the simple steps in the documentation: `https://applitools.com/tutorials/selenium-javascript.html`.

Basically, you need to create an account and obtain an Applitools API Key, and then install the node package by running the following command:

```
npm install @applitools/eyes-selenium –save-dev
```

The SDK offers a few easy APIs to visually analyze the web applications under test. Developers can use `eyes.open();`, `eyes.check();`, and `eyes.close();` within their Selenium test code and report all captures onto the cloud-based dashboard. There is a ready-to-use open source project offered by Applitools on GitHub (available at `https://github.com/applitools/tutorial-selenium-javascript-basic`) that can be used to get started with the SDK.

Accessibility testing with Selenium

As highlighted in *Chapter 7, Core Capabilities of the Leading JavaScript Test Automation Frameworks*, all leading test automation frameworks can easily integrate with the leading axe accessibility SDK provided by Deque and create accessibility tests within their functional test code.

A very useful GitHub repository is offered by Deque with access to the accessibility engine (axe-core), code samples, and so on at `https://github.com/dequelabs`.

To install the engine, simply run the following command in the folder where you have the Selenium project:

```
npm install axe-core --save-dev
```

In addition to the preceding installation, you will need to specify within your JavaScript test code the path to the axe accessibility spec file (in the following code example, the file is `axe.min.js`):

```
const {Builder, By, Key, until} =
  require('selenium-webdriver');
const fs = require('fs')
const by = require('selenium-webdriver/lib/by');
(async function helloSelenium() {
let driver = await new Builder().forBrowser(
  'MicrosoftEdge').usingServer(
  'http://192.168.1.157:4444/wd/hub').build();
await driver.get('https://www.packtpub.com');
const data = await fs.readFileSync(
  'node_modules/axe-core/axe.min.js','
utf8'
)
await driver.executeScript(data.toString());
let result = await driver.executeAsyncScript('var callback
  = arguments[arguments.length -1];axe.run().then(results
  => callback(results))');
await fs.writeFileSync('tests/report.json',
                       JSON.stringify(result));
await driver.getTitle(); // => "Packt"
```

```
let searchBox = await driver.findElement(By.name('q'));
let searchButton = await driver.findElement(
  By.className('magnifying-glass'));
await searchBox.click();
await searchBox.sendKeys('UI Testing with Puppeteer');
await searchButton.click();
await driver.getTitle().then(function(title) {
console.log("The title is: " + title)
});
console.log
await driver.quit();
})();
```

This spec file holds the relevant accessibility checks, based on which the test will run and report the results back to the user. If we take the preceding `test1.js` source code and add the bold marked lines, it will not only open the Packt website and search for the *UI Testing with Puppeteer* book but will also perform an accessibility check via the `axe.run()` method and store the entire results in a `report.json` file.

After the preceding test completes and a `report.json` file is generated, it will include a set of arrays broken by the `violations`, `passes`, `incomplete`, and `inapplicable` results, as follows:

s NT 10.0; Win64; x64) AppleWebKit/537.36 (KHTML, like Gecko) Chrome/97.0.4692.71 Safari/537.36 Edg/97.0.1072.55","windowHeight"
"https://www.packtpub.com/","violations":[{"description":"Ensures buttons have discernible text","help":"Buttons must have disce
id":"button-name","impact":"critical","nodes":[{"all":[],"any":[{"data":null,"id":"button-has-visible-text","impact":"critical",
":"serious","message":"aria-label attribute does not exist or is empty","relatedNodes":[]},{"data":null,"id":"aria-labelledby","

Figure 9.9 – A sample accessibility violation, detected by running Selenium with the axe SDK on the Packt website

The entire preceding project is also available in my GitHub repository, which you can clone and build from here: `https://github.com/PacktPublishing/A-Frontend-Web-Developers-Guide-to-Testing/tree/master/Selenium_examples`.

Upgrading your Selenium code to Selenium 4

This is not an advanced feature of Selenium. However, to enjoy the new features of Selenium 4, you will need to upgrade your version to the latest one. With any such upgrade, you will need to ensure that your test code is W3C-compliant and adheres to the new syntax of a framework. Here, we will not provide a complete guide to migrate Selenium 3 and below to Selenium 4. If you need information for the complete changes that need to be considered as part of the migration, please refer to this link: `https://www.selenium.dev/documentation/webdriver/getting_started/upgrade_to_selenium_4/`. As an example, let's focus on the changes to the most used feature of Selenium, which is the `findElement` method. This is used to identify an object within a web application and perform any kind of action on it. Within the preceding link, you will find a consolidation of changes that need to happen to your **Maven** and **Gradle** dependencies within your IDEs and changes to the desired capabilities, such as **platform**, **browserName**, and others. In addition, the preceding guide covers changes that you need to know and perform to your waits and timeout usage, and deprecation of old APIs that aren't supported anymore.

With the preceding accessibility summary, we can wrap up the highlights of Selenium framework capabilities. Selenium is, of course, richer than just the preceding features and includes the **Page Object Model** (**POM**) design pattern (you can learn more about POM here: `https://learn-automation.com/page-object-model-using-selenium-webdriver/`), different waiting methods, and other useful APIs that can be learned and used outside of this chapter.

Now that we have covered both the Selenium project components, and its core and important features that we need to be familiar with, let's explore the future of the Selenium project and how it will stack up against other advanced frameworks and the rise of AI and low-code technologies.

The future of the Selenium framework

While Selenium 4 marks a phenomenal milestone for this framework and cross-browser testing technology, as highlighted in the book, frontend developers have other options and competitive frameworks to choose from. To remain relevant and shine as it has over the many years since it was launched, Selenium and its community need to think about the future of modern web applications such as **PWAs**, **Flutter**, and **React Native**.

In the age of intelligent testing and analysis, with digital apps also becoming more complex and demanding, test automation frameworks including Selenium and others must also become richer and more capable. In Selenium 4, the community launched a modified version of Selenium IDE that records all the user actions in a browser, including all the web elements, and can export the recorded script into code. Projects such as Healenium that were covered in this chapter should not be created, and instead, the abilities within Healenium should be part of the Selenium core project.

In future releases, such tools should be able to perform more complex test creation activities, generate reports, ensure no flakiness in the resultant script, and much more. With Cypress's experimental project called **Cypress Studio**, the Cypress team is already aiming higher in its test recording technology.

The core pillars of a futuristic test automation framework such as Selenium should be able to also match all business roles that are doing test automation. Developers, SDETs, and manual testers should find it easier to work and set up the test framework. At the time of writing, Selenium isn't considered the easiest ramping-up test automation framework to use compared with Cypress and Playwright.

Selenium, as a great multichannel framework that can support both web platforms and mobile ones, should continue evolving its APIs and capabilities and run its roadmap in parallel with the Appium tools so that it remains a unique offering for such application types.

To conclude this section, the hope of practitioners that use Selenium is to have a more advanced AI-based, self-healing, and very capable testing technology that can ease the ramping up, maintenance, and analysis of test runs across web and mobile apps of any kind.

Summary

In this chapter, we started by providing a recap of the Selenium project core pillars and how to get started with the basic Selenium framework. We then zoomed in and went deeper into the core features and abilities of the Selenium test automation framework. We highlighted the features with a practical example on how to get started and use these features, as well as providing some ready-to-use code samples that can help you build an advanced testing project for your web application.

We also offered a more futuristic vision for such a test automation framework, looking at desirable capabilities that practitioners are lacking today and could find useful going forward.

That concludes this chapter! In the following chapter, we will do the exact same analysis as we did for Selenium but for the Cypress test automation framework.

10

Working with the Cypress Framework

As highlighted in *Chapter 3, Top Web Test Automation Frameworks*, **Cypress** is the fastest-growing cross-browser and developer-friendly test automation framework. Focused on JavaScript and TypeScript development languages, the framework offers an end-to-end web application testing ability. While Cypress is an open source framework, as opposed to Selenium and other featured frameworks in this book, Cypress also has a paid functionality through its dashboard (`https://docs.cypress.io/guides/dashboard/introduction#Features`) and reporting platform. In this chapter, you will get a technical overview of the framework with a focus on its advanced capabilities, including time travel, component testing, network control, API testing, supported plugins, cloud testing, and support for **Behavior-Driven Development (BDD)** testing.

The chapter will cover the following topics:

- Getting started with Cypress and running a first test scenario
- Highlighting the most advanced and important-to-know capabilities of the framework
- Understanding where the framework is heading in the future

The goal of this chapter is to help frontend developers enrich their test automation coverage with more advanced capabilities of the framework, whether they are built-in features or plugins.

Technical requirements

The code files for this chapter can be found here: `https://github.com/PacktPublishing/A-Frontend-Web-Developers-Guide-to-Testing`.

Getting started with Cypress

As explained in *Chapter 3, Top Web Test Automation Frameworks*, to get started with the Cypress (`https://www.cypress.io/`) framework, you need to install the node package through the following command line:

```
npm install cypress -D
```

After the installation is complete, you can use both the Cypress GUI and the IDE (in our case, we will use Visual Studio Code) to run your Cypress tests.

Launching the Cypress GUI is done by running the following command:

```
npx cypress open
```

The Cypress GUI

After launching the Cypress GUI using the preceding command, you will be presented with three windows:

- **Tests**: This gives an overview of scripts and execution. In this window, you can either launch a single JavaScript or TypeScript test against any of your local browsers.

- **Runs**: In this window, a user can log in to the dashboard and run tests in parallel, identify test flakiness and debug failures, manage multiple users and organizations, integrate easily with the Jira defect management tool as well as CI tools, and get more scaled analytics on the overall test suites.

- **Settings**: In this window, a user can review their Cypress workspace configuration, the Node.js version used, the proxy settings configuration, the file opener preference, and so on:

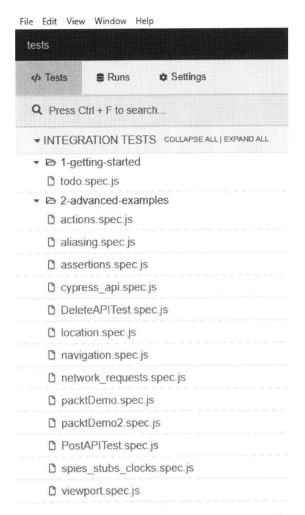

Figure 10.1 – The Cypress GUI main window with a focus on the Tests tab

When running a test script from the GUI runner, the practitioner sees in real time all the steps running side by side on the browser and the website under test. It provides a unique time-travel ability that shows upon each step in the test what happened, what the website status was, and so on:

Figure 10.2 – The Cypress test execution window with the time-travel ability demonstrated

Another great feature that can be used within the GUI runner is the **Cypress selector**. The Cypress selector is an advanced built-in object spy that can be used to analyze the DOM elements, as well as provide the element locator IDs to be used in test code creation:

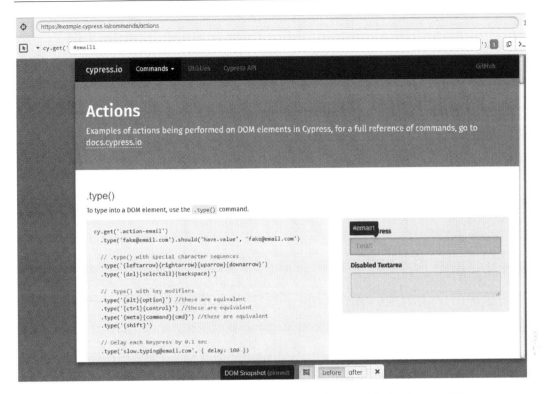

Figure 10.3 – The Cypress element selector capabilities within the Cypress GUI

In the preceding Cypress selector screenshot, a user can analyze and copy and paste the textbox element locator into their JavaScript test code (in this case, the element ID is #email1).

Cypress IDE and command-line executions

Alternatively, to run the Cypress tests from the command line within an IDE such as Visual Studio Code and utilize the Cypress dashboard, you will need to log in with a valid email and place the generated project ID in the cypress.json file. You will also receive a new private generated key. Running the following command will execute and present in the web-based dashboard your test results:

```
npx cypress run --record --key ["private key"]
```

If all was properly set up, you should see in your command-line output the execution progress, as well as the results being populated on your Cypress dashboard:

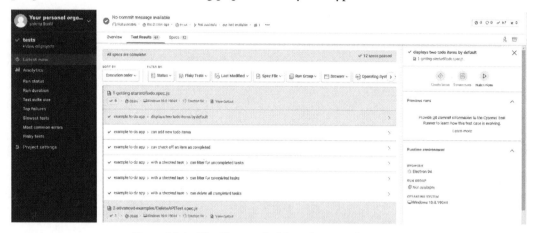

Figure 10.4 – The Cypress dashboard test results output

As you can see from the preceding dashboard screenshot, there are a few pillars of the platform that include the test results (passed, failed, pending, and so on) and the test execution insights, covering test duration, the slowest tests, test suite size, and so on. In the paid version, users can also obtain much deeper insights from their suite as well as more test analysis and scale.

To run Cypress tests in parallel, you will need to set up local machines with the supported CI servers (**Jenkins**, **Bitbucket Pipelines**, **GitLab**, **GitHub Actions**, **CircleCI**, and so on), and pass the `--parallel` command-line option at the end of the aforementioned execution command (`https://docs.cypress.io/guides/guides/parallelization#Overview`).

To get the feel for a simple Cypress JavaScript test scenario that navigates to the Packt website and checks the different viewport visuals when changing screen resolutions, we have created the following test code. The first validation is to provide the test with a very small screen resolution that will collapse the main home page navigation bar, then expand the size to various sizes, and assert the screen's UI.

To execute all of your test code from the command line, you will need to use the following option from your IDE command line:

```
npx cypress run --headed
```

To specifically run a JavaScript test spec, you will need to add the `--spec` command-line option with the path to the specific test file:

```
/// <reference types="cypress" />

context('Viewport', () => {
  beforeEach(() => {
    cy.visit('https://www.packtpub.com')
  })

  it('cy.viewport() - set the viewport size and dimension',
    () => {
    // https://on.cypress.io/viewport

    cy.get('#search').should('be.visible')
    cy.viewport(320, 480)
    cy.viewport(2999, 2999)

    cy.viewport('macbook-15')
    cy.wait(200)
    cy.viewport('macbook-13')
    cy.wait(200)
    cy.viewport('macbook-11')
    cy.wait(200)
    cy.viewport('ipad-2')
    cy.wait(200)
    cy.viewport('ipad-mini')
    cy.wait(200)
    cy.viewport('iphone-6+')
    cy.wait(200)
    cy.viewport('iphone-6')
    cy.wait(200)
    cy.viewport('iphone-5')
    cy.wait(200)
    cy.viewport('iphone-4')
    cy.wait(200)
    cy.viewport('iphone-3')
```

```
    cy.wait(200)


    // cy.viewport() accepts an orientation for all presets
    // the default orientation is 'portrait'
    cy.viewport('ipad-2', 'portrait')
    cy.wait(200)
    cy.viewport('iphone-4', 'landscape')
    cy.wait(200)


    // The viewport will be reset back to the default
    // dimensions in between tests (the  default can be set
    // in cypress.json)
  })
})
```

After running the preceding **functional** test spec from the Cypress GUI, we will see how the Packt home page looks with various screen sizes and resolutions. Specifically, as shown in the following screenshot, we can see what the page will look like in an **iPhone 6+** smartphone screen resolution:

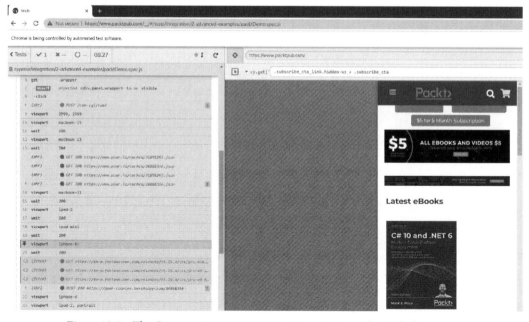

Figure 10.5 – The Cypress viewport test execution output on the Packt homepage

Now that we successfully have set up a Cypress test environment and explored the two main methods of running Cypress test code (the GUI and the IDE command line), let's explore the most advanced features of the Cypress framework.

Cypress's advanced test automation capabilities

In *Chapter 9*, *Working with the Selenium Framework*, we explored the advanced features of the framework that frontend developers and SDETs can use, and we will now do a similar overview of the most advanced features of Cypress.

Note that measuring code coverage is also considered a powerful capability within software test automation; however, since we covered the abilities of code coverage with **Istanbul** and **Babel** in *Chapter 8*, *Measuring Test Coverage of the Web Application*, we will not repeat it here.

Cypress test retries

When creating test automation scenarios, one of the most complex cases as well as the most time-consuming is test stability and flakiness. Tests can often fail due to platform availability, environmental issues such as loss of network connectivity on the test machine, synchronization issues on the web application under tests, and so on. For such cases, Cypress offers a test retry mechanism (https://docs.cypress.io/guides/guides/test-retries#How-It-Works) that, in cases of failures, will attempt to rerun tests up to three times prior to marking them as failed.

To enjoy this useful feature globally for all your tests, you will need to add a short block of code to the cypress.json file, as shown here:

```
{
  "retries": {
    // Configure retry attempts for 'cypress run'
    // Default is 0
    "runMode": 2,
    // Configure retry attempts for 'cypress open'
    // Default is 0
    "openMode": 0
  }
}
```

Alternatively, to use this feature on a test-by-test case basis, you will need to include this code block within the JavaScript test spec:

```
It (
'do something',
{
    retries: {
        runMode: 2,
        openMode: 1,
    },
},...
```

When using the retry mechanism, all flaky and retried test executions are visible in the Cypress web-based dashboard. Users can go to the project test suite menu, and within the **Flaky tests** option, they can look at the identified flaky test cases, as well as see the overall percentage of flakiness within the project. Users can then analyze and decide what the next steps are for these unstable test scenarios.

Using stubs, spies, and clocks with Cypress

When it comes to developing units, APIs, and integration tests, having the ability to manipulate output or force different behaviors of your web application can expand your test coverage and uncover defects earlier in the cycle. For that purpose, Cypress comes equipped with stubbing, spying, and mocking tools through its bundled **Sinon. js** (https://sinonjs.org/), **Lolex** (https://github.com/sinonjs/fake-timers), and **Sinon-chai** (https://github.com/domenic/sinon-chai) libraries.

To better understand the use of the Cypress network control and specifically the cy.clock() method, here is a short code sample that goes to a Cypress web page (https://example.cypress.io/commands/spies-stubs-clocks), which is used for demonstration purposes, and validates the time by moving the clock 10 seconds forward through the cy.tick() method:

```
/// <reference types="cypress" />

const now = new Date(Date.UTC(2017, 2, 14)).getTime()

context('Viewport', () => {
  beforeEach(() => {
```

```
        cy.visit('https://example.cypress.io/commands/
                spies-stubs-clocks')
  })
    it('set timer', () => {
  cy.clock(now)
      cy.get('#tick-div').click().should('have.text',
                                    '1489449600')
  cy.tick(10000) // 10 seconds passed
  cy.get('#tick-div').click().should('have.text',
                                  '1489449610')
  cy.wait(2000)
  cy.clock()
  cy.tick(60000)
  cy.clock().invoke('restore')
  })
  })
```

In the preceding code snippet, we are setting the date in **Coordinated Universal Time**
(UTC) (https://en.wikipedia.org/wiki/Coordinated_Universal_Time)
to keep it consistent and the same for each test run (we are using February 14, 2017).
Within the test, we are initiating the clock to the current time and then validating the time
prior to using the cy.tick(10000) method and afterward to assert that 10 seconds
moved by running the command.

After running the preceding test code, we can see in the following screenshot (taken from the Cypress GUI runner) the before and after time change after using the `clock` and `tick` commands:

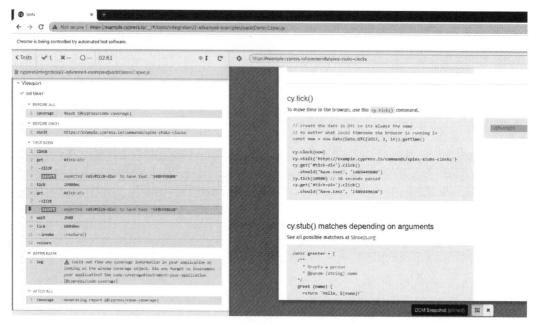

Figure 10.6 – The Cypress clock and tick methods used to push the actual time 10 seconds forward

Within Cypress, you can also use `cy.stub()` inherited from the SinonJS library to validate different outputs for a test, as well as use the various SinonJS matchers (`https://sinonjs.org/releases/latest/matchers/`).

Capabilities such as stubbing and network/clock control are very beneficial for test coverage expansion with more negative and boundary conditions, as well as different test case conditions. If you need to validate a web page's output if there is a specified time change or other input to the page, you can use the preceding capabilities and make the proper assertions.

Lastly, for this section, it is very important to be familiar with the `cy.intercept()` method. This capability is super-powerful in routing API calls from the original/expected and often cached routes to a "controlled" and specific one. This helps to test more often, across different scenarios, and sometimes prior to the real production API being available for testing (`https://docs.cypress.io/api/commands/intercept#cy-intercept-and-request-caching`). As documented in detail on the Cypress website (`https://docs.cypress.io/api/commands/intercept#Matching-url`), using the intercept option can provide greater flexibility to test against production, QA, staging, and other environments within a single test code.

Running Cypress within CI

Creating test automation is great; however, within Agile teams and to save time, a lot of tests are being integrated into a CI process that runs them upon a specified trigger. Such a trigger can be any code change made within the source code repository or at a specific time within a day. Cypress integrates perfectly with most of the CI server tools (`https://docs.cypress.io/guides/continuous-integration/ci-provider-examples`), including CircleCI, Jenkins, GitHub Actions, GitLab, AWS CodeBuild, and Bitbucket Pipelines. You can also configure a local Docker image (`https://github.com/cypress-io/cypress-docker-images`) that will run your tests via a GitHub action in a container. Note that Cypress already provides ready-made Docker images on Docker Hub. A step-by-step guide on how to configure and run a set of Cypress tests through GitHub Actions is available at `https://github.com/marketplace/actions/cypress-io` and basically provides a list of .YML configuration files for each of the CI servers supported by Cypress.

In the following file, we specify that any code or repository change driven by the `[push]` command will trigger a Cypress test run against a `Chrome` browser:

```yaml
name: E2E on Chrome
on: [push]
jobs:
  cypress-run:
    runs-on: ubuntu-20.04
    # let's make sure our tests pass on Chrome browser
    name: E2E on Chrome
    steps:
      - uses: actions/checkout@v2
      - uses: cypress-io/github-action@v2
        with:
          browser: chrome
```

Figure 10.7 – A sample YML GitHub Actions configuration file
(source – `https://github.com/marketplace/actions/cypress-io`)

Based on the CI server that is adopted by the development and testing team, you should select the workflow and configure the respective .YML files accordingly.

Component testing

An innovative and unique testing method is being introduced and driven by Cypress. Component testing (`https://docs.cypress.io/guides/component-testing/introduction`) aims to bridge the gap between **unit** and **integration** testing and offers a test engineer focused and isolated component-based testing to expedite feedback and identify core defects more effectively. This feature is still at an experimental stage at the time of writing; however, it already has great documentation and code samples for practitioners to get started with it.

The key fundamentals for testing a component within a web application is not to use the usual `cy.visit()` method that will navigate to a specified web page but instead utilize the **mount** capability, and home in on a target feature or component on the web page under test. Using the mount capability allows the test engineer to perform assertion directly on the rendered component from within the website.

The component testing structure utilizes the **webpack** JavaScript technology (`https://webpack.js.org/concepts/`) to process and "bundle" the web application into modules. On top of your existing Cypress installation, you will need to install both the webpack node module as well as the relevant web development framework that you are using for your web application development (**React** or **Vue.js**).

In the following command, we will assume that Vue.js is the framework used for web application development:

```
npm install --save-dev cypress @cypress/vue @cypress/webpack-dev-server webpack-dev-server
```

After the preceding installation, add the following block to your local `cypress/plugins/index.js` file:

```
module.exports = (on, config) => {
  if (config.testingType === 'component') {
    const { startDevServer } =
      require('@cypress/webpack-dev-server')

    // Your project's Webpack configuration
    const webpackConfig =
      require('../../webpack.config.js')

    on('dev-server:start', (options) =>
      startDevServer({ options, webpackConfig })
```

```
        )
    }
}
```

Now that the setup is ready, we can create a basic component test in a similar way, as provided by the Cypress documentation (we'll name the file `Button.spec.jsx`):

```
import { mount } from '@cypress/vue'
import Button from './Button'

it('Button', () => {
  // with JSX
  mount(() => <Button>Test button</Button>)

  // ... or ...
  mount(Button, {
    slots: {
      default: 'Test button',
    },
  })

  cy.get('button').contains('Test button').click()
})
```

Running the tests is done by opening the Cypress GUI runner with the `-ct` command-line option and, from the GUI, selecting the spec file to run. In the preceding example, it would be the `Button.spec.jsx` file:

```
npx cypress open-ct
```

Alternatively, you can run all of your component tests from your IDE command line using the following command:

```
npx cypress run-ct
```

That's it!

Cypress Studio

Similar to component testing, Cypress Studio (`https://docs.cypress.io/guides/core-concepts/cypress-studio`) is under development. This capability is evolving and is aimed at providing a low-code option for frontend developers and SDETs. It comes with a recorded GUI-based test that automatically generates JavaScript test specs.

To use this feature, it needs to be enabled within the `cypress.json` file. Simply include the following line in that file:

```
{
    "experimentalStudio": true
}
```

At the time of writing, Cypress Studio supports the `.click()`, `.type()`, `.check()`, `.uncheck()`, and `.select()` commands.

The Cypress community provides a preparatory project that leverages an open source web application called Real World App (`https://github.com/cypress-io/cypress-realworld-app`).

One of the great benefits of the studio is the ability to record directly against the web application under test without writing any lines of code. Another benefit is simply to use the studio as an entry-level point and a learning experience of the Cypress technology.

Let's take the preceding code sample from our Cypress clock demonstration and run it using the Cypress GUI runner. After clicking on the edit test step, we will then see the studio platform enabled, and we can interact with the web application under test as well as record new steps, as shown in the following screenshot:

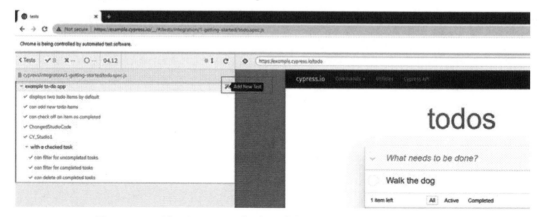

Figure 10.8 – The Cypress Studio launch button within the Cypress GUI

Upon any test launch from the GUI, users will have the ability to click on the **Add New Test** button, as highlighted in *Figure 10.8*, and start the test recording process:

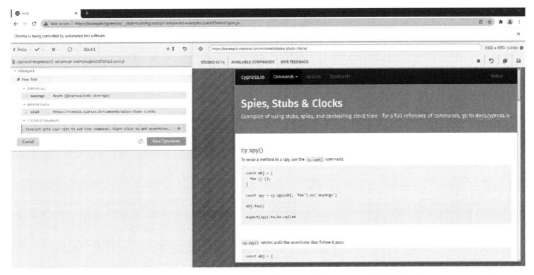

Figure 10.9 – The Cypress Studio UI in action from within an available JavaScript test spec

When I used the recorder on the preceding existing test, I was able to generate in seconds a new test scenario that was added as "studio commands," as shown in the following screenshot:

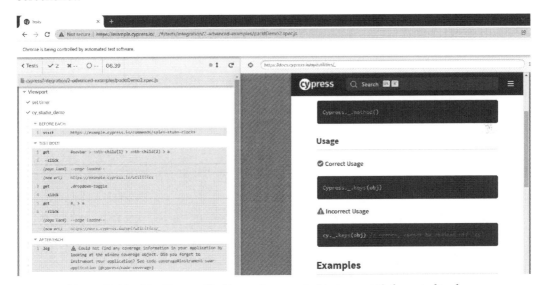

Figure 10.10 – The Cypress Studio newly generated test spec, titled cy_studio_demo

To realize what code was generated by the studio in the current test spec, here is a screenshot of the test code. You can see that the code is annotated with a message that says it was created with Cypress Studio:

```
/* ==== Test Created with Cypress Studio ==== */
it('cy_studio_demo', function() {
    /* ==== Generated with Cypress Studio ==== */
    cy.get('#navbar > :nth-child(1) > :nth-child(2) > a').click();
    cy.get('.dropdown-toggle').click();
    cy.get('#_ > a').click();
    /* ==== End Cypress Studio ==== */
});
```

Figure 10.11 – The Cypress Studio-created code snippet example

Cypress plugins

Cypress alone is a great and powerful testing framework; however, as an open source framework, it enjoys the benefit of external contributors. Among the contributions to Cypress, there is a rich set of available plugins (https://docs.cypress.io/plugins/directory) that can extend the core capabilities of the framework towards code coverage measurements, accessibility testing using the AXE tool (https://github.com/component-driven/cypress-axe), visual testing with Applitools (https://applitools.com/tutorials/cypress.html), code analysis using ESLint (https://github.com/chinchiheather/cypress-eslint-preprocessor), webpack for component testing (as described earlier in this chapter), and so on.

A very useful plugin that is also supported by Cypress is the cucumber plugin (https://github.com/TheBrainFamily/cypress-cucumber-preprocessor). It enables you to utilize BDD for test automation. As with any other Cypress plugin, with cucumber, you will need to install the relevant node package through this command:

```
npm install --save-dev cypress-cucumber-preprocessor
```

Then, you will need to declare it in the cypress/plugins/index.js file accordingly:

```
const cucumber = require('cypress-cucumber preprocessor').
default
module.exports = (on, config) => {
    on('file:preprocessor', cucumber())
}
```

In addition, within the `cypress.json` file, you will need to specify that the test files are BDD feature files, as follows:

```
{
"testFiles": "**/*.feature}
```

Lastly, and specifically for cucumber within Cypress, you will need to add this configuration to the `package.json` file:

```
"cypress-cucumber-preprocessor": {
   "nonGlobalStepDefinitions": true
}
```

The following is a screenshot of Cypress with a cucumber BDD test spec (a `feature` file) that I developed while running on a web-based designer tool called Gliffy (`https://www.gliffy.com/`). The entire test while using underneath the `feature` file **JavaScript step definitions** is fully built using the **Gherkin** syntax of Given, When, and Then:

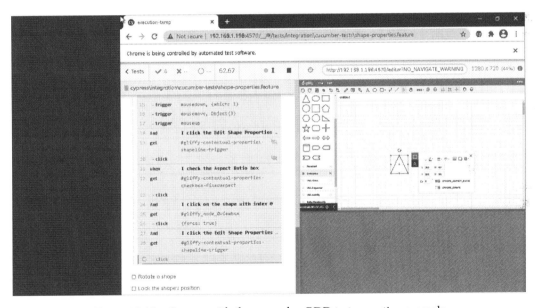

Figure 10.12 – Cypress with the cucumber BDD test execution example

Another invaluable option within Cypress is the ability to create simple but powerful plugins. A good example is a plugin that can help switch between test environments. If you are running tests and wish to control the target environment (whether it is staging, QA, production, and so on), you can use Cypress to generate a configuration plugin that will redirect your test to the right environment. Filip Hric wrote a nice blog that explains the process (`https://filiphric.com/create-a-configuration-plugin-in-cypress`).

That's it!

Cypress API testing

Among all the features of Cypress, there is also a built-in capability to create and execute API testing that covers the core methods of an API – GET, PUT, POST, DELETE, and so on.

Using the `cy.request()` commands, you can create rich API tests and perform API assertions with Cypress in JavaScript. A nice guide that was created by one of the leading CI vendors, CircleCI (`https://circleci.com/blog/api-testing-with-cypress/`), showcases how to not only create an API test with Cypress but also how to run it through CI.

In addition to the preceding guide, you can take this ready-to-run JavaScript Cypress test spec and, upon creating a username and a token through the **Register** menu item on the open source website (`https://docket-test.herokuapp.com/`), run these API POST test scenarios. An alternative website to use for API testing is `https://jsonplaceholder.typicode.com/`.

Basically, the following code sample uses the API POST method to add a few to-do items to the free web application (`https://docket-test.herokuapp.com/`). It consists of two test scenarios that add a to-do item with the text `Walk cat` and a to-do item called `Packt publishing`. It validates that the response status for both requests is OK (200):

```
/// <reference types="cypress" />
describe("Docket Post Test", () => {
    it("Should create a Todo item", () => {
        cy.request({
            method: "POST",
            url:
                "https://docket-test.herokuapp.com/api/Todo/",
            headers: {
```

```
                    token: "[YOUR TOKEN ID",
                },
                body: {
                    Body: "Walk cat",
                },
            })
                .its("status")
                .should("be.ok");
        });
    });
describe("Docket Post Test 2", () => {
    it("Should create a Todo item", () => {
        cy.request({
            method: "POST",
            url:
                "https://docket-test.herokuapp.com/api/Todo/",
            headers: {
                token: "YOUR TOKEN ID",
            },
            body: {
                Body: "Barclays Demo",
            },
        })
            .its("status")
            .should("be.ok");
    });
});
});
```

In this section, we explored many of the advanced capabilities of the Cypress framework, including component testing, Cypress Studio, network control, code coverage measurements, BDD, running tests within CI, the rich plugin archive, API testing, and the test retries. While these are not all the features in this massive framework but it is a great list to focus on and utilize within tour test development activities.

We will now move on to explore where Cypress might be heading in the future and some of the expected directions for this framework.

The future of the Cypress framework

While Cypress has made amazing progress in a very short amount of time in this industry, it is already looking at some transformational capabilities in the shape of the studio and component testing. For Cypress to mature even further, it will need to tick a few more boxes for the expected capabilities of a test automation framework:

- Support for **all browser types** and versions, including Safari's WebKit on macOS.
- Support for **web applications on mobile platforms**.
- Potentially expand to testing more easier **multiple tabs and windows** as Selenium 4 does.
- There is a rise in the adoption of **languages** such as Python, so more language support by Cypress could expand its usage within the community.
- Better support for **modern application** types such as the **Progressive Web Apps (PWAs) Flutter** and **React Native**.

In addition to the preceding, if the Cypress framework can develop its low-code studio solution with more intelligent capabilities driven by **Machine Learning (ML)**, it will stand out compared with the Selenium IDE and Selenium framework extension called **Healenium**, which was covered in the previous chapter, *Chapter 9, Working with the Selenium Framework*.

Another great opportunity for Cypress to advance through its dashboard is reporting and test analysis. The ability to identify flaky test cases, tests that take longer than others to execute, and so on is a huge productivity boost for frontend developers and SDETs. Investing in these features and making them easier to adopt would allow this framework to stand out from the alternatives.

What is also important to find within a modern frontend web application testing framework from a capability standpoint is **performance testing**. As we know, all the featured test frameworks in this book do not come with built-in performance testing capabilities and are either integrating and relying on open source **JMeter** or are staying away from such types of tests. As this framework matures, this type of non-functional testing should be given equal consideration within this framework.

The way that Cypress has partnered with **cloud vendors** and supported the development of SDKs to scale up and run Cypress tests in the cloud was a great initiative, which many large enterprise organizations adopted. It would be very beneficial to deepen these partnerships and see how cloud solutions can contribute to the Cypress ecosystem with features such as reporting and scale. Currently, Cypress works well with a set of reporters that includes **JUnit** and **TeamCity** (`https://docs.cypress.io/guides/tooling/reporters`); however, when expanding partnerships with other technology vendors, Cypress can benefit from a much more meaningful reporting solution.

Finally, investing in more security testing of web applications in the age of cyberattacks and denials of service would be a huge advantage for Cypress. Currently, Cypress users can work with **Auth0** authentication features (`https://docs.cypress.io/guides/testing-strategies/auth0-authentication#Auth0-Application-Setup`) and other authentication solution providers such as **Okta**, **Google**, **GraphQL**, and **Amazon**; however, this is only one aspect of security, which isn't sufficient.

With these suggestions and opportunities for enhancements, we will conclude this section and provide a summary for this chapter.

Summary

In this chapter, we covered the fundamentals of the Cypress framework and learned how to get started, and run a JavaScript Cypress test in both IDE mode and from the GUI runner. We then dived deeper into the most advanced features of the Cypress framework and provided code samples, references, and insights on how to use them and for what benefits. Among the core features that we touched upon were the network control capabilities, running from CI, Cypress Studio, component testing, and API testing. We then tried to project the future of Cypress through capabilities that are currently experimental as well as the missing and greatly needed features for this framework.

The two main code examples from this chapter that show the use of the clock and the API test are in the following GitHub repository, forked from the Cypress master repository: `https://github.com/PacktPublishing/A-Frontend-Web-Developer-s-Guide-to-Testing/tree/master/Cypress_examples`.

That concludes this chapter! In the following chapter, we will perform the exact same analysis we did for Cypress for the Playwright test automation framework.

11
Working with the Playwright Framework

As highlighted in *Chapter 3, Top Web Test Automation Frameworks*, **Playwright** is among the newest and most modern frontend test automation frameworks. Being built on top of **CDP** (the Chrome Debugger Protocol) allows the framework to acquire the deep coverage and testing abilities of any web application across all browser types. With CDP (`https://chromedevtools.github.io/devtools-protocol/`), frontend web application developers can better inspect their web applications, debug them, cover the network and performance aspects of the app, scan the app for accessibility and PWA compliance, and much more besides. As opposed to the **Cypress** and Google **Puppeteer** frameworks, which only come with JavaScript and TypeScript language support, Playwright comes with more language binding support, including Python, Java, and .NET.

The framework is maintained by Microsoft and led by the same team that built the Google Puppeteer framework. With rich built-in capabilities that include an inspector, test generator, visual testing, parallel testing and sharding, API testing, a retry mechanism, page object model practice, and more, this framework is positioning itself quite high on the candidate's list for frontend developers.

In this chapter, you will get a technical overview of the framework with a focus on the advanced capabilities with working examples that can be used out of the box, some core differences between Playwright and the other leading frameworks covered in this book, and much more.

The chapter is designed to cover the following areas:

- Getting started with Playwright and running a first test scenario
- Highlights of the most advanced and important capabilities of the framework
- Understanding where the framework is heading in the future

The goal of the chapter is to help frontend developers enrich their test automation coverage with the more advanced capabilities of the framework, whether these are built-in features or plugins.

Technical requirements

You can find complete code examples on GitHub under the following repository:

```
https://github.com/PacktPublishing/A-Frontend-Web-Developers-
Guide-to-Testing
```

Getting started with Playwright

As explained in *Chapter 3*, *Top Web Test Automation Frameworks*, to get started with the Playwright (`https://playwright.dev/`) framework, you need to install the node package through the following command lines:

```
npm install -D @playwright/test
npx playwright install
```

Once the preceding package has been installed, together with its dependencies, you are ready to start writing and running your first test locally in either **Headed** or **Headless** mode, as explained in *Chapter 1*, *Cross-Browser Testing Methodologies*.

To get right down to the code, simply use the JavaScript test code depicted below that performs a login scenario on the GitHub website:

```
const { test, expect } = require('@playwright/test');
test('basic test', async ({ page }) => {
  await page.goto('https://github.com/login');
  await page.fill('input[name="login"]', 'USER NAME');
```

```
await page.fill('input[name="password"]', 'PASSWORD');
await page.click('text=Sign in');
});
```

To run the simple script above, which logs in to GitHub across three browsers in parallel, you would use a configuration file, as shown below. This configuration file will launch three workers through Playwright and validate the login scenario on Chrome, Firefox, and Edge. The config file should be placed in the project root folder and not in the tests folder.

As you will see in *Figure 11.1* at the end of the execution, Playwright uses **workers** to run tests in parallel across one type of browser or many browser platforms. You can think of workers as processes that are executed in parallel to expedite the test execution time as well as coverage:

```
// playwright.config.js
const { devices } = require('@playwright/test');
/** @type {import('@playwright/test').PlaywrightTestConfig} */
const config = {
  forbidOnly: !!process.env.CI,
  retries: process.env.CI ? 2 : 0,
  use: {
    trace: 'on-first-retry',
  },
  projects: [
    {
      name: 'chromium',
      use: { ...devices['Desktop Chrome'] },
    },
    {
      name: 'firefox',
      use: { ...devices['Desktop Firefox'] },
    },
    {
      name: 'edge',
      use: { ...devices['Desktop Edge'] },
    },
  ],
```

```
};
module.exports = config;
```

At the end of the execution of the script in parallel, you should get the following output on your IDE terminal. You can also observe in the following screenshot that the entire parallel execution only took 4 seconds:

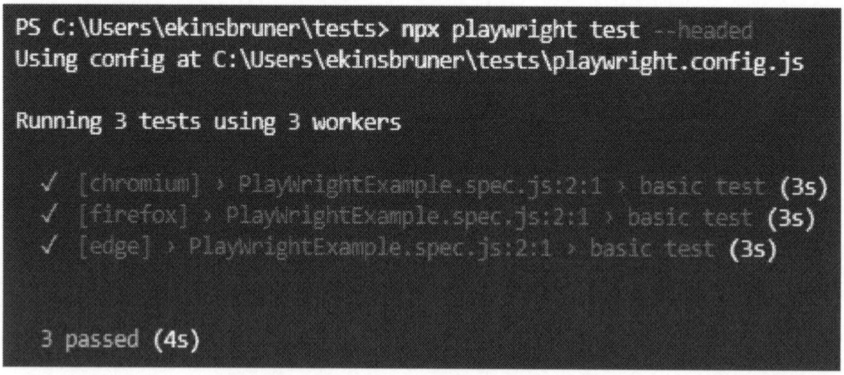

```
PS C:\Users\ekinsbruner\tests> npx playwright test --headed
Using config at C:\Users\ekinsbruner\tests\playwright.config.js

Running 3 tests using 3 workers

  ✓ [chromium] › PlaywrightExample.spec.js:2:1 › basic test (3s)
  ✓ [firefox] › PlaywrightExample.spec.js:2:1 › basic test (3s)
  ✓ [edge] › PlaywrightExample.spec.js:2:1 › basic test (3s)


3 passed (4s)
```

Figure 11.1 – Playwright command-line interface output for parallel testing

If you only want to run a single test or a few tests on one of the browsers within your Playwright configuration file, just like the one above, you will add --project with the browser name that you are interested in testing. For example, running just the preceding test in Headed mode on the *Firefox* browser is done through the following command line:

```
npx playwright test --headed --project=firefox
```

In addition to the keyword used for parallel testing called **workers,** Playwright uses the keyword expect to perform test assertions. Also, Playwright performs all its actions on a **page**, which is one of the several fixtures that are part of the framework. The Page component within Playwright (https://playwright.dev/docs/api/class-page) provides all the methods needed to interact with a single tab within a browser to test your web application. Other fixtures supported by the framework in addition to Page are **context** (https://playwright.dev/docs/test-configuration), **browser**, and **browserName**.

If, for example, you wanted to validate the fact that after logging in to your GitHub account, you can see the **Pull requests** tab, and by clicking on that tab, you will get a list of your **Created** pull requests, you would simply add the following two lines of code to the preceding JavaScript test:

```
await page.click('text=Pull requests');
await expect(page.locator(
  'text=Created').first()).toBeVisible();
```

Many of the testing capabilities of Playwright use, and are derived from, the Test class and its underlying APIs (`https://playwright.dev/docs/api/class-test`). In the next sections, we will cover some of the key methods that a practitioner needs to be familiar with.

Playwright also allows its users to record all the test executions within a video file. To do so, you will need to add a few lines to the configuration used above:

```
Use: {
    Video: ' on',
},
```

Lastly, like the Cypress framework, with Playwright, you can specify up to three test execution retries in the event of failure. You can either specify them in the preceding sample configuration file or within the command line through a parameter:

```
npx playwright test --retries=3
```

Another powerful built-in capability that comes with the Playwright framework is the auto-waiting feature, which ensures less flaky and more synchronized test execution (`https://playwright.dev/docs/actionability`). The framework automatically waits for elements to be visible, stable, and in a ready state within the **Document Object Model (DOM)** prior to performing an action such as `click`, `tap`, or `check`.

In addition, and unlike the Cypress framework, the Playwright framework can work with multiple frames within a web application through the `page.frame()` APIs that support actions such as interacting with specific elements through `frame.fill()` and other options (`https://playwright.dev/docs/frames`).

Now that we have briefly covered the first installation and execution steps of a single piece of JavaScript test code within Playwright, let's start reviewing the other core capabilities, including the most advanced ones.

Playwright's advanced test automation capabilities

Just as we explored the advanced features of the Selenium and Cypress frameworks that frontend developers and SDETs can, and should, use in *Chapter 9, Working with the Selenium Framework*, and *Chapter 10, Working with the Cypress Framework*, respectively, we will carry out a similar overview of the most advanced features of Playwright.

> **Note**
>
> Measuring code coverage (`https://playwright.dev/docs/api/class-coverage`) is also considered a powerful capability within software test automation. However, since we've covered the abilities of code coverage with Istanbul and Babel in *Chapter 8, Measuring Test Coverage of the Web Application*, we will not repeat it here. Keep in mind that for Playwright, the code coverage with **Istanbul** is currently only supported on **Chromium**-based browsers.

Playwright Inspector

The Playwright framework provides a GUI tool that can facilitate test automation creation and debugging. The **Inspector** tool (`https://playwright.dev/docs/inspector`) allows users to view the DOM elements and debug the tests through breakpoints or test stops. It also allows the **DevTools** browser to be used for additional debugging and analysis of the web application under test.

To launch the Inspector tool in a **PowerShell** (`https://code.visualstudio.com/docs/languages/powershell`) command line, simply run the following command (note that on non-Microsoft machines, PowerShell must be installed separately):

```
$env:PWDEBUG=1
```

After running the preceding command, you will launch the Playwright test execution using the normal command:

```
npx playwright codegen wikipedia.org
```

The browser will launch with the Inspector tool running in a separate window, as you can see in the following screenshot. From the **Inspector** window, you can now record your test steps and perform a step over from an existing action to the next.

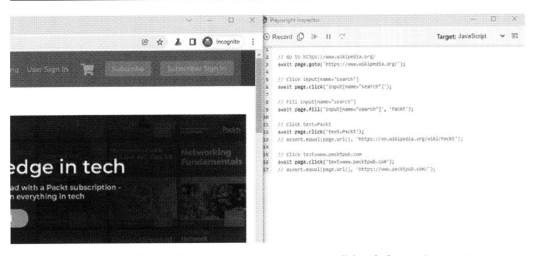

Figure 11.2 – Playwright Inspector tool running in parallel with the JavaScript test

Users of the Inspector tool can step through the test code line by line and see in real time the behavior of the web application under test. In the example below, we are looking at the **Firefox** browser in a simple login test scenario with a simple step into the input of the username.

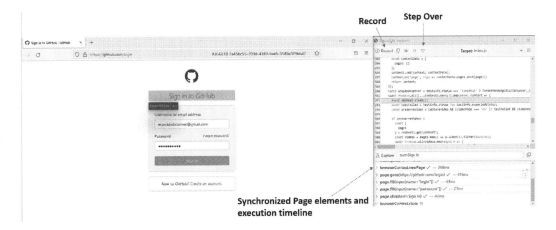

Figure 11.3 – Synchronized Page elements and execution timeline

The GUI has the *step-over* option, along with a **Record** button that allows the addition of more steps to an existing test scenario. In the bottom GUI of the Inspector, users can see the elements that the test is interacting with and view all their properties.

When a user clicks on the **Explore** button on the bottom part of the Inspector GUI, they will get the option to mouse hover the elements on the browser as well as launch and use the browser DevTools mentioned earlier.

When running the test with the Inspector tool enabled, you can launch the *Test Generator* (`https://playwright.dev/docs/codegen`) option by clicking on the **Record** button. Any action performed by the user when the **Record** button is **ON** will be converted into test code added to the existing script.

This tool is an awesome addition to the framework that can be leveraged as frontend developers are creating their test code and during debugging processes.

Emulating mobile devices

As opposed to the Cypress framework (which is not mobile-friendly at this stage), Playwright offers built-in mobile device emulation capabilities that can validate against the mobile device *viewports* and *color schemes* to show how a web application will look and behave. While it doesn't replace a real mobile device test, it does extend the test coverage capabilities within Playwright. Additional mobile-specific capabilities center on specifying the geolocation, time zones, and locales of the web application under test.

In the code snippet screenshot that follows, you can see how, by using Playwright, you can navigate to the Google website on an iPhone 13 Pro smartphone while setting a **German locale** (de-DE).

When running the following command, it will open in an iPhone 13 Pro viewport size:

```
const { webkit, devices } = require('@playwright/test');
const iPhone = devices['iPhone 13 Pro'];
(async () => {
  const browser =
    await webkit.launch({headless: false, slowMo: 300});
  const context = await browser.newContext({
    ...iPhone,
    locale: 'de-DE'
  });
  const page = await context.newPage();
  await page.goto('https://www.google.com/');
  // other actions...
  await page.screenshot({path: 'DE-Google.png'})
  await browser.close();
})();
```

The preceding code from your IDE terminal can be run by node and the path to the preceding JavaScript source file.

Figure 11.3 – Playwright code snippet that emulates the Google home page on an iPhone 13 Pro device in the German locale

As explained in this section, with Playwright, you can emulate many viewports and mobile devices and cover to some extent your web application responsiveness across these different layouts.

Playwright test annotations

In addition to the above capabilities, the Playwright framework also offers annotations (https://playwright.dev/docs/test-annotations) such as skipping tests, focusing, grouping tests, tagging, and conditionally skipping a group of tests. Such abilities can provide more control and governance within a test suite. A very cool and unique annotation within the Playwright framework is test.fixme(). This annotation marks a test that is constantly failing and lets Playwright ignore it; so, it does not appear as a failure case.

Let's see how we can use the `fixme` annotation in the earlier code sample of the GitHub login scenario:

```javascript
const { test, expect } = require('@playwright/test');
test.fixme('basic test', async ({ page }) => {
await page.goto('https://github.com/login');
await page.fill('input[name="login"]', 'EMAIL ADDRESS');
await page.fill('input[name="password"]', 'PASSWORD');
await page.click('text=Sign in');
});
```

As you can see in the preceding code snippet, `.fixme` has been added at the beginning of the test and, upon running the test, you will see that it gets skipped.

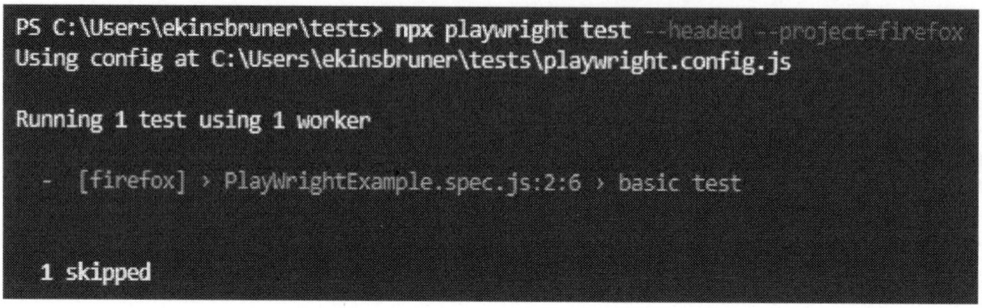

```
PS C:\Users\ekinsbruner\tests> npx playwright test --headed --project=firefox
Using config at C:\Users\ekinsbruner\tests\playwright.config.js

Running 1 test using 1 worker

  -  [firefox] › PlaywrightExample.spec.js:2:6 › basic test


  1 skipped
```

Figure 11.4 – Playwright fixme annotation example – IDE terminal output

If you had three test cases in your test suite after adding the `.fixme` annotation, Playwright would only execute two tests and skip the third annotated one, marking it in yellow with the tag **skipped,** as shown in the preceding screenshot.

You can also enhance the preceding `.fixme` annotation by adding a condition, for example, ensuring that you only skip a specific browser if it is not supported by the web application (`https://playwright.dev/docs/api/class-test#test-fixme-1`).

Playwright API testing

Playwright, similar to the Cypress framework, supports API testing activities. We have clarified in *Chapter 10, Working with the Cypress Framework*, the importance of API testing within the test pyramid as well as the additional layer of coverage that such a testing type adds to the overall testing activities. With Playwright, frontend developers and SDETs can develop API testing (`https://playwright.dev/docs/test-api-testing`) for their web applications. As with Cypress, you can use the GET, POST, DELETE, and other API methods to send API requests and validate their responses. You can learn more about the common RESTful API methods supported by Playwright in the context of automating expected versus actual results of service API tests here: `https://www.restapitutorial.com/lessons/httpmethods.html`.

Developing API tests with Playwright can be done through the specified methods of `request.get()`, `request.post()`, `request.delete()`, and so on, or by means of a request context that you create through the following code.

When using a request context, the newly created context, `const`, is the one that drives all of the API methods through `context.get()`, `context.post()`, and so on:

```
const context = await request.newContext({
    baseURL: 'https://api.github.com',
});
```

Based on the context created above, which will trigger the HTTP requests, we can create a GitHub API **POST** test scenario:

```
await context.post('/user/repos', {

    headers: {

        'Accept': 'application/vnd.github.v3+json',

        // Add GitHub personal access token.

        'Authorization': 'token ${process.env.API_TOKEN}'    },

    data: {

        name: REPO
```

```
    }


  });
```

In the same way as we perform a **POST** command on the GitHub website, Playwright provides more code examples that cover all other API methods.

As an additional example in the context of GitHub source control capabilities, the following code snippet will create a new **feature request** on a repository that resides in GitHub. In the following code block, the test performs an **API POST** request to a specific user (${USER}) and repository (${REPO}) that are configurable as environment variables for the test, with a given title and body for this request:

```
test('should create a feature request', async ({ request })
  => {

  const newIssue = await request.post(
    '/repos/${USER}/${REPO}/issues', {

    data: {

      title: '[Feature] request 1',

      body: 'Feature description',

    }

  });
```

This code simply creates a new repository on GitHub via a user API token based on the baseURL that we provided in the preceding short code snippet.

Playwright assertions

Like many test automation frameworks, Playwright also comes with built-in assertion capabilities. Such assertions are used for test scenario validations across positive and negative use cases, as well as for test anchoring or synchronizations. To know that the test step reached its target web page and has the proper title or text, you can use the framework assertions such as `expect()` and `assert.equal()`, and also visual assertions using `expect(await page.screenshot()).toMatchSnapshot('image name');`.

To understand a bit more about assertions, we can use the code snippet provided by Playwright that simply navigates to the Playwright home page and validates the page title and text through the `expect` method.

We are using assertions on the page URLs to ensure that we have landed on the right pages within the test flow:

```javascript
const { test, expect } = require('@playwright/test');

test('my test', async ({ page }) => {
  await page.goto('https://playwright.dev/');

  // Expect a title "to contain" a substring.
  await expect(page).toHaveTitle(/Playwright/);

  // Expect an attribute "to be strictly equal" to the
  // value.
  await expect(page.locator('text=Get Started')
    .first()).toHaveAttribute('href', '/docs/intro');

  // Expect an element "to be visible".
  await expect(page.locator('text=Learn more')
    .first()).toBeVisible();

  await page.click('text=Get Started');
  // Expect some text to be visible on the page.
  await expect(page.locator(
    'text=Introduction').first()).toBeVisible();
});
```

Instead of the URL assertions, we could have taken screenshots and validated against the saved visuals that we are on the right page, or used `expect()` with specific web page locators.

Playwright network mocking

We covered network mocking and network control abilities in *Chapter 10, Working with the Cypress Framework*, where we covered the use of `cy.intercept()`, `cy.clock()`, and more. Playwright also has built-in network testing abilities (`https://playwright.dev/docs/test-configuration#network`) that support network mocking, specifying proxy settings, ignoring **HTTPS** errors during test navigation, and more.

A simple example that Playwright provides its users with is to automatically abort any CSS requests within the test file by adding this command in the `beforeEach()` method that is inherited and used as part of the Mocha test runner (`https://mochajs.org/`) in Playwright. You can see more fundamental examples of the **MochaJS** framework and its supported features here: `https://www.tabnine.com/code/javascript/functions/mocha/beforeEach`:

```
await context.route(/.css/, route => route.abort());
```

In addition, using the network capabilities within the Playwright framework, you can add to your test network request monitoring or use the `waitForResponse()` method as a preliminary step before performing an action on your web page under test (this method also has the equivalent `waitForRequest()`):

```
page.waitForResponse('SOME RESPONSE')
page.click('ACTION')
```

Within the documentation and API reference (`https://playwright.dev/docs/test-api-testing#configuration`), you can see additional capabilities and code samples on top of the aforementioned ones.

Playwright POM (Page Object Model)

As described earlier in the book, modern test automation frameworks support the **POM** design pattern. Such a tool helps simplify the test development as well as the test maintenance by storing all web application page elements in a code-based class as a centralized hub for other tests to use. With Playwright, you can also create a POM (`https://playwright.dev/docs/test-pom`) to store and maintain all the web elements across all your test scenarios. In the above reference link that Playwright provides, you can see in a simple way how, by creating a JavaScript class that, in this example, is named `playwright-dev-page.js` (`https://playwright.dev`), which defines the home page elements, a test scenario separate class named `example.spec.js` simply utilizes these elements in much cleaner test code. This design pattern makes frontend web application developers' lives easier from the perspective of source code maintenance. In case some element locators change, you only need to change their properties in the main POM class, and all the dependent test classes will inherit these changes.

Playwright test reporting

In stark contrast to Cypress and Selenium, which provide nice test reports with flakiness filtering and more either through plugins such as Allure or their own dashboard, for Playwright, test reporting is not as advanced at the time this book is being developed. Several test reporters can be used out of the box (`https://playwright.dev/docs/test-reporters`); however, they are either console outputs with pass and fail results, or if you wish to utilize JUnit test reports, you can set this environment variable through the following Microsoft Windows PowerShell command:

```
$env:PLAYWRIGHT_JUNIT_OUTPUT_NAME="results.xml"
```

For non-Microsoft Windows operating systems, `$env:PLAYWRIGHT` should be replaced with `env=PLAYWRIGHT`.

And upon running the test with `--reporter=junit`, the output report of the execution will be saved in a `results.xml` file:

```
npx playwright test --reporter=junit
```

```
▼<testsuites id="" name="" tests="3" failures="0" skipped="0" errors="0" time="5.653">
  ▼<testsuite name="PlayWrightExample.spec.js" timestamp="1642373192921" hostname="" tests="1" failures="0" skipped="0" time="3.122" errors="0">
    ▼<testcase name="basic test" classname="[chromium] > PlayWrightExample.spec.js:2:1 > basic test" time="3.122">
        <system-out> [[ATTACHMENT|test-results\PlayWrightExample-basic-test-chromium\4d3894382014bd47cf69be26ac67b466.webm]] </system-out>
      </testcase>
    </testsuite>
  ▼<testsuite name="PlayWrightExample.spec.js" timestamp="1642373192921" hostname="" tests="1" failures="0" skipped="0" time="3.423" errors="0">
    ▼<testcase name="basic test" classname="[firefox] > PlayWrightExample.spec.js:2:1 > basic test" time="3.423">
        <system-out> [[ATTACHMENT|test-results\PlayWrightExample-basic-test-firefox\699c0efe-efb8-4951-8b92-b2710eed9960.webm]] </system-out>
      </testcase>
    </testsuite>
  ▼<testsuite name="PlayWrightExample.spec.js" timestamp="1642373192921" hostname="" tests="1" failures="0" skipped="0" time="3.117" errors="0">
    ▼<testcase name="basic test" classname="[edge] > PlayWrightExample.spec.js:2:1 > basic test" time="3.117">
        <system-out> [[ATTACHMENT|test-results\PlayWrightExample-basic-test-edge\7cab657372608d6999f8c2e63a3137c9.webm]] </system-out>
      </testcase>
    </testsuite>
  </testsuites>
```

Figure 11.5 – Playwright test report output in a JUnit XML format

As the Playwright framework evolves, it would be expected that the test reporting features will also mature, either through built-in reporters or better integrations that can provide better and actionable test data to frontend developers.

Playwright test runners

Like the Selenium and Cypress frameworks, Playwright also integrates and can be easily used with many of the JavaScript test runners (`https://playwright.dev/docs/test-runners`), including **Mocha**, **Jest**, **Jasmine**, and **AVA**. Mocha (`https://mochajs.org/#getting-started`) is the most well-known and commonly used test runner along with Jest (`https://jestjs.io/`); however, Playwright offers its own test runner (`https://playwright.dev/docs/intro`) that gets installed within the initial installation steps that we covered earlier in the chapter. To use the built-in Playwright test runner, you have to specify the following at the beginning of your **JavaScript** file:

```
const { test, expect } = require('@playwright/test');
```

If you wish to use **Jest** and **Jasmine** in your test code, which allow you to use methods such as `expect()`, you will need to specify the following at the beginning of your source code file:

```
const {chromium} = require('playwright');
const expect = require('expect');
```

For **Mocha** to be used in your JavaScript code to enable capabilities such as `before()`, `after()`, `beforeEach()`, and more, you will need the following lines added at the beginning of your file:

```
const {chromium} = require('playwright');
const assert = require('assert');
```

To utilize the AVA (`https://playwright.dev/docs/test-runners#ava`) test runner within Playwright, you need to install the `NODE` package first, and then include it as a required capability in your JavaScript code:

```
npm install --save-dev ava
```

```
Const test = require(' ava').default
```

With the inclusion of AVA (`https://github.com/avajs/ava`), the test code will run by default, concurrently and quite quickly. The AVA test runner has some unique capabilities regarding code simplicity, test execution speed as a result of the aforementioned concurrency, reporting abilities, resolving the **promise** challenges (`https://github.com/avajs/ava/blob/main/docs/01-writing-tests.md#promise-support`), creating test assertions, and much more.

Playwright trace viewer

Playwright offers frontend developers a GUI tool (`https://playwright.dev/docs/trace-viewer`) that can help explore and visualize the test execution traces once the test run is complete. Users are offered an online viewer (`https://trace.playwright.dev/`) that can open the trace recorded files for further analysis.

You can also open the trace recorded files in your IDE terminal command-line tool by running this command:

```
npx playwright show-trace trace.zip
```

To record a trace during a test run, you will need to enable tracing in your Playwright config JavaScript file by adding the following option:

```
Use: {
    Trace: ' on',
},
```

You can either record a trace for each test execution or in the event of failure by setting the option to be **on-first-retry** instead of **on**.

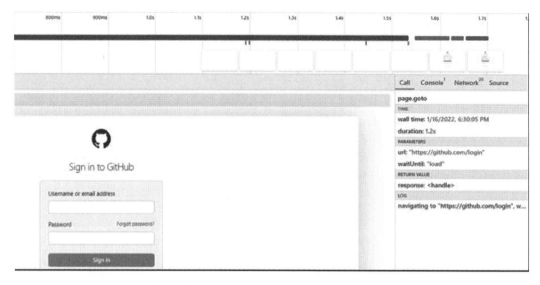

Figure 11.6 – Playwright trace viewer tool following test execution completion

As you can see in the preceding screenshot taken from the Playwright web-based trace viewer, users can examine each step within the test execution and gather timing, network analysis, and other insights. The trace.zip file that is created also includes screenshots, log files, network trace files with all requests and responses, snapshots taken before and after, and other useful artifacts for debugging and analyzing test runs.

Playwright advanced configurations

Within the Playwright framework, users can also enjoy a wide range of useful testing configuration capabilities (https://playwright.dev/docs/test-advanced).

Within the `TestConfig` object that comes with Playwright (`https://playwright.dev/docs/api/class-testconfig`), users can make very useful and productive changes to their test suites, test execution cadence, and much more. Being able to configure your browser under test conditions, your security options, including `ignoreHTTPSErrors`, viewports for different platforms screen resolutions, the base URL for your tests, the number of test retries, the number of workers for parallel execution, and other test environment variables, are key for testing at scale and testing efficiently. These are all supported through the `TestConfig` component.

Please refer to the framework configuration documentation section to review the wide range of configuration options (`https://playwright.dev/docs/test-configuration`).

If we configure the `playwright.config.js` file used previously and add specific test scenarios to run through the `testMatch` and `testIgnore` options, we can really orchestrate a single suite to run a subset of tests versus other tests with and without retries.

In the following screenshot of a **JavaScript** configuration file, we are specifying the Playwright execution to ignore tests that start with the word *Playwright* when running on the mobile Chrome platform (a Pixel 5 device in the following example).

The following configuration file includes five platform configurations that mix both mobile and desktop web configurations. The maximum number of test executions for 2 test specifications would be 10.

We are going to run each of our tests against a desktop Chrome browser, Firefox, Pixel 5, Edge, and iPhone 12 on Safari mobile. Note that for the mobile Chrome configuration with the Pixel 5 platform, we added the following line:

```
testIgnore: '/.*Playwright*.spec.ts/',
```

That line will ensure that for each test in my suite that starts with Playwright characters, the test runner will ignore them and not execute them. This means that if, in my suite, I have two test cases, I will only run them against the four remaining configurations instead of all five.

```javascript
1   // playwright.config.js
2   const { devices } = require('@playwright/test');
3
4   /** @type {import('@playwright/test').PlaywrightTestConfig} */
5   const config = {
6     retries:1,
7     use: {
8       trace: 'on',
9     },
10    projects: [
11      {
12        name: 'chromium',
13        use: { ...devices['Desktop Chrome'] },
14      },
15      {
16        name: 'firefox',
17        use: { ...devices['Desktop Firefox'] },
18        testMatch: '/.*Config*.spec.ts/',
19      },
20      {
21        name: 'edge',
22        use: { ...devices['Desktop Edge'] },
23      },
24      {
25        name: 'Mobile Chrome',
26        use: devices['Pixel 5'],
27        testIgnore: '/.*Playwright*.spec.ts/',
28      },
29      {
30        name: 'Mobile Safari',
31        use: devices['iPhone 12'],
32      },
33    ],
34  };
35
36  module.exports = config;
```

Figure 11.7 – Playwright advanced configuration using the testMatch and testIgnore options

To run the two test specifications, `ConfigTestExample.spec.js` and `PlayWrightExample.spec.js`, based on the following configuration, we can use the usual command:

```
npx playwright test
```

After running the two test files with the preceding configuration, this is the output that you will get on your IDE terminal (**Visual Studio Code**).

As you can see in the following screenshot, we have a total of **eight test executions** out of possible 10, since Playwright is ignoring the two test cases on the mobile Chrome platform:

```
PS C:\Users\ekinsbruner\tests> npx playwright test
Using config at C:\Users\ekinsbruner\tests\playwright.config.js

Running 8 tests using 6 workers

  ✓ [chromium] › ConfigTestExample.spec.js:3:1 › New test (3s)
  ✓ [edge] › ConfigTestExample.spec.js:3:1 › New test (4s)
  ✓ [Mobile Chrome] › ConfigTestExample.spec.js:3:1 › New test (3s)
  ✓ [chromium] › PlayWrightExample.spec.js:3:1 › basic test (3s)
  ✓ [edge] › PlayWrightExample.spec.js:3:1 › basic test (3s)
  ✓ [Mobile Chrome] › PlayWrightExample.spec.js:3:1 › basic test (3s)
  ✓ [Mobile Safari] › ConfigTestExample.spec.js:3:1 › New test (2s)
  ✓ [Mobile Safari] › PlayWrightExample.spec.js:3:1 › basic test (2s)


  8 passed (7s)
```

Figure 11.8 – Playwright terminal output upon execution with an advanced configuration

The two specification files and the configuration used above are on a public GitHub repository for you to clone and use (`https://github.com/ek121268/PlaywrightExamples`).

The `TestConfig` class is very extensive and rich, and we only looked at a few of its capabilities. However, there are many other useful options, including `testConfig.grep` and `testConfig.reporter`. The entire set of options that are part of this class is well documented here: `https://playwright.dev/docs/api/class-testconfig`.

Playwright integration with CI

Like Cypress, Selenium, and the next framework in the book, Puppeteer, the Playwright framework also integrates with **continuous integration (CI)** servers (https://playwright.dev/docs/ci) to expedite the testing and feedback loop. Among the CI servers that Playwright works with are **GitHub Actions**. As with Cypress, you will need to configure a .yml file that will install and run the Playwright test specs on the target new web application build.

The following is a sample GitHub Actions configuration file that will install all the Playwright dependencies and execute an end-to-end Playwright test in the event of a successful deployment state:

```yaml
name: Playwright Tests
on:
  deployment_status:
jobs:
  test:
    timeout-minutes: 60
    runs-on: ubuntu-latest
    if: github.event.deployment_status.state == 'success'
    steps:
    - uses: actions/checkout@v2
    - uses: actions/setup-node@v2
      with:
        node-version: '14.x'
    - name: Install dependencies
      run: npm ci
    - name: Install Playwright
      run: npx playwright install --with-deps
    - name: Run Playwright tests
      run: npm run test:e2e
      env:
        # This might depend on your test-runner/language
        binding
        PLAYWRIGHT_TEST_BASE_URL:
          ${{ github.event.deployment_status.target_url }}
```

In addition to GitHub Actions, frontend developers can alternatively use **Docker**, **Azure Pipelines**, **Travis CI**, **Circle CI**, **Jenkins**, **GitLab CI**, and **Bitbucket Pipelines**.

In case you are using CI tools other than GitHub Actions, you can find the dedicated configuration for each of the supported tools here: `https://playwright.dev/docs/ci`.

With the above CI section, we have concluded our overview of the advanced features of the Playwright testing framework. In this section, we've covered the various supported test runners, the retry mechanism, advanced configuration abilities, POM design patterns, how to use Playwright Inspector, API testing, annotations, reporters, and a few more capabilities that can help expand web application testing coverage.

Now that we've completed our review of these capabilities, let's explore where Playwright is heading in the future and what we can expect to see.

The future of the Playwright framework

Even though Playwright is the newest open source test automation framework in the marketplace, it has matured fast and offers unique as well as advanced capabilities that some of the other older frameworks do not support. Its ability to cover the major development languages, including Java, .NET, and Python, in addition to JavaScript, as well as all the browser platforms, gives it the flexibility and capability to fit into any web application testing project. This framework can perform complete end-to-end testing with visual comparisons, API testing, and network mocking abilities, as well as use the unique Inspector and **CodeGen** options to autogenerate test code in various languages. From a frontend test development perspective, the test creation process is accompanied by a powerful debugger tool and a set of stabilization features including autowaiting and the retry mechanism.

From a future standpoint, Playwright is very promising as far as frontend web application developers are concerned because, unlike Selenium and Cypress, this framework is 100% backed and owned by **Microsoft**. That means a few things: huge community support, great funding resources, potential merges, and acquisitions to expand the richness and testing capabilities of the framework.

It is anticipated that in the future, Playwright will better support the following areas of testing:

- **Mobile platform advanced support testing abilities**: While Playwright can already emulate mobile viewports and other parameters, such as locale, geolocation, and others, this is not sufficient in the growing digital landscape. Expanding to more mobile-specific testing of a web application will position this framework higher than its competitors. The only alternative today for testing web apps on mobile platforms is a combination of Selenium + Appium.

- **Visual and user experience testing**: There is a great opportunity to build more user experience testing capabilities into this framework. From visual analysis through network virtualization, to performance testing and other end user-specific traits coverage, this framework can lead the way for this kind of testing.

- **Modern web application testing**: None of the frameworks featured in this book properly support **Progressive Web Apps (PWAs), or modern Flutter and React Native** apps. Having dedicated abilities to test such apps would make the framework future-proven technology.

- **Low code and intelligent testing**: As highlighted in this book through the Inspector and CodeGen features, Playwright is already well positioned to take the low-code generation functionality to the next level. Building reliable JavaScript and other language-based test automation can be a game-changer if it can reliably support the creation of more advanced testing scenarios and scale them across platforms upon recording completion.

- **Test reporting**: The current test reporter of Playwright is too basic and not informative enough for users. Playwright needs to try and match the Cypress dashboard or properly integrate with **Allure** or other good test reporters so that users get proper feedback from their test execution and can analyze their test failures at scale.

- **Performance testing**: While Selenium integrates and recommends using the **JMeter** open source framework for performance testing, with Playwright, it is challenging to cover this type of testing. It is important for Playwright and **Microsoft** to invest and offer such capabilities within Playwright, either through built-in features or through integrations.

- **Static code analysis**: Investing in enhanced security testing of web applications in the age of cyber attacks and denials of service would be a huge advantage for Playwright. Within the Playwright framework, users can cover basic authentication testing (`https://playwright.dev/docs/test-auth`); however, this is not a **software application security testing (SAST)** capability. With a recent launch from **Perforce SAST**, the **Klocwork** (`https://www.perforce.com/products/klocwork`) product that now supports **JavaScript** static code analysis, teams can use such add-ons within their IDEs and get more code-quality insights within their pipelines. The benefit of SAST (`https://en.wikipedia.org/wiki/Static_application_security_testing`) is to provide code security coverage in earlier development stages of the application, either from the local developer workstation, or through the CI.

Summary

In this chapter, we covered the fundamentals of the Playwright framework and learned how to get started and run a JavaScript Playwright test in both IDE mode and in debugging mode through the GUI **Inspector**. We then dived deeper into the most advanced features of the Playwright framework and provided code samples, references, and insights on how to use them and for what benefits. Among the core features that we touched on were API testing, test retries, test annotations, network control capabilities, running from CI, Playwright's **CodeGen** tool, advanced configuration, auto-retries, and more. We then concluded the chapter by looking into the future of Playwright through capabilities that are only just emerging, such as the low-code ones, as well as those features that are missing and very much required by this framework. ·

By reading through this chapter, you should have received a thorough overview of Playwright as well as an understanding of how the Playwright framework is different from other testing frameworks, as well as some useful code samples and references to help you get started with writing your test code for your web application.

The two main code examples from this chapter are stored in this GitHub repository for you to use as baseline and learning material: `https://github.com/ek121268/PlaywrightExamples`.

That concludes this chapter!

In the following chapter, we will do the exact same analysis as we did for Playwright but for the Puppeteer test automation framework and conclude the advanced guides for all frameworks covered in this book.

12
Working with the Puppeteer Framework

As highlighted in *Chapter 3*, *Top Web Test Automation Frameworks*, Google Puppeteer is the baseline framework that was built by the Microsoft team that is now responsible for Playwright. Both frameworks are node libraries based on the CDP, and that obviously allows the Puppeteer framework to acquire deep coverage and testing abilities for any web application. Unlike the Playwright framework, which supports most web browsers as well as other language bindings, Google's Puppeteer framework only works on **Chromium**-based browsers and only supports JavaScript.

The framework runs by default in Headless mode, but can also be run with the browser UI (in Headed mode). With rich built-in capabilities that support the generation of screenshots and PDFs from web pages, network HAR file creation, and the automation of complex web applications, including keyboard inputs, UI, capturing timeline traces of the website under test, and much more, this framework is a great option for frontend web application developers.

In this chapter, you will get a technical overview of the framework, with a focus on the advanced capabilities with some code-based examples that can be used out of the box. In addition, and since this framework is older than Playwright, but was the foundation of that framework, we will also uncover some core differences between Puppeteer and Playwright.

The chapter is designed to cover the following topics:

- Getting started with Puppeteer
- Learning about Puppeteer's advanced test automation capabilities
- The future of the Puppeteer framework

The goal of the chapter is to help frontend developers enrich their test automation coverage with more advanced capabilities of the framework, whether these are built-in features or plugins.

Technical requirements

The code files for this chapter can be found here: `https://github.com/PacktPublishing/A-Frontend-Web-Developers-Guide-to-Testing`.

Getting started with Puppeteer

As explained in *Chapter 3*, *Top Web Test Automation Frameworks*, to get started with the Puppeteer framework, you need to install the node package through the following command line:

```
npm install puppeteer
```

Once the preceding package, together with its dependencies, is installed, you are ready to start writing and running your first test locally in either Headed or Headless mode.

To see the full documentation of the Puppeteer framework along with code samples, API descriptions, release notes, and more, please see `https://pptr.dev/`.

Like the Playwright framework, Puppeteer also drives its automation through the **Browser** object, which then drills down into the multiple **browserContext** sessions that can operate on multiple **pages, extensions** (`https://pptr.dev/#?product=Puppeteer&version=v13.1.0&show=api-working-with-chrome-extensions`), and **frames**.

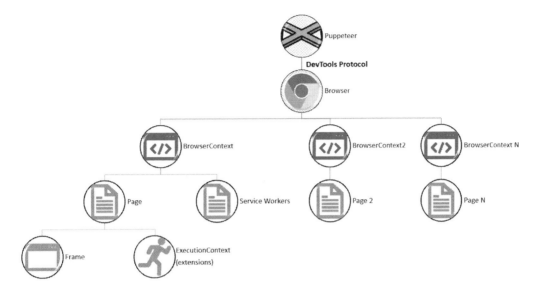

Figure 12.1 – Google Puppeteer high-level architecture diagram

Since Google is the leader in **progressive web applications** (**PWAs**) and was the first technology provider to launch such application types, within this framework, you will be able to use built-in methods to test such application types. In the preceding architecture diagram, you can see the **Service Workers** support under the **BrowserContext** component within the web applications.

In this chapter, we will expand on the Puppeteer JavaScript class from *Chapter 3*, *Top Web Test Automation Frameworks*, so here is the code for it again (note that to run this code, you will also need to install the puppeteer-har node module):

```
npm install puppeteer-har
```

```
const puppeteer = require('puppeteer');
const PuppeteerHar = require('puppeteer-har');
(async () => {
  const browser = await puppeteer.launch();
  const page = await browser.newPage();
  const har = new PuppeteerHar(page);
  await har.start({ path: 'book_demo.har' });
  await page.goto('https://www.packtpub.com/');
  await har.stop();
  await browser.close();
})();
```

The preceding code snippet, as explained previously, navigates to the Packt website and generates an HAR file for frontend developer review.

After running the preceding test code using the following command, a new HAR file under the name book_demo.har is generated:

```
node [filename.js] //depends on the JavaScript file name given
above
```

The default Puppeteer node library that Google provides comes built-in with Chromium's latest browser locally installed. However, with this technology, frontend developers can also install the **puppeteer-core** package, which is mostly the same as the default Puppeteer framework, just without the installation of the browser on your local machine.

As with the default Puppeteer installation, to get the core package, simply run this command:

```
npm install puppeteer-core
```

With the preceding installation, also make sure to replace the first line in your source code with this code:

```
const puppeteer = require('puppeteer-core');
```

Since JavaScript and the tests written in that language within Puppeteer are **asynchronous** when we write our tests across all frameworks, we need to make sure that all actions and **promises** are resolved as a condition to move to the next step in the code (https://web.dev/promises/?gclid=Cj0KCQiAraSPBhDuARIsAM3Js4orqfiLBv1p_jh76YWTW40rTL1yf6HNgeR31knsv7WlAWVJio06XZgaAkjqEALw_wcB).

> **Promise**
> **Promise** in JavaScript is an object and a way to manage the asynchronous nature of the language within the frameworks that use it. To ensure that code can move from one action or a step to the next, promises ought to be **resolved** by returning a **value**, or if not resolved, throw an **error**. Only after they have been resolved can the next block of code be executed. Promises consist of three possible states: **Fulfilled**, **Rejected**, or **Pending**.

Let's better understand this important concept through a short JavaScript example.

In the following code snippet, we are using a web application with a file chooser button that allows users to upload files to the website. We are using the `Promise.all()` method to ensure that all of the code is running properly and in sequence. We can see that only after the file chooser button has been clicked is the promise code block closed and then the file upload operation will take place, followed by the browser closing.

To run the following code, please make sure to also install the `selenium-webdriver` module through the following command:

```
npm install selenium-webdriver
```

```
const puppeteer = require('puppeteer');
const { waitForUrl } =
  require('selenium-webdriver/http/util');
(async () => {
  const browser = await puppeteer.launch({headless:false,
    args: ['--window-size=1920,1080']});
  const page = await browser.newPage();
  await page.goto('https://uppy.io/examples/xhrupload/',
    {"waitUntil": 'networkidle2'});
  const [fileChooser] = await Promise.all([
    page.waitForFileChooser(),
    page.click('.uppy-FileInput-btn')
  ])
  await fileChooser.accept(['Packtpub.png']);
  await page.screenshot({ path: 'FileChooser.png' });
  await browser.close();
})();
```

After running the preceding code on the XHR file and uploading a screenshot of the Packt Publishing home page, this is what the website looks like:

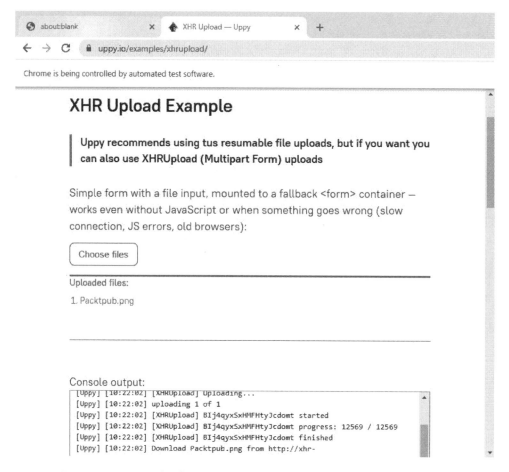

Figure 12.2 – Example of Puppeteer with Promise and the FileChooser method

As highlighted with the other test automation frameworks in this book, Puppeteer also supports common JavaScript test runners such as **Jest** and **Mocha** (https://www.npmjs.com/package/mocha-puppeteer). Such frameworks extend the richness of the test scenarios with methods such as expect(), assert(), and much more, which allow improved coding flexibility.

To install both Mocha and Jest (https://jestjs.io/docs/puppeteer) and work with them in Puppeteer, simply install the node library accordingly:

```
npm install jest-puppeteer
```
```
npm install mocha-puppeteer
```

In the next section of this chapter, we will dive deeper into the core features and some of the advanced capabilities of the Puppeteer framework.

Learning about Puppeteer's advanced test automation capabilities

Following *Chapter 11, Working with the Playwright Framework*, we will cover the advanced capabilities of Google Puppeteer.

Note that measuring code coverage (`https://pptr.dev/#?product=Puppeteer& version=v13.1.0&show=api-class-coverage`) is also considered a powerful capability within software test automation; however, since we covered the abilities of code coverage with Istanbul and Babel in *Chapter 8, Measuring Test Coverage of the Web Application*, we will not repeat it here. Keep in mind that, like Playwright, Puppeteer JavaScript and CSS code coverage with Istanbul (`https:// github.com/istanbuljs/puppeteer-to-istanbul`) is only supported on Chromium-based browsers.

Puppeteer namespaces

Within the Puppeteer framework, frontend web application developers can utilize the device's methods, network conditions, and error-handling capabilities.

To perform web application testing on specific devices, including **mobile** viewports, you can utilize the `puppeteer.devices['DEVICE NAME']`, `page. emulateNetworkConditions()`, and `page.emulate()` methods (`https:// pptr.dev/#?product=Puppeteer&version=v13.1.0&show=api- pageemulateoptions`). From the preceding URL, you can find all of the supported `page.emulate()` APIs with code samples and useful documentation.

Now, let's try navigating to the Packt website using the following code:

```
const puppeteer = require('puppeteer');
const iPhone = puppeteer.devices['iPhone 11'];


(async () => {
  const browser =
    await puppeteer.launch({headless: false});
  const page = await browser.newPage();
  await page.emulate(iPhone);
  await page.goto('https://www.packtpub.com');
```

```
await page.screenshot({path: 'packtpub.png'});
await browser.close();
})();
```

The preceding code snippet simply navigates to the Packt Publishing website and emulates it on an iPhone 11 device through a slow 3G network profile specified within the Puppeteer framework. Here is the 3G network profile spec used in the test:

```
'Slow 3g' {
Download: ((500 * 1000) /8) *0.8,
Upload: ((500 * 1000) / 8) * 0.8,
Latency: 400 *5,
},
```

Prior to closing the browser session, the code for navigating to the Packt website performs a screen capture that is saved under Packtpub.png:

```
'Slow 3g' {
Download: ((500 * 1000) /8) *0.8,
Upload: ((500 * 1000) / 8) * 0.8,
Latency: 400 *5,
},
```

In the context of mobile testing, you can use the page.setViewport() methods and specify a screen resolution using the width and height as required. From the following device descriptor page, you can see the built-in mobile device specifications: https://github.com/puppeteer/puppeteer/blob/main/src/common/DeviceDescriptors.ts. For example, for the iPhone 11 used in the preceding code snippet, the test uses the specification for that iPhone platform from the preceding descriptor to virtualize a slow 3G network connection.

Puppeteer working with elements

To interact with web page elements, Puppeteer uses the `page` APIs to type text, click, scroll, and conduct other events on the web application under test.

In the following code sample, still on the Packt website, we are clicking on the book search box and performing a search of JavaScript books together with a screenshot of the JavaScript books landing page. We are using both the `type` method and `waitForNavigation` to ensure that the landing page is loaded prior to taking a screenshot (refer to the next page):

```
const puppeteer = require('puppeteer');
const { waitForUrl } =
    require('selenium-webdriver/http/util');


(async () => {
    const browser = await puppeteer.launch({headless:false});
    const page = await browser.newPage();
    await page.goto('https://www.packtpub.com');
    const searchElement = await page.$('#search');
    await searchElement.type("JavaScript");
    await page.type('#search',String.fromCharCode(13));
    await Promise.all([
        await page.waitForNavigation({waitUntil: 'load'})
    ]);
    await page.screenshot({ path: 'Packtpub.png' });
    await browser.close();
})();
```

The following is the screenshot taken from the JavaScript landing page on the Packt website:

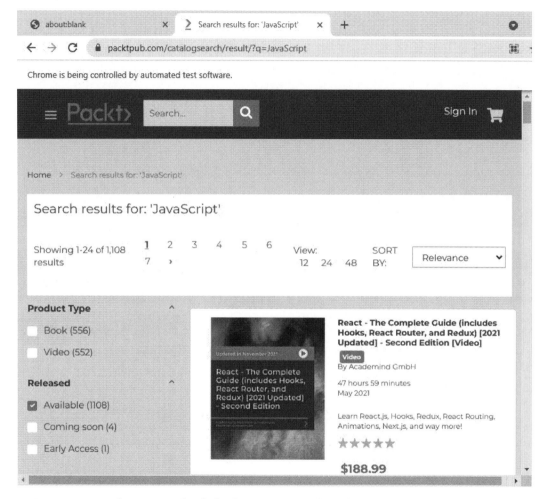

Figure 12.3 – Packt JavaScript books landing page screenshot taken by Puppeteer at the end of the preceding test

To take Puppeteer to a new level, please refer to this elegant and free demo code provided by Google to test their online PacMan game:

```
const readline = require('readline');
const puppeteer = require('puppeteer');
(async() => {
const browser = await puppeteer.launch({
  headless: false,
  args: ['--window-size=800,500']
});
const page = await browser.newPage();
await page.setViewport({width: 800, height: 500,
  deviceScaleFactor: 2});
await page.goto(
  'https://www.google.com/logos/2010/pacman10-i.html');
process.stdin.on('keypress', async (str, key) => {
  // In "raw" mode, so create own kill switch.
  if (key.sequence === '\u0003') {
    await browser.close();
    process.exit();
  }
  if (['up', 'down', 'left', 'right'].includes(key.name)) {
    const capitalized =
      key.name[0].toUpperCase() + key.name.slice(1);
    const keyName = 'Arrow${capitalized}';
    console.log('page.keyboard.down('${keyName}')');
    await page.keyboard.down(keyName);
  }
});
readline.emitKeypressEvents(process.stdin);
process.stdin.setRawMode(true);
})();
```

As you can see in the preceding JavaScript code sample, the code navigates to the Google PacMan game site and, once loaded in its set viewport sizes, a user can play the game via the keyboard's arrow keys.

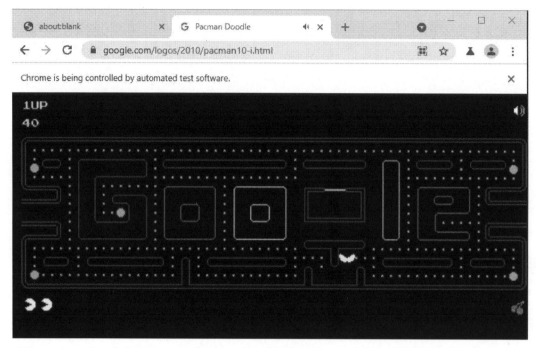

Figure 12.4 – Google PacMan game being executed within a browser through keyboard arrows driven by Puppeteer test code

To perform more actions using elements through the keyboard APIs, you can also refer to some nice code samples provided by the *Tabnine* website (https://www.tabnine.com/code/javascript/functions/puppeteer/Page/keyboard).

Puppeteer load test option

Google Puppeteer offers a powerful node library that can be installed and used to run multiple instances in parallel on any JavaScript test against your web application and perform load testing (https://github.com/svenkatreddy/puppeteer-loadtest).

Simply install that package using this command:

```
npm install -g puppeteer-loadtest
```

Once installed, you should include the package as required within the JavaScript test code:

```
const startPuppeteerLoadTest =
  require('puppeteer-loadtest');
```

Running a specific test is possible through various command-line options as follows:

- `--file` – Provides a path to your JavaScript test file.
- `--s` and `--c` – This is the sample size configuration for the load (such as `--s=100 --c=25` will run a total of 100 specified scripts across 25 concurrent Chrome headless instances).

Running a load test using the preceding command-line option can be triggered through the following:

```
npx puppeteer-loadtest --file=./test/sample.js --s=100 --c=25
```

To view a generated JSON performance test report, please refer to this GitHub repository: `https://github.com/svenkatreddy/puppeteer-loadtest/blob/master/test/performance.json`.

Puppeteer and Cucumber BDD

As with Cypress and Selenium, you can also implement BDD testing with Puppeteer through a feature file written in Gherkin and step-definition functions in JavaScript.

To use Cucumber BDD with Puppeteer, please install the node library for `cucumber-js` by means of the following command:

```
npm install @cucumber/cucumber
```

Following the installation, you should be able to use a folder structure that includes both step-definition files as well as Gherkin feature files.

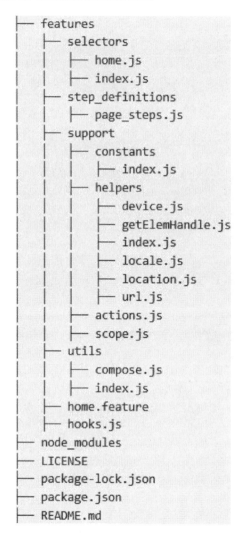

Figure 12.5 – Puppeteer and Cucumber BDD directory structure example (source: `https://github.com/mlampedx/cucumber-puppeteer-example`)

A full open source project that showcases BDD and Puppeteer can be obtained from the following GitHub repository: `https://github.com/mlampedx/cucumber-puppeteer-example`.

With the help of the preceding code samples, you can easily get started with this agile testing method.

Puppeteer accessibility testing

You can create accessibility testing with Puppeteer and the common Deque axe (https://www.deque.com/axe/) open source accessibility analyzer library. To do so, simply install the axe-puppeteer node library and add it to your source code using the following command. It will allow you to utilize the AxePuppeteer.analyze APIs and report back to the console and create an output file with the accessibility results and issues identified:

```
npm install axe-puppeteer
```

Running the short code sample on the Packt Publishing website will report accessibility issues back to the console using the following code:

```
const puppeteer = require('puppeteer');
const { waitForUrl } =
    require('selenium-webdriver/http/util');
const {AxePuppeteer} = require ('axe-puppeteer');
(async () => {
    const browser = await puppeteer.launch({headless:false,
        args: ['--window-size=1920,1080']});
    const page = await browser.newPage();
    await page.setBypassCSP(true);
    await page.goto('https://www.packtpub.com');
    const accessibilityResults =
        await new AxePuppeteer(page).analyze();
    console.log(accessibilityResults);
    await page.close();
    await browser.close();
})();
```

The preceding code execution output to the console will look as follows:

```
{
  id: 'table-duplicate-name',
  impact: null,
  tags: [Array],
  description: 'Ensure that tables do not have the same summary and caption',
  help: 'The <caption> element should not contain the same text as the summary attribute',
  helpUrl: 'https://dequeuniversity.com/rules/axe/3.5/table-duplicate-name?application=axe-puppeteer',
  nodes: []
},
{
  id: 'td-headers-attr',
  impact: null,
  tags: [Array],
  description: 'Ensure that each cell in a table using the headers refers to another cell in that table',
  help: 'All cells in a table element that use the headers attribute must only refer to other cells of that same table',
  helpUrl: 'https://dequeuniversity.com/rules/axe/3.5/td-headers-attr?application=axe-puppeteer',
  nodes: []
},
```

Figure 12.6 – Using Puppeteer with axe-puppeteer for an accessibility audit on the Packt website

Alternatively, you can also use basic accessibility APIs that are built into the Puppeteer framework, `https://pptr.dev/#?product=Puppeteer&version=v13 .1.0&show=api-class-accessibility`, which will provide you with the `accessibility.snapshot()` capabilities on a given page on your website under testing; however, it will be much more basic than the axe tool coverage.

Puppeteer web app tracing

Within Puppeteer, we have already reviewed the ability to generate an HAR file through the `har.start()` and `har.stop()` capabilities. However, Puppeteer also provides the ability to generate JSON trace files from a web application under test through the `tracing.start()` and `tracing.stop()` APIs. Such an ability enables frontend developers to gain insights regarding page loading times, performance issues such as slow loading resources on the page, and more.

The following code will generate two output files, `trace_demo.har` and `traceDemo. json`, for frontend developers to analyze and debug their network traffic, its performance, and other traffic that is happening on their website:

```javascript
const puppeteer = require('puppeteer');
const PuppeteerHar = require('puppeteer-har');
(async () => {
    const browser = await puppeteer.launch({headless:false});
    const page = await browser.newPage();

    const har = new PuppeteerHar(page);
```

```
    await har.start({ path: 'trace_demo.har' });
    await page.tracing.start({path: 'traceDemo.json'});
    await page.goto('https://www.packtpub.com/');
    await har.stop();
    await page.tracing.stop();
    await browser.close();
})();
```

The preceding two output files can be opened in a GUI manner through the Google-provided URL: `https://chromedevtools.github.io/timeline-viewer/`.

Puppeteer for API testing

As we covered earlier in this book with Cypress in *Chapter 10, Working with the Cypress Framework*, and Playwright in *Chapter 11, Working with the Playwright Framework*, frontend web application developers can also create API tests within the Puppeteer built-in APIs. To do so, they can utilize the Puppeteer `httpRequest()` and `httpResponse()` set of methods. All options are well documented in the Google documentation portal (`https://devdocs.io/puppeteer/index#class-httprequest`). Advanced API calls for network interceptions and the mocking of responses are supported. In addition, retrieving page header-request methods, getting a response back from the website cache, and much more besides can be used within test code.

Puppeteer with Google DevTools

As we know, Google owns the Chrome browser **DevTools**, which enables users to debug their web applications, launch the Lighthouse tools, measure performance and accessibility, and much more. Within Puppeteer, users can easily integrate with DevTools (`https://developers.google.com/web/tools/puppeteer/debugging`) and maximize their testing activities. From the preceding URL, you can learn more about the debugging process that is enabled through **DevTools** and how to slow down the test execution for further analysis of the web application under test.

To use DevTools within your test code, simply call the `puppeteer.launch()` method, with `devtools` set to `true` accordingly:

```
const browser = await puppeteer.launch({ devtools: true });
```

The preceding settings will allow you to utilize the `page.evaluate()` method and leverage the DevTools debugger.

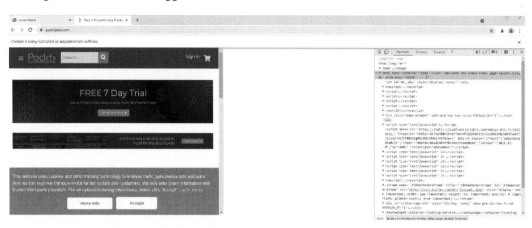

Figure 12.7 – Puppeteer test execution with the DevTools debugger enabled on the Packt home page

Within the aforementioned Chrome browser DevTools, there is a rich automated inspection tool called Lighthouse. Lighthouse is basically an open source automation tool that can be used either interactively or through test automation frameworks such as Puppeteer and others. With this tool, web application developers and testers can validate web application accessibility, performance, compliance with PWA guidance, network calls, and much more.

The Lighthouse tool can also be used from the command-line interface (`https://developers.google.com/web/tools/lighthouse#cli`). Using the command-line interface, frontend developers can launch the Google Lighthouse audit against their web application from any command-line interface. To install the tools for use within the command line, run the following command:

```
npm install -g lighthouse
```

To perform an audit on a web application once the tool is installed, run this command:

```
lighthouse <url>
```

To use Google DevTools with the Puppeteer framework, you may refer to this great documentation: `https://github.com/GoogleChrome/lighthouse/blob/master/docs/puppeteer.md`.

Puppeteer and CodeceptJS integration

A notable third-party integration that is available and worth considering is the one between Puppeteer and **CodeceptJS**. The CodeceptJS framework (`https://codecept.io/`) allows users to easily create end-to-end acceptance testing for web applications in JavaScript (`https://codecept.io/puppeteer/#setup`).

To add CodeceptJS to your testing environment, simply install the node library using these commands:

```
npm install codeceptjs
npx codeceptjs init
```

This library, together with Puppeteer, will allow you to build rich end-to-end testing with the unique and easy-to-understand code syntax of CodeceptJS.

Upon the `Init` command, you will need to specify your JavaScript test file path as well as the framework with which you want to work. In our case, we are selecting Puppeteer; however, as you can see in the following screenshot, CodeceptJS also works with the Playwright framework:

```
Installing to C:\Users\ekinsbruner\puppeteer
? Where are your tests located? ./*_test.js
? What helpers do you want to use?
  Playwright
  WebDriver
> Puppeteer
  TestCafe
  Protractor
  Nightmare
  Appium
```

Figure 12.8 – The output from the CodeceptJS initialization process for Puppeteer framework selection

Upon completion of the initialization process of CodeceptJS, a simple JavaScript configuration file will be created together with sample JavaScript test code as a baseline for your development.

In the following code, we are performing a simple and invalid login process to the Dribble website using CodeceptJS syntax.

Note that this code must be saved with the file extension that is defined in `codecept.conf.js`. By default, that is the following:

```
tests: './*_test.js'
Feature('login');
```

```
Scenario('Login to dribble page', ({ I }) => {
    I.amOnPage('https://dribbble.com/')
    I.click('Sign in');
    I.fillField('login', "erank@email.com");
    I.pressKey('Tab');
    I.fillField('password', "pass12345");
    pause();
    I.pressKey('Enter');
    I.see('We could not find an account matching');
});
```

As you can see, it uses plain and meaningful commands such as `I.amOnPage()` and `I.see()`. Running the preceding code is achieved through the following command:

```
npx codeceptjs run --steps
```

Upon running the preceding code sample, a Puppeteer browser is launched, and the test code gets executed.

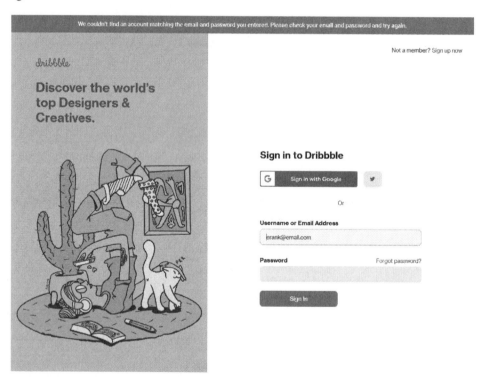

Figure 12.9 – CodeceptJS and Puppeteer code execution example on the Dribble website

Puppeteer testing within CI

You can integrate your Puppeteer JavaScript testing with many of the CI servers that are available on the market, including **CircleCI**, **GitLab** (`https://touch4it.com/blog/ui-testing-with-puppeteer-and-gitlab-ci`), **GitHub Actions**, **Jenkins**, and **Azure DevOps**. In this section, we will provide a single example of how to use Puppeteer with **GitHub Actions**.

I am using my own GitHub Puppeteer examples repository and will create a new action workflow with a **Node.js** type through the web UI from GitHub. This step will generate a `.yml` configuration file that will be used to run my Puppeteer tests upon a CI trigger or schedule.

Upon committing the new GitHub action, a new `.YML` file with the selected name will be generated and placed under the `.github/workflows` directory in my repository.

As you can see in the screenshot from the creation of the GitHub action file in *Figure 12.10*, there is a list of generated steps that will define this specific workflow and sequence of actions:

```
name: Node.js CI

on:
  push:
    branches: [ main ]
  pull_request:
    branches: [ main ]

jobs:
  build:

    runs-on: ubuntu-latest

    strategy:
      matrix:
        node-version: [12.x, 14.x, 16.x]
        # See supported Node.js release schedule at https://nodejs.org/en/about/releases/

    steps:
    - uses: actions/checkout@v2
    - name: Use Node.js ${{ matrix.node-version }}
      uses: actions/setup-node@v2
      with:
        node-version: ${{ matrix.node-version }}
        cache: 'npm'
    - run: npm ci
    - run: npm run build --if-present
    - run: npm test
    env:
        CI: true
```

Figure 12.10 – Screenshot of the GitHub Actions .YML file created on the Puppeteer repository (source: `https://github.com/ek121268/PuppeteerExamples`)

With this new workflow, in the event of any change to the repository, such as merging a branch into the master, this will trigger the execution of GitHub Actions (`https://docs.github.com/en/actions/quickstart`), as you can see in the following screenshot, which was taken in the event of a source code change.

From the preceding Quickstart guide provided by GitHub, you can learn how to create and customize actions to your CI process, create new workflows, and analyze the workflow results.

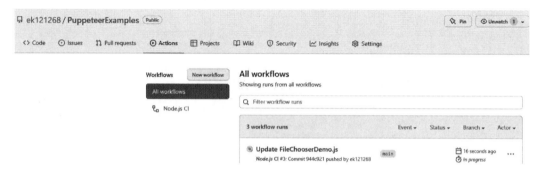

Figure 12.11 – GitHub Actions workflow execution example

Successful DevOps teams typically shift their test automation activities into their CI/CD processes. By doing it right and using tools such as GitHub, Jenkins, and others, teams are able to expedite feedback and identify issues as early as they commit their code changes. In addition, such a method of shifting testing left allows more frequent releases of new functionality and innovation.

With the preceding section, we have wrapped up the Puppeteer features overview. The framework has, of course, a wider range of APIs and other capabilities and integrations that can be reviewed through the Puppeteer documentation page (`https://pptr.dev/`).

We will now look at the opportunities and the future of the Puppeteer framework while considering the other mature and advanced frameworks that we've covered in this book.

The future of the Puppeteer framework

Google's Puppeteer framework is quite mature and has been on the market since January 2018 (`https://github.com/puppeteer/puppeteer/releases/tag/v1.0.0`). As mentioned earlier in this chapter, it is the baseline for the Playwright framework. The fact that this framework has been on the market longer than Playwright and Cypress is not well reflected in its maturity and capabilities. As we've learned in this chapter, there are some very useful and unique capabilities for this CDP-based framework, such as generating `traces`, `HAR` files, grabbing screenshots, working seamlessly with the DevTools APIs, performing advanced audits of websites through Lighthouse tool integration, working with BDD, integrating with CI tools and third-party frameworks such as CodeceptJS, and more. While these are very great features that allow frontend web application developers to test and debug their websites, this framework lacks some important capabilities that, unless implemented by Google, will position this framework lower in the marketplace.

Features that are missing in Puppeteer as this book is being developed consist of the following:

- **Cross-browser testing support**: Puppeteer only supports Chromium browsers, which includes Chrome and Edge. Without supporting all other browsers, such as Firefox and Safari, developers will have to utilize other tools.

- **Limited language bindings**: While JavaScript is the dominant language for web application development, testers' skillsets vary, and they often seek alternatives, such as Java, Python, and C#. Playwright and Selenium in that regard cover more language bindings and provide more flexibility for testers.

- **Mobile testing**: Testing web applications and network conditions across many mobile platforms is possible through Appium, which is built on top of Selenium. With Puppeteer, users can emulate basic network conditions and a very limited number of mobile platforms. With Google behind *Flutter* and *PWA*, the expectation is for better mobile landscape coverage within the testing tool stack.

- **Low-code support**: Most test frameworks have built-in test code generation. Selenium has its Selenium IDE, Cypress has its Cypress Studio, and Playwright has its codegen within `Inspector`. Puppeteer does not have a built-in capability other than automated audits through DevTools and Lighthouse.

- **Test reporting**: The ability to generate actionable and meaningful test reports is a weakness of this framework, especially when compared to the Cypress dashboards, and Selenium with Allure integration. Puppeteer will need to find a better and easier way to report test results with richer artifacts if it wishes to compete in this space with the other frameworks.

From a future standpoint, Puppeteer will have to make a few investments in its framework to close some of the aforementioned gaps and provide new cutting-edge features that will convince developers to continue using it over the other options.

An impressive opportunity from a codeless and intelligent testing perspective has emerged through a project called Puppetry (`https://puppetry.app/`). This project facilitates the creation of codeless, end-to-end Puppeteer-based test automation without the need to write any lines of JavaScript code. With such a tool incorporated into the Puppeteer project, this solution can close one of Puppeteer's gaps and provide a nice alternative to both developers and non-developers who wish to develop test automation. Getting started with this project can be done through the following GitHub repository: `https://github.com/dsheiko/puppetry/releases`. This project also extends support to the Firefox browser. In the case of code generation, users can export the recorded tests to *Jest* JavaScript code.

With these suggestions and opportunities for enhancement, we will conclude this section and provide a summary for this chapter.

Summary

In this chapter, we covered the fundamentals of the Puppeteer framework and learned how to get started and run a JavaScript Puppeteer test. We reviewed Puppeteer's core capabilities; both the basic ones as well as the advanced ones, such as API testing, network mocking, BDD, accessibility, DevTools, CI integrations, working with elements, emulating mobile platforms, and more.

We then concluded the chapter by looking into the future of Puppeteer, while covering the framework's currently missing, and very much needed, features, along with emerging opportunities, such as the codeless solution, complementing web testing with support for PWA and Flutter within Puppeteer, reporting, and more.

With the core skills that were introduced in this chapter, you can now get started with your own Puppeteer project in JavaScript, create web application assertions, including monitoring network traces, run Lighthouse audits, create performance testing from your own workstation, and be more familiar with the rich set of Puppeteer APIs that Google provides.

In the following chapter, we will focus solely on the intelligent cross-browser test automation landscape and learn what is supported within the top four test automation frameworks, and what can be extended through other commercial low-code and AI-based tools.

13

Complementing Code-Based Testing with Low-Code Test Automation

While the open source community offers a wide range of coding test frameworks as highlighted in this book, there are also new and emerging intelligent testing solutions that can base their record-and-playback abilities with self-healing **machine learning (ML)**-driven features to provide an additional layer of test automation coverage. In this chapter, we will learn about the available options in the market, the relevant places and use cases to use such tools within a development pipeline, and caveats or pitfalls to be aware of.

Through our study of the four leading testing frameworks that we've covered in this book, **Selenium**, **Playwright**, **Cypress**, and **Puppeteer**, we've seen that each of these frameworks have some level of low-code/no-code capabilities. Within this chapter, we will highlight these specific capabilities but mostly provide an overview of the additional intelligent codeless test automation tools for web applications. We will look into **Perfecto codeless web** (https://www.perfecto.io/products/scriptless), **Testim** (https://www.testim.io/), **Mabl** (https://www.mabl.com/), and a few other tools that are new and emerging.

The chapter is designed to cover the following:

- Learning about the fundamental features of low-code testing tools for web applications

- Providing a technical overview of the leading codeless tools within the open source frameworks

- Providing an overview of commercial **artificial intelligence** (**AI**)-based codeless tools for web application testing

- Understanding when to use low-code over code-based solutions and what some of the trade-offs are

The goal of the chapter is to help frontend developers and testers consider additional tools that can support their overall test coverage objectives, as well as realizing in which cases such tools are more useful than the core open source tools.

Fundamental features of low-code/codeless testing tools

Over the past few years, we've seen tremendous growth and investment in codeless and low-code software testing tools. Some of these advancements occurred within the open source landscape community (for example, **Selenium integrated development environment** (**IDE**), **Playwright CodeGen Inspector**, and so on), while other advancements were seen within the rise of commercial intelligence tools.

Prior to exploring the available options, let's first understand what it takes from a features perspective for a codeless or low-code testing tool to compete in the cross-browser testing landscape.

As we have explored throughout this book, properly testing a modern web application across all relevant browser configurations and mobile viewports requires massive coverage and thorough planning. Functional testing, non-functional testing—such as performance, security, and accessibility—through visual and **user interface** (**UI**) testing, **application programming interface** (**API**) testing, mocking capabilities, scaling, and testing in parallel and within **continuous integration** (**CI**) are all critical pillars of a web application testing plan. Most of the open source test automation frameworks that we've covered in this book support in one way or the other the aforementioned capabilities, either as built-in features or through third-party integrations. For a codeless testing tool to equally be considered a competitor, such a tool needs to have most of these capabilities built in as well, and with high reliability and maintainability. Web applications change often and changing source code is relatively easy. Code is being managed within **version control systems** (**VCSs**), hence keeping up with changes and maintaining the code base is manageable. With codeless solutions where there are typically no code artifacts, it is critical to have an easier method to scale and version the test scenarios in between changes.

Have a look at the following diagram:

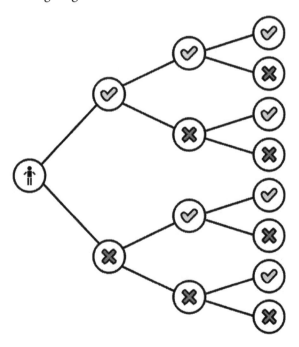

Figure 13.1 – Decision tree visualization

These are the high-level pillars and features that we would expect from a low-code/codeless web testing solution:

- **Test methodologies coverage**

  - Functional testing

  - API testing and mocking capabilities

  - Visual testing

  - Accessibility testing

  - Performance testing

- **Testing at scale/parallelization**

  - Grid executions

  - Cloud integrations

  - CI server integrations (GitHub Actions, Jenkins, and so on)

- **Test development capabilities**

  - Advanced scenario support (**inline frames (iFrames)**, multi-tabs, dynamic locators, varying authentication options, and so on)

  - Working with elements across test scripts

  - Support for Agile testing methods (for example, **behavior-driven development**, or **BDD**)

  - Test scenario editing and maintenance

- **Complementing code-based suites with codeless**

  - Exporting codeless to code

  - Extending codeless with code modules for advanced cases

- **Test reporting and analysis**

  - Test result artifacts

  - Trends and analysis

  - Integration of test reports to code-based reporting dashboards

- **Ease of use and ramp-up**

  - Time to get started with easy and more advanced test scenario development

  - Solid documentation with recommended practices

  - Ongoing and online support

- **Cost of ownership**

  - Compared to open source, how costly are such tools?

  - **Return on investment (ROI)** models for such tools compared to open source

As highlighted in the preceding list, there are quite a lot of considerations that practitioners and managers need to deal with when selecting technology for testing their web applications. With code-based open source frameworks, it is a bit simpler to choose, since these frameworks are all JavaScript-based, backed by large communities, proven for several years, and clearly valuable from a test automation creation and execution perspective. When looking into the low-code/codeless marketplace, these tools are newer and less flexible to modify to the needs of an organization; they come with a cost, and they are often limited from a test coverage perspective.

> **Note**
> With the preceding information in mind, this raises the following question: *So, why do we need codeless intelligent testing tools anyway?*

In the next section, we will uncover the leading codeless testing tools for web applications and highlight their core features and added value on top of the open source frameworks. It is important to realize that these codeless tools are still new and emerging, and this needs to be considered as teams adopt such tools.

Codeless tool overview within the open source landscape

In this section, we will cover the leading codeless testing tools that are available and supported for free within the open source testing frameworks.

Open source codeless tool lineup

Selenium, **Playwright**, **Cypress**, and even **Puppeteer** provide a level of codeless testing abilities through recording and playing back the test scenarios.

Let's provide a brief overview of codeless open source tools, starting with Selenium.

Selenium IDE codeless tool overview

Selenium offers a browser plugin, Selenium IDE (`https://github.com/ SeleniumHQ/selenium-ide/releases`), which is a basic record-and-playback solution to help new users of the Selenium project get started with the technology. The evolution of this IDE has led to it being a multi-browser extension (Chrome and Firefox) with a built-in element locator tool and a nice recorder with export-to-code abilities. It is not even close to the capabilities of a codeless AI-based testing tool but provides an entry-level option to Selenium.

Getting Selenium IDE for the Chrome browser can be done from here:

`https://chrome.google.com/webstore/detail/selenium-ide/ mooikfkahbdckldjjndioackbalphokd`

Once you install the browser extension for Selenium IDE, you can immediately start recording a test scenario against your web application, as illustrated in the following screenshot:

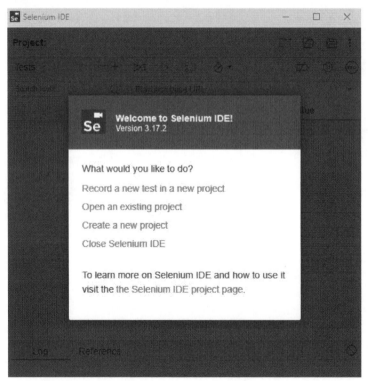

Figure 13.2 – Selenium IDE browser extension main UI

If you simply record a navigation scenario to the *Packt Publishing* home page, search for *JavaScript books*, and open a secondary tab, the generated test script will resemble the one shown in *Figure 13.3*.

As you can see, the IDE is built out of commands that are being performed on the web application, the target, which consists of the element locators, and the value that is being sent when relevant. All Selenium IDE projects are exported and saved under the `*.side` file format, which is basically the Selenium command-line runner (`https://www.selenium.dev/selenium-ide/docs/en/introduction/command-line-runner`). A saved Selenium IDE project that has been created can be executed through the command line with the saved `*.side` file as the target.

You will need to install the node library to run such saved projects by running this command:

```
npm install -g selenium-side-runner
npx selenium-side-runner [path to *.side test file]
```

Figure 13.3 shows a simple recorded scenario with the Selenium IDE browser plugin. It performs a navigation to the Packt homepage and records a few actions on the website.

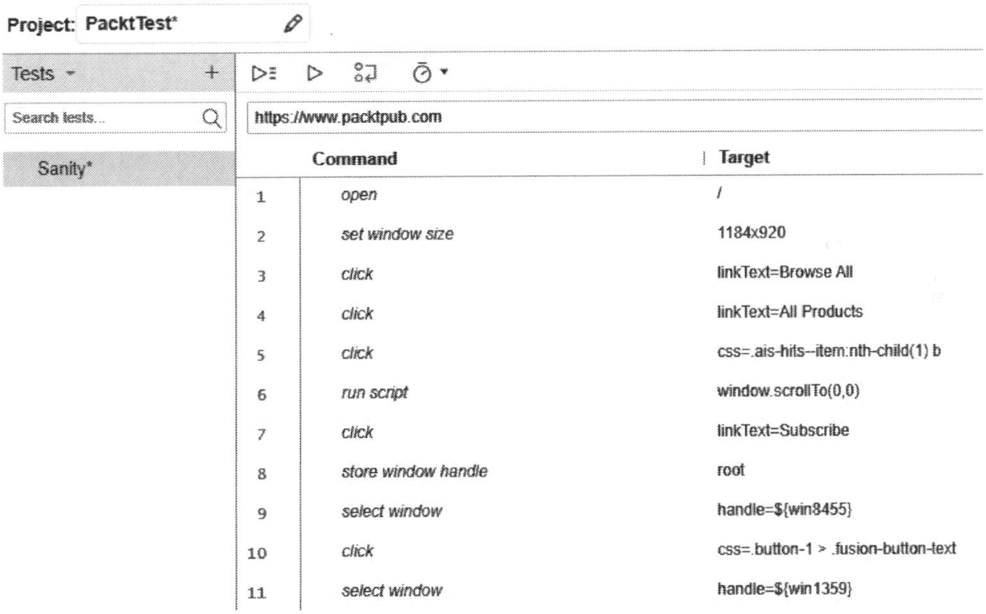

Project: PacktTest*		
Tests ▾ +	▷≣ ▷ ⏱▾	
Search tests... 🔍	https://www.packtpub.com	
Sanity*	Command	Target
	1 open	/
	2 set window size	1184x920
	3 click	linkText=Browse All
	4 click	linkText=All Products
	5 click	css=.ais-hits--item:nth-child(1) b
	6 run script	window.scrollTo(0,0)
	7 click	linkText=Subscribe
	8 store window handle	root
	9 select window	handle=${win8455}
	10 click	css=.button-1 > .fusion-button-text
	11 select window	handle=${win1359}

Figure 13.3 – Selenium IDE-generated test scenario example

Under the **Target** menu item, users can change and use different locators such as ID, Name, CSS, XPATH, and any other exposed property of the object.

After generating the sample codeless Selenium script within the IDE, you can easily export it to any of the Selenium language bindings that are supported, as shown in the following screenshot, by hovering over the test name and clicking on the three vertical dots:

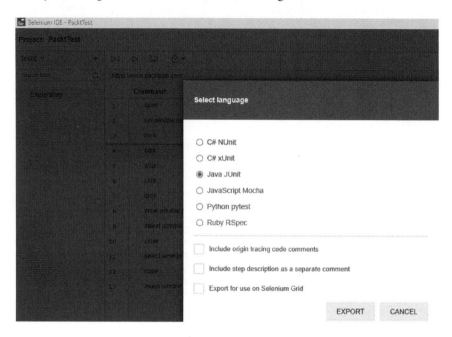

Figure 13.4 – Selenium IDE codeless test scenario export feature to language bindings

The generated code in JavaScript will look like this and will have the upper header line stating that this code was generated through Selenium IDE:

```
// Generated by Selenium IDE
const { Builder, By, Key, until } = require('selenium-webdriver')
const assert = require('assert')

describe('Exploratory', function() {
  this.timeout(30000)
  let driver
  let vars
  beforeEach(async function() {
    driver = await new Builder().forBrowser('chrome').build()
    vars = {}
  })
  afterEach(async function() {
    await driver.quit();
  })
  async function waitForWindow(timeout = 2) {
    await driver.sleep(timeout)
    const handlesThen = vars["windowHandles"]
    const handlesNow = await driver.getAllWindowHandles()
    if (handlesNow.length > handlesThen.length) {
      return handlesNow.find(handle => (!handlesThen.includes(handle)))
    }
    throw new Error("New window did not appear before timeout")
  }
  it('Exploratory', async function() {
    await driver.get("https://www.packtpub.com/")
    await driver.manage().window().setRect({ width: 1184, height: 920 })
    await driver.findElement(By.id("search")).click()
    await driver.findElement(By.id("search")).sendKeys("JavaScript")
    await driver.findElement(By.css(".magnifying-glass > .fa")).click()
    await driver.findElement(By.css(".ais-hits--item:nth-child(1) b")).click()
    vars["windowHandles"] = await driver.getAllWindowHandles()
    await driver.findElement(By.linkText("Free Learning")).click()
    vars["win9595"] = await waitForWindow(2000)
    vars["root"] = await driver.getWindowHandle()
    await driver.switchTo().window(vars["win9595"])
    await driver.close()
    await driver.switchTo().window(vars["root"])
    await driver.close()
    await driver.switchTo().window(vars["undefined"])
  })
})
```

Figure 13.5 – Selenium IDE-generated code in a JavaScript language binding

As mentioned previously, Selenium IDE is a very basic tool to generate Selenium scripts, but it does provide a quick ramp-up to generate codeless tests that can be then exported into different languages.

Playwright CodeGen Inspector overview

As highlighted in *Chapter 11, Working with the Playwright Framework*, this framework also offers a nice entry-level codeless solution (`https://playwright.dev/docs/codegen`) that can record web applications through a GUI-based tool and export the generated script into code.

You can start the tool by running the following command from your command line or the **Visual Studio Code (VS Code)** IDE terminal window:

```
npx playwright codegen [website under test URL], e.g.,
packtpub.com
```

Upon running this command from your local **Playwright** installation folder path, you will get a browser window with the web page, and you can perform actions on the page while they are being recorded and converted in real time to JavaScript. You can see in the following screenshot that the recording already generates test code without any need to manually export the code, as you would need to do in Selenium IDE. This obviously enables better maintenance of the code, editing, and much more flexibility:

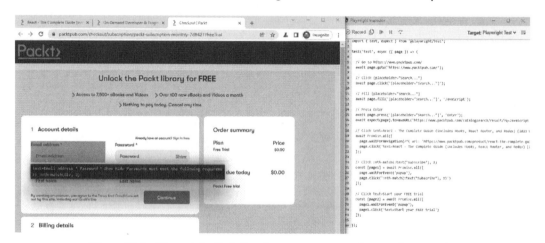

Figure 13.6 – Playwright CodeGen Inspector-generated test code example

The default test is generated in JavaScript **Playwright test** syntax; however, you can easily convert the code through the upper-right menu into the other language bindings supported by Playwright, as seen in the following screenshot, including JavaScript, Java, Python, and C#:

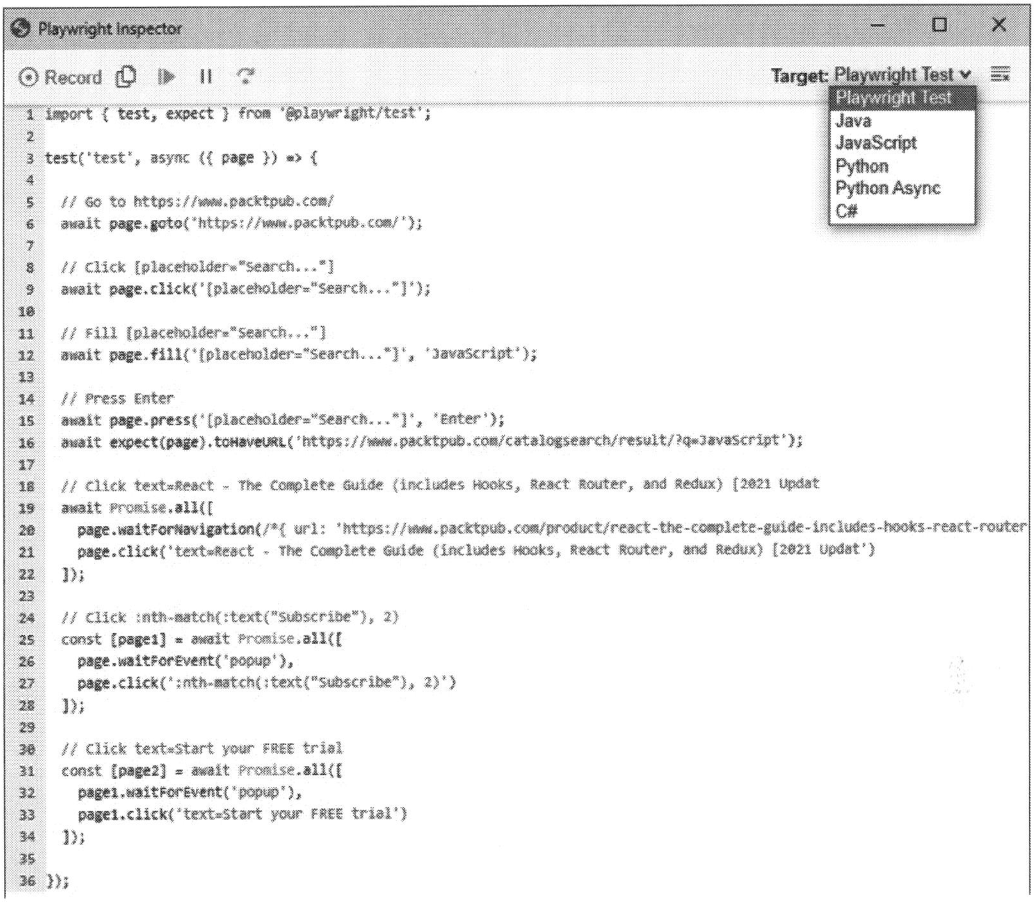

Figure 13.7 – Playwright-generated code: supported exporting language bindings

Compared to Selenium IDE, the Playwright CodeGen tool seems more modern and more frontend developer-friendly, as well as more capable. It can easily cope with complex websites, multiple tabs, and other challenging elements. It doesn't use self-healing or advanced AI capabilities, but it is a solid, codeless, free-to-use tool that comes with the Playwright open source installation.

Cypress Studio codeless tool overview

As we highlighted in *Chapter 10, Working with the Cypress Framework*, users of the Cypress framework can also benefit from the emerging **Cypress Studio** codeless tool (https://docs.cypress.io/guides/core-concepts/cypress-studio).

To get started with the Cypress Studio tool, you will need to enable its usage through the `cypress.json` file by adding the following lines of code:

```
{
    "experimentalStudio": true
}
```

Once you enable this feature, when you run the **Cypress** framework in GUI mode, you will get the option to click on the **Edit** button near your existing test code in JavaScript on the left panel, and it will enable the Cypress Studio test-recording capabilities. Alternatively, you can start a new test using Cypress Studio by placing a test specification JavaScript file under your local Cypress integration folder, as specified in the following instructions: `https://docs.cypress.io/guides/core-concepts/cypress-studio#Using-Cypress-Studio`.

In the following screenshot, I took the *getting started* basic JavaScript test code and used Cypress Studio to add a step to the test. As you can see, as of the time of writing this book, there are several commands that are supported by the tool, such as `.check()`, `.click()`, `.select()`, `.type()`, and `.uncheck()`:

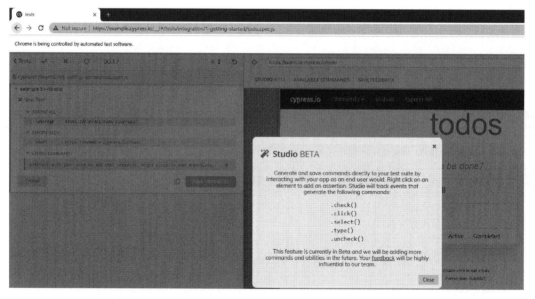

Figure 13.8 – Cypress Studio (beta) in action on an existing JavaScript test specification file

Simply interfering with the existing test code and recording a few more actions generated the following code block in the existing JavaScript file:

```
144    /* ==== Test Created with Cypress Studio ==== */
145    it('ChangedStudioCode', function() {
146      /* ==== Generated with Cypress Studio ==== */
147      cy.get(':nth-child(1) > .view > label').click();
148      cy.get(':nth-child(1) > .view > .toggle').check();
149      cy.get('.filters > :nth-child(2) > a').click();
150      /* ==== End Cypress Studio ==== */
151    });
```

Figure 13.9 – Cypress Studio-generated JavaScript code block example

Such a tool can easily extend in a short amount of time the test coverage and the time it takes to write code in JavaScript. As this tool is still evolving as this book is being written, it will be interesting to see how it matures and which advanced features will be added to this tool. As with the Selenium and Playwright frameworks covered previously, this tool is free and comes within the Cypress open source framework, which is quite nice.

Now that we've covered the main open source codeless tools within the leading test frameworks, let's explore some of the leading commercial web testing tools that are available in the market at this time.

Leading commercial codeless testing tools for web applications

In the commercial landscape, there are a few leading tools that should be known to frontend web application developers, **software development engineers in test** (**SDETs**), and manual testers. While we will only focus on three tools in this section, there are a few others that are not in the scope of this chapter, including Katalon Studio and Tricentis Tosca.

This section will feature the following three commercial tools:

- **Perfecto scriptless web** (based on the acquired TestCraft solution)
- **Testim** codeless testing solution for the web
- **Mabl** codeless testing solution for the web

These three tools are quite different in their features and capabilities, as well as the vision that the companies behind these tools have.

Perfecto scriptless web overview

The **Perfecto** scriptless solution is an integration of a codeless web testing AI-driven solution that was acquired by Perfecto's owning company Perforce (`https://www.perforce.com/press-releases/perforce-expands-portfolio-testcraft`). After TestCraft was acquired, it was fully integrated into the Perfecto cloud-based continuous testing platform for web and mobile (`https://www.perfecto.io/products/scriptless`). With this tool, users can easily record any type of web application and generate keyword-driven test scenarios without writing a single line of code. At the backbone of the implementation, Perfecto scriptless utilizes the **Selenium** framework to perform actions on the web application under test; however, it also provides a wide range of testing capabilities, as listed here:

- Test creation and recording

- Test management and cloning

- Self-healing and element locator weighting

- Running tests within CI, schedulers, and in parallel

- A unique feature called **Selenium-Based Extended Module (SBEM)** for importing code into the codeless solution

- Fully integrated into the Perfecto platform with access to the code/codeless reporting and manual testing of web applications

You can see an example of a Perfecto scriptless test scenario in the following screenshot:

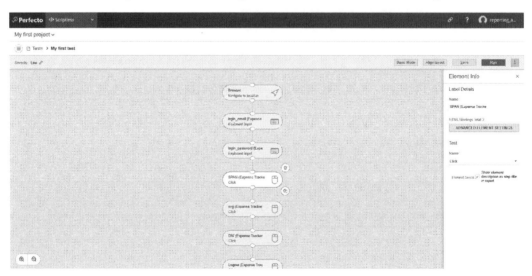

Figure 13.10 – Perfecto scriptless test scenario example

In the preceding screenshot, you can see the high-level and keyword-driven syntax of a test scenario that is available to view and edit after it has been recorded on the canvas. Developers can change sequence, add steps, modify the element locators used in the script, and much more. In addition, if there is a need to extend the test beyond what's supported in the codeless tool, developers can import JavaScript code into the tool via the SBEM, as seen in the following screenshot. Such an ability can add a command to the GUI recorder and expand the test flow:

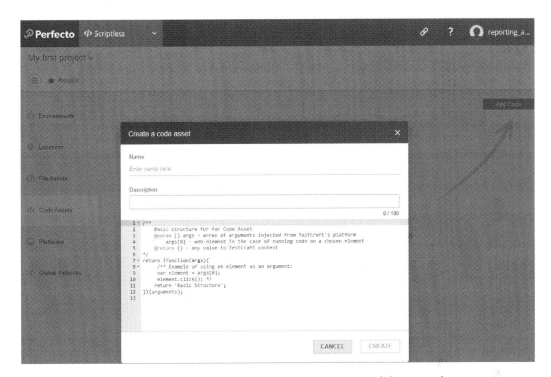

Figure 13.11 – Perfecto scriptless SBEM extension capability example

Perfecto scriptless also encapsulates a self-healing mechanism that, through learning and continuous analysis of the web application DOM, can weight each of the elements on the page and use the highest-rated and most probable element during the test execution, as illustrated in the following screenshot:

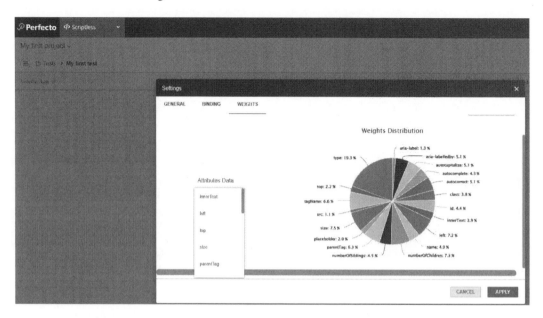

Figure 13.12 – Perfecto scriptless advanced element locators weighting algorithm

In the preceding screenshot, the `type` attribute has the highest weight distribution, with 19.3%. Unless a user manually overrides the use of this element, this is the element that the tool will use in the script by default. From one test run to the next, the algorithm keeps learning and adjusting these weights to always use the ones that have the highest chances of being found and interacted with.

Test execution at scale, in parallel, and within CI is key for Agile testing and velocity. With Perfecto scriptless, users can use a built-in scheduler, connect to CI, and run the tests in the Perfecto cloud, as illustrated in the following screenshot:

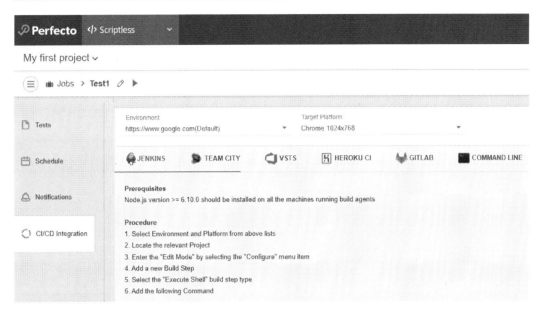

Figure 13.13 – Perfecto scriptless CI/CD integration option and configuration window

Clearly, Perfecto scriptless provides rich and complete **end-to-end** (**E2E**) test framework abilities from the creation standpoint, through execution, maintenance, and integration to CI/CD.

Another capability of the **Perfecto scriptless** solution is to create and execute **API** tests on the web application under test. As we will learn later in this chapter, Mabl can also cover API testing.

It will be interesting to follow this product and see how it evolves, expands to mobile app testing as well, and enriches its AI abilities beyond element self-healing.

Testim codeless web tool overview

Testim has a great codeless solution for web application testing. Unlike Perfecto scriptless, which is fully cloud-based and embedded into the wider Perfecto platform, Testim (https://www.testim.io/) is a browser extension that allows practitioners to point to a web application under test and record the action on the app. The test scenarios are converted into keyword sets of sequential commands. After registering with a company account or your personal GitHub account, you will be redirected to download the Testim browser extension (https://chrome.google.com/webstore/detail/testim-editor/pebeiooilphfmbohdbhbomomkkoghoia). Once the extension is installed, you can start by recording a new test scenario on any web application.

With the acquisition by Tricentis (`https://www.tricentis.com/news/ tricentis-acquires-ai-based-saas-test-automation-platform- testim/`), it will be interesting to see how this tool evolves and integrates into the overall portfolio Tricentis has.

You can see an example of a Testim-generated test flow here:

Figure 13.14 – Testim-generated test flow on the Packt Publishing home page

Each step in the exploratory test flow that was recorded and shown in the preceding screenshot is attached to a dedicated screenshot and element locator properties with options and conditions, such as when to mark the step as failed, options to run the step only when an element is visible, and more.

You can see an example for a specific recorded step here:

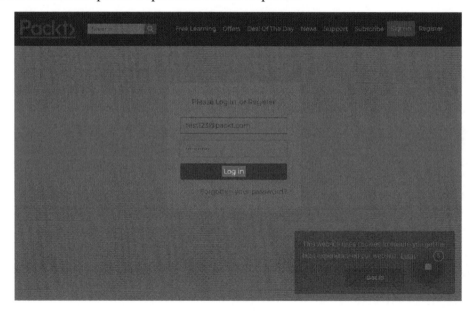

Figure 13.15 – Testim-generated screenshot for a specific recorded step with a highlight of the element under test

At the end of a test recording, if you like, you can click from the menu on **export to code**, and the tool will convert the high-level test scenario into source code using a tool called the **Dev Kit**. A nice feature of the Testim product is the ability to branch from a recorded test suite, as well as copying and pasting an existing test.

The tool also offers a nice structure for managing single test cases, test suites—which are groups of single test cases—test plans, labels to use per test case (for example, **Nightly**), and shared steps that can be used by other test scenarios. You can see an example of this in the following screenshot:

Figure 13.16 – Testim GUI options for managing test cases and test suites

An additional set of capabilities within Testim is the ability to use data-driven tests through spreadsheets, **JavaScript Object Notation** (**JSON**) files, or other test data configuration options to maximize test coverage, including happy path testing, negative scenarios, and boundary cases. You can see an example of this here:

```
1   return [{
2       "username": "tomsmith" + Date.now(),
3       "password": "SuperSecretPassword!"
4   },{
5       "username": "david",
6       "password": "SecretPassword?"
7   }];
```

Figure 13.17 – Testim Test Data capabilities: built-in example

Also, Testim provides the ability to perform network mocking, as we've seen in code-based testing frameworks such as Cypress, Playwright, and Puppeteer. To use the mock features, users need to record an **HTTP Archive** (**HAR**) format file and upload it to the system. You can see an overview of this here:

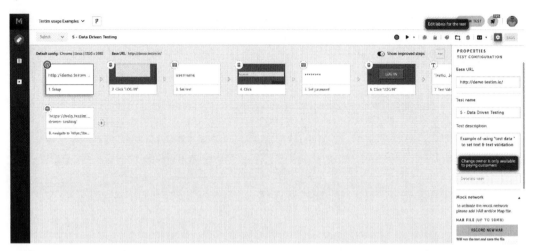

Figure 13.18 – Testim project settings options and mocking network capability

At the end of executions, whether they are triggered from the Testim GUI or from CI, users have a dedicated reporting portal within the tool to view all their test results and filter the test data based on their results. From this view, users can also change and create new test configurations such as browser version, **operating system** (**OS**), screen resolution, and step timeouts.

A newly created offer from Testim is their TestOps dashboard (https://www.testim. io/testops/). This dashboard offers granular governance across all test cases within the Agile team, an additional layer of test management at scale, and allows developers and testers to better analyze trends and failures.

Two additional and notable features of the product are outlined here:

- Testim Dev Kit
- Testim recorder for Playwright and Puppeteer frameworks

The **Testim Dev Kit** (https://help.testim.io/docs/index) provides a set of JavaScript APIs that allow frontend developers to create and edit test code.

To get started with this solution, you need to install a dedicated node library through this command:

```
npm install -g @testim/testim-cli
```

This library connects through your Testim credentials to the Testim tool.

The installation and initiation of the library creates a skeleton of a JavaScript test case that you can then edit and expand (`https://help.testim.io/docs/getting-started`). Once you finish coding, you can run it locally or within CI. Also, recorded tests from the Testim GUI can be exported to the Dev Kit framework and be used as a quick jumpstart to coding web test automation.

The **Testim recorder** for *Playwright* and *Puppeteer* is called **Playground**. After you have your Testim account created and the browser extension installed, simply go to `https://www.testim.io/playground/`, which consists of two tabs—Playwright and Puppeteer. You can record within the relevant tab an E2E scenario, and the code will be generated in the background and can be copied and pasted into your IDE of choice, such as VS Code, IntelliJ, and so on. From that point, you can continue editing the code from the IDE itself. This is a free offering from *Testim*.

The nice thing about Testim is that it provides a hybrid model of web application test automation that is both codeless-driven by AI to self-heal elements through the use of visual layers, automated waits, and support for smart locators (`https://www.testim.io/test-stability/`), as well as through code via its **Dev Kit** and **Playground** tools.

To learn more and even get Testim certifications, go to this resource and register:

`https://www.testim.io/education/`

Mabl codeless web testing tool overview

The third and last codeless tool that we will cover in this section is **Mabl** (`https://www.mabl.com/`). After registering for a free trial with Mabl, you will be asked to download the desktop application called **Mabl trainer**. This tool allows users to record and generate web application codeless test scenarios. There are two main views and interfaces for Mabl users: the **trainer** and the web platform. The **trainer** is where you record and generate tests, and the web view is where you run tests either locally or in the *Google* cloud. Tests can be executed either **headed** or **headless**.

The execution report also supports downloading autogenerated HAR files and testing logs. You can see an example of the Mabl application here:

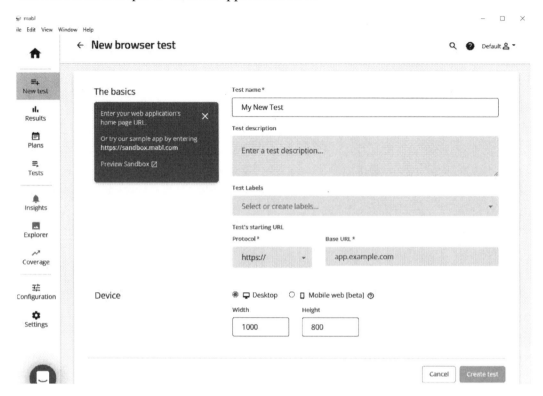

Figure 13.19 – Mabl trainer desktop application main GUI

After filling in the initial details in the desktop application from Mabl, you can get started with recording your test flow. As you can see in the preceding screenshot, you can configure the web application URL and the screen resolution for desktop, and even mobile web is supported in the early stages.

When clicking on the **Create test** button on the app, a Chrome browser will launch and start recording all the user actions, as illustrated in the following screenshot:

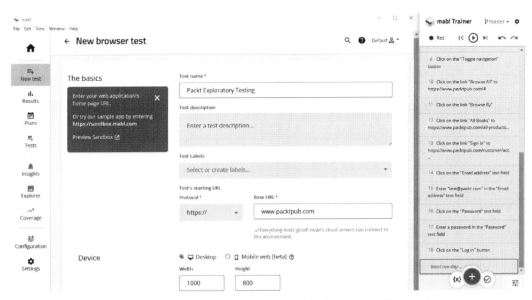

Figure 13.20 – Mabl trainer side by side with the generated test script

After the recording is completed, the trainer application allows you to edit tests, as well as adding assertions. After saving the newly created test scenario, you can view it in the application GUI. Within the Mabl tool, users can also inspect their web application's single-user performance through the built-in speed index (`https://help.mabl.com/docs/speed-index`), as well as performing coverage analysis of their tests against the web application under test. As you can see in the following launch console, the Mabl execution engine uses Playwright to run the tests:

Figure 13.21 – Mabl test execution console in runtime

Here is the generated test scenario in a keyword-based syntax. The test can be added to a plan or executed within CI or a defined schedule:

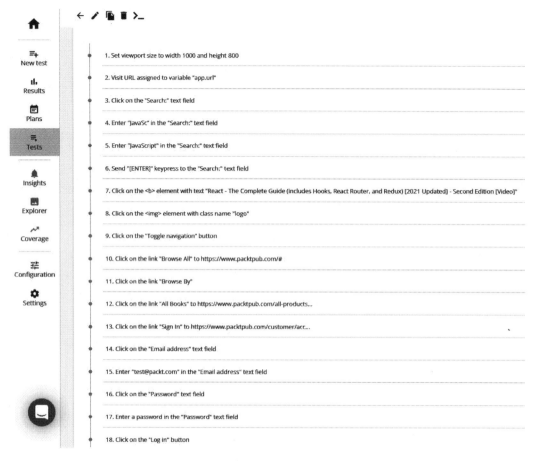

Figure 13.22 – Mabl-generated test flow example

Executing the tests from the Mabl application can be done, as mentioned previously, locally or through the Google cloud, as shown in the following screenshot. Users can add loops (`https://help.mabl.com/docs/using-loops`), conditions, mouse hovers, page refreshes, environment variables, and other abilities to their test scenarios:

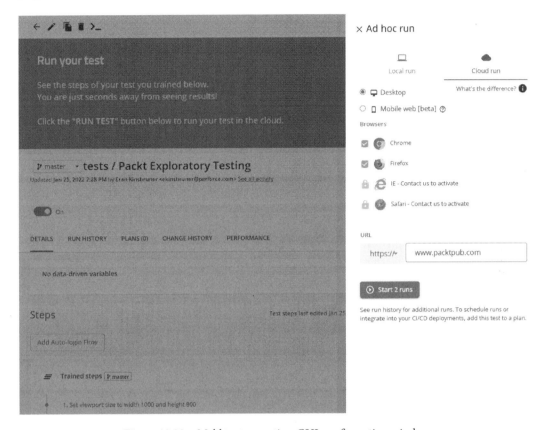

Figure 13.23 – Mabl test execution GUI configuration window

In addition, and in parallel with functional E2E testing, Mabl also supports API test creation and execution. Users can define a set of API calls and use them within the test suite, as well as within the overall test coverage analysis that is provided by Mabl. This is illustrated in the following screenshot:

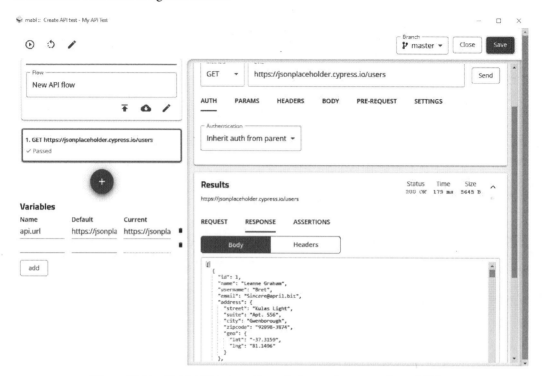

Figure 13.24 – Mabl API test creation window and supported capabilities

Mabl is indeed a rich product that supports functional, API, single-user performance, and visual testing (`https://help.mabl.com/docs/visual-testing-and-monitoring`). It has various integrations into many **development-operations (DevOps)** tool stacks including CI tools such as *Jenkins*, *Azure Pipelines*, *GitLab*, *CircleCI*, *Slack*, *Jira*, *Microsoft Teams*, and others.

Mabl, as with Testim and Perfecto scriptless, also uses its AI algorithm within the element locators and self-healing functionality (`https://www.mabl.com/auto-healing-tests`). However, as opposed to the other tools, with Mabl, users cannot export the recorded scripts into code, and that's a limitation.

With the upcoming support for mobile web testing, this solution can also be a solid complementary tool to the code-based testing frameworks that were covered in this book.

Now that we have covered the major commercial codeless tools in the market, let's provide a summary and conclude this chapter.

Summary

In this chapter, we focused 100% on codeless tools that are offered by the open source community, as well as commercial tools. We looked at the capabilities of such tools and what to look for in such tools from a feature set perspective and provided a quick getting started guide for each of the tools. We dived deeper into the three main commercial codeless and AI-based tools and explored their core capabilities. While these tools mark a transformation milestone in the marketplace, they are still new and emerging, and there are still major gaps in using them. As opposed to open source codeless tools, commercial tools are licensable and paid products, and the expectations are high. From my evaluation of all the commercial tools, it was clear that they provide great value and can complement code-based testing tools with exploratory and mid-level complex test creations. However, the level of stability in such tests as the scenario becomes more advanced and the ability to playback the tests are not always consistent. In addition, the scaling of test execution in most of the tools (excluding Perfecto scriptless) is not straightforward and requires additional cloud licenses and a separate paid package.

To place all three commercial tools in a comparison table, they look like this:

Capabilities	Perfecto scriptless	Testim	Mabl
Self-healing with smart locators	✘	✘	✘
E2E functional testing (loops, assertions, data-driven testing, and so on)	✘	✘	✘
Export script to code	✘	✔	✘
Import code into codeless tool	✔	✔	✘
Support for API testing	✔	✘	✔

Capabilities	Perfecto scriptless	Testim	Mabl
Parallel/cloud testing at scale	✓	☰	☰
Support single-user performance testing	✗	✗	✓
Documentation and support	✓	✓	✓
Ability to work with advanced scenarios	☰	☰	☰
Support for visual testing	✗	✗	✓

With the preceding summary table in mind, you can get an understanding of the weak spots and strengths, as well as commonalities between the three commercial tools.

The future of web application testing across desktop platforms and mobile is promising, and when combining open source code-based testing frameworks with codeless commercial tools, teams can really maximize the test coverage, stability, and maintainability of their test assets.

That concludes this chapter!

With this chapter, we conclude this book. The next chapter will provide a summary of the book and some predictions for the future, as well as expectations of this dynamic marketplace.

14
Wrapping Up

In this very thorough book that is aimed mainly at web application frontend developers, we've provided a complete compilation of all testing aspects that are important to keep web applications at high quality and performance. The book was divided into three parts, each building upon the ones before it.

To achieve continuous software delivery performance, both frontend developers and SDETs must keep evaluating their testing assets, reviewing their results, and maintaining and adding to their existing suites. In addition, knowing all options in the marketplace, both open source and commercial, can help practitioners to make better decisions and even combine multiple technologies to enhance testing coverage and capabilities.

In *Part 1* of the book, we provided a deep overview of the web application testing types, the marketplace for frontend web application developers and testers, the key testing objectives, and the main roles that need to be concerned about these marketplaces. We also covered, in the first part, the variety of web application types, both legacy and emerging, such as **PWAs**, **Flutter**, **React Native**, and **responsive**.

In *Part 2* of the book, we dived deeper into the world of frontend developers and provided instructions on building an efficient test plan from the ground up, as well as tools to measure success within the continuous testing of web applications. We then broke down the core capabilities of the leading JavaScript testing frameworks and covered items such as visual testing, accessibility testing, and API testing. We concluded the second part of the book with a dedicated chapter around code and test coverage analysis for web applications.

In *Part 3*, we dedicated most of the content to the most advanced features of the four leading open source web testing frameworks: **Selenium, Cypress, Playwright**, and **Puppeteer**. We concluded that part with an overview of intelligent web testing solutions that are based on low-code and codeless from within both the open source and commercial landscapes. We provided an overview for getting started with the three leading codeless tools on the market: **Perfecto Codeless**, **Testim**, and **Mabl**.

Throughout the entire book, I provided basic and advanced code samples with **GitHub** repository pointers and other references to help practitioners from all levels to get started or advance their testing skills and knowledge.

Major takeaways from the book

While writing this book, I solidified my belief that while there are many other open source test automation frameworks for web applications that are great and have nice capabilities, such as **Robot** (`https://robotframework.org/`), **TestCafe** (`https://testcafe.io/`), **WebdriverIO** (`https://webdriver.io/`), and **CodeceptJS** (`https://codecept.io/`), the most valuable and rich frameworks for frontend web application developers that should be considered are the four that we've covered.

The main insights to keep in mind are as follows:

- The web application testing marketplace is divided into **three architecture-based frameworks**:

  - **Chrome debugging protocol** (CDP)-based, including Playwright and Puppeteer

  - WebDriver protocol frameworks, including Selenium (as well as WebdriverIO)

  - In-browser JavaScript testing, including Cypress

- There are **many commonalities between the four covered frameworks**; however, each brings a unique value that the others don't. Hence, *combining more than a single framework within the testing strategy might be a productive decision*. For multi-skillset teams, consider the use of Selenium, which comes with more language bindings, and Playwright or Cypress, which add additional features, such as API testing, built-in code coverage, ease of debugging, and stronger codeless creation abilities.

- The future of web application testing will depend on the *synergy between new and emerging commercial codeless tools and open source frameworks*. If they can complement each other and maintain a proper balance of test coverage, stability, and maintainability, teams that adopt both types of solutions will be highly successful.

- Continuous testing for web applications must consider the entire digital landscape, which is both web and mobile platforms, PWAs, Flutter, React Native, and other types of modern applications. To remain competitive in the market across verticals (healthcare, insurance, finance, and so on), teams have to build stronger and higher-coverage test suites and *shift left all testing types, including security, accessibility, APIs, and performance.*

The software testing world for both web and other digital apps, including mobile and IoT, is constantly evolving and advancing. As a takeaway from this book, I recommend all developers and testers keep an eye on digital transformation-related trends, follow their industry-specific trends, and learn/adopt things that can improve their daily work and contribute to greater application quality.

You can find an additional set of references and links as follows to expand your knowledge and skills around web application testing with the aforementioned open source testing frameworks.

I do hope that this book will continue to contribute to your overall testing practices throughout the software development life cycle and beyond.

GitHub main repository – `https://github.com/PacktPublishing/A-Frontend-Web-Developers-Guide-to-Testing`

Useful references and bookmarks

For future reference and more examples and best practices, I recommend bookmarking the following.

Cypress framework-specific

- Cypress ambassadors – `https://www.cypress.io/ambassadors/`
- Cypress Gitter – `https://gitter.im/cypress-io/cypress#`
- Marie Drake's personal blog – `https://www.mariedrake.com/blog`
- Gleb Bahmutov – `https://glebbahmutov.com/blog/`
- Filip Hric's blog – `https://filiphric.com/`
- Cypress Courses by Gleb Bahmutov - `https://cypress.tips/courses`

Playwright framework-specific

- Microsoft Playwright documentation – `https://docs.microsoft.com/en-us/microsoft-edge/playwright/`

- Playwright community documentation – `https://playwright.tech/`

- A basic but useful *getting started with Playwright* guide – `https://dev.to/leading-edje/automate-your-testing-with-playwright-1gag`

- Extending Playwright testing with C# support – `https://medium.com/version-1/playwright-a-modern-end-to-end-testing-for-web-app-with-c-language-support-c55e931273ee`

- Execute automation YouTube Playwright tutorial – `https://www.youtube.com/watch?v=2_BPIA5RgXU`

- Playwright Slack channel – `https://playwright.slack.com/join/shared_invite/zt-smuwd93l-Itgcv8IKYaF~wRnLQl4UMg#/shared-invite/email`

Selenium framework-specific

- Online Selenium tutorial – `https://artoftesting.com/selenium-tutorial`

- Selenium testing guide by Mozilla – `https://developer.mozilla.org/en-US/docs/Learn/Tools_and_testing/Cross_browser_testing/Your_own_automation_environment`

Puppeteer framework-specific

- Google Developers Puppeteer guides:

  - `https://developers.google.com/web/tools/puppeteer/get-started`

  - `https://pptr.dev/`

- Puppeteer official documentation – `https://devdocs.io/puppeteer/`

- Getting started with Puppeteer: an insightful blog – `https://codoid.com/puppeteer-tutorial-the-complete-guide-to-using-a-headless-browser-for-your-testing/`

Index

Packt.com

Subscribe to our online digital library for full access to over 7,000 books and videos, as well as industry leading tools to help you plan your personal development and advance your career. For more information, please visit our website.

Why subscribe?

- Spend less time learning and more time coding with practical eBooks and Videos from over 4,000 industry professionals

- Improve your learning with Skill Plans built especially for you

- Get a free eBook or video every month

- Fully searchable for easy access to vital information

- Copy and paste, print, and bookmark content

Did you know that Packt offers eBook versions of every book published, with PDF and ePub files available? You can upgrade to the eBook version at packt.com and as a print book customer, you are entitled to a discount on the eBook copy. Get in touch with us at customercare@packtpub.com for more details.

At www.packt.com, you can also read a collection of free technical articles, sign up for a range of free newsletters, and receive exclusive discounts and offers on Packt books and eBooks.

Other Books You May Enjoy

If you enjoyed this book, you may be interested in these other books by Packt:

API Testing and Development with Postman

Dave Westerveld

ISBN: 978-1-80056-920-1

- Find out what is involved in effective API testing
- Use data-driven testing in Postman to create scalable API tests
- Understand what a well-designed API looks like
- Become well-versed with API terminology, including the different types of APIs
- Get to grips with performing functional and non-functional testing of an API
- Discover how to use industry standards such as OpenAPI and mocking in Postman

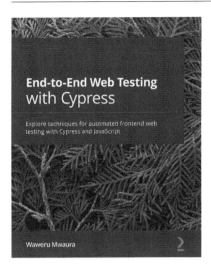

End-to-End Web Testing with Cypress

Waweru Mwaura

ISBN: 978-1-83921-385-4

- Get to grips with Cypress and understand its advantages over Selenium

- Explore common Cypress commands, tools, and techniques for writing complete tests for web apps

- Set up and configure Cypress for cross-browser testing

- Understand how to work with elements and animation to write non-flaky tests

- Discover techniques for implementing and handling navigation requests in tests

- Implement visual regression tests with Applitools eyes

Packt is searching for authors like you

If you're interested in becoming an author for Packt, please visit `authors.packtpub.com` and apply today. We have worked with thousands of developers and tech professionals, just like you, to help them share their insight with the global tech community. You can make a general application, apply for a specific hot topic that we are recruiting an author for, or submit your own idea.

Hi!

I Eran Kinsbruner, author of *A Frontend Web Developer's Guide to Testing*, I really hope you enjoyed reading this book and found it useful for increasing your productivity and efficiency in ensuring web application quality.

It would really help us (and other potential readers!) if you could leave a review on Amazon sharing your thoughts on *A Frontend Web Developer's Guide to Testing*.

Go to the link below or scan the QR code to leave your review:

`https://packt.link/r/1803238313`

Your review will help us to understand what's worked well in this book, and what could be improved upon for future editions, so it really is appreciated.

Best wishes,

Eran Kinsbruner

Printed in Great Britain
by Amazon

79766820R00174